Growing Up Young

By

Allen Young   Jimmy Flynt

We would like to dedicate this book to:

Raymond and Ruby Young

&

Pete and Opal Young Flynt.

Each of you have instilled in our lives the importance of family and through your love we are blessed to be a small part of this great family.

Table of Contents

With each generation that passes we lose the knowledge of history, stories, and family traditions that have been put aside and forgotten. Our goal in writing this book is to instill in the readers and future generations the legacy and history that has been passed down to each member of the Young Family for over 350 years.

The Young family roots can be traced back to England in the seventeenth century when Henry Young was born in 1626. Three generations later Benjamin Young was born in 1733. He would travel to America by ship as a teenager and land in Annapolis, Maryland in 1744. Benjamin would be the first to bring our family to what would later become the United States. Soon after his marriage he moved his family to North Carolina and would become the first Young to own land in the new world. He settled down in the small community known as Townfork near present day Walnut Cove. It was a long trip for the young couple but their journey was only beginning. They would visit the nearby town of Salem for supplies and fight to protect their family from the Indians on their own property. They cleared a portion of their property and started a tradition of farming that would be passed down for generations in the family. Five generations later Elias and Alma Young were tending their own tobacco farm just 10 miles away from where Benjamin's family first settled. Elias and Alma made several moves during their lifetime and raised their family in the small farming community of Oak Ridge. They lived and raised their family through some of the most trying times and some of the greatest moments in our country's history. Through their love, support, and hard work they raised nine wonderful children during their 54 years of marriage. The Young family has left a rich history in North Carolina over the last 250 years and continues to leave their legacy today.

We would like to thank each member of the family who took the time to share their memories and photographs with us as we worked together through the process of writing this book. Special thanks to Bill and Loretta Young Hauser for advising and sharing with us their years of genealogical research. There are too many names to list everyone that has helped in completing this book. From family members, to friends, and even people we have never met, your stories, suggestions and kind words are what made this possible.

Opal, Elsie, Clyde, and Juanita were instrumental in making this book a reality. Thank you for reliving your childhood and telling the stories for the members of the family who are no longer with us. Without each of you this book would not have been possible. We hope that through reading this book it brings back special memories of your parents and siblings from a simpler time.

Often times with family history we tend to focus on our ancestors who came to the new world as settlers from other countries or our ancestors from the civil war era and we forget about recent history. Not 200 years ago but 100 or even 50 years ago. These are the stories that are usually put aside and forgotten in our busy lives. As a child or grandchild the simplest stories are often some of the greatest treasures. While reading this book we hope you will remember to stop and share these little moments in life with your family and help preserve a special moment in time as we are *Growing up Young*.

Thank You!

Allen Young   Jimmy Flynt

Chapter One

"The Great Wagon Road"

The Early Ancestry of
Elias Linville Young

*T*his book will tell the story of the Elias Linville Young and Grace Alma McGee Young family. Married in 1910, this book will tell about their early life, their struggles of living through the Great Depression, and the nine wonderful children they raised. Although life was not always easy during the early 1900's Elias and Alma taught their children the power of hard work, love, and prayer.

The first chapter is devoted to Elias Young's direct early family ancestry and will explain in detail how they left England, lived for several decades on the island of Barbados, and then made their way to what is now the United States of America.

We will continue their journey from the time they first settled on American soil briefly in Maryland and then migrated south to north central North Carolina. Several generations would live and prosper in this central North Carolina area before Elias Young was born.

It all started with Henry Young who was born in Somersetshire, England in 1626. He would be the first of the direct family line to leave England and begin the trek to America.

Henry Young was born in turbulent times. Four European countries were in a power struggle to rule the world. Those countries were England, Spain, Portugal, and France. Their main areas of conquest were the North and South American continents and the Islands of the South Atlantic.

Sailing ships constantly sailed to the new world in hopes of finding a new territory of land that could be claimed for their nation. One such discovery for England was the Island of Barbados.

English ship Captain, John Powell, first came to Barbados on May 14, 1625 as he was sailing from Brazil back to England. His ship went off course due to a navigational error and he discovered the uninhabited island and placed a wooden cross on the beach and carved "James K. of E." into the cross to claim the island in the name of King James I of England.

When Captain Powell returned to England he told the owner of his ship, Sir William Courteen, about his find and how he had staked a cross marker to claim it for King James.

Courteen saw the potential of the island and sent 80 English settlers to lay claim to the land for England. The settlers named the settlement Jamestown in honor of King James I.

The group of settlers quickly began clearing land and built small simple houses for each family. They received help from 40 experienced settlers from Guyana who taught them what would grow and flourish in the tropical island climate. They helped the settlers grow crops such as Indian corn, yams, cotton, sugar cane, and tobacco.

Although the first Young descendent, Henry Young, was born in 1626 it would be 1663 before he sailed from his home in Somersetshire, England to the island of Barbados.

We do know he was married while living in Barbados; however we have no history of his wife's name.

The financial arrangements for the earlier settlers in Barbados were quite simple.

The settlers never owned any land. Sir William Courteen, the financial power behind the settlement, owned all of the land and the settlers worked for him. Although all of the profits were sent back to Courteen he paid the settlers a generous salary and provided them with supplies from England and protection from the Indians or Spanish who may try to attack. As a result of Courteen's generosity toward the settlers everyone remained happy and the island of Barbados became profitable for Courteen and for England.

Three years after his arrival to Barbados Henry Young and his wife had a son, George Young, who was born on July 5, 1666. *George is in the direct lineage of Elias Young's ancestry.*

Our first forefather, Henry Young died four years later in 1670 and was most likely buried in Barbados. His wife and son continued living in Barbados after Henry passed away. George spent his youth learning how to farm the major crops of the island. As a teenager George met Alice Powell and they were married on August 2, 1683 in St. Michael's Parrish in the southwest portion of the island. The two continued living on the island where George farmed the land raising cotton, sugarcane and tobacco.

On July 13, 1690, George and Alice became the proud parents of a son, William Young. William would be in his late 20's before he meet and fell in love with Rebecca Lewis of the island. They were married on February 13, 1718. Over the years William and Rebecca became the proud parents of five children. Those children were Martha, William, Jr., John, James and Benjamin.

Benjamin, who is next in the direct lineage of Elias Young's ancestry, was born to William and Rebecca on April 28, 1733.

Benjamin has the distinction of being the first Young in our family to travel to and live in what is now the United States of America. Benjamin received his opportunity in 1744 when he was 11 years old.

Benjamin boarded a ship in the town of Holetown in Barbados. Holetown was formally known as Jamestown when it was first claimed for King James in 1625. The town gets its name from a stream they called "The Hole", which provided a safe landing place for the early settlers to arrive and depart from the island. It is located in the Parrish of Saint James on the sheltered west coast of the island.

Most likely Benjamin traveled on a cargo ship with his parents from Barbados to the port of Annapolis, Maryland carrying a ship load of cotton, sugar, tobacco, and possibly slaves. It would have been a long, hot, and crowded ship sailing for 30 days or more through the Atlantic Ocean. Passengers would sleep below deck where they remained safe from the dark nights at sea. If they were sailing during the fall or winter months it would have turned extremely cold on the open ocean as the ship traveled north and neared the colonial state of Maryland.

The ship sailed from the blue waters of the Atlantic Ocean into the slow moving waters of the Severn River. It is on the banks of this river that Benjamin first stepped foot on land that would one day become the United States. Peter Coldham's book, "Settlers of Maryland" tells us that Benjamin Young arrived in Annapolis, Maryland in 1744. Annapolis was Maryland's major port of entry during this era and they were known to have a wealthy and cultivated society. Baltimore, Maryland, which was a mere six miles away, would not take away the distinction of being Maryland's major port for another 40 years.

William and Rebecca Young returned to Barbados and records show they were both buried there when they passed away years later. Their son, Benjamin, appears to have stayed in Annapolis.

While living in Annapolis Benjamin became acquainted with a young lady named Zipporah Gist and her family. Zipporah belonged to a prominent Maryland family. Her Great Grandfather, Christopher

Richard Gist, was the surveyor of Maryland's western shore and one of the original commissioners who laid out Baltimore town in 1729.

After a courtship of several months Benjamin and Zipporah were married in 1751. They were both 18 years old and ready to face life's challenges and adventures.

Benjamin and Zipporah would not live in Annapolis for long after getting married. Instead they packed up all of their belongings and moved south to a new community in north central North Carolina known as Townfork. This rural community had rich farm land and would be great for Benjamin's first farm.

Townfork was located in what is now northern Forsyth County and southern Stokes County, North Carolina. Townfork Creek ran through the community and fed into the nearby Dan River. This meant there was plenty of water for the new settlers.

The trip south from Annapolis to Townfork would not be easy. After purchasing a horse or mule, a sturdy wagon, and necessary supplies. Benjamin and Zipporah loaded up their wagon and started their journey south.

While this trip would only take about seven hours by car today, at the time the 400 mile journey took at least two months by wagon. If they were lucky they rode horses but for a majority of the journey they would have walked on foot alongside their wagon at a pace of 5 miles a day.

The reason it would take so long was because of the poor road systems of the 1750's. For the most part roads consisted of old Indian paths that had been walked by local tribes over the years.

Benjamin and Zipporah did have one major wagon path to follow on their journey. It was known as The Great Wagon Road. Fortunately for them it would take them straight to their Central North Carolina destination. The Great Wagon Road brought many settlers to the open lands of the south. In 1751 the road ended in central North Carolina but by 1760 it extended from Philadelphia to Augusta, Georgia for about 735 miles. You can still travel on parts of the Great Wagon Road today in North Carolina. Highway 311 from Madison to Walnut Cove follows the route today. This would have been the same route Benjamin and Zipporah traveled on as they neared their new home.

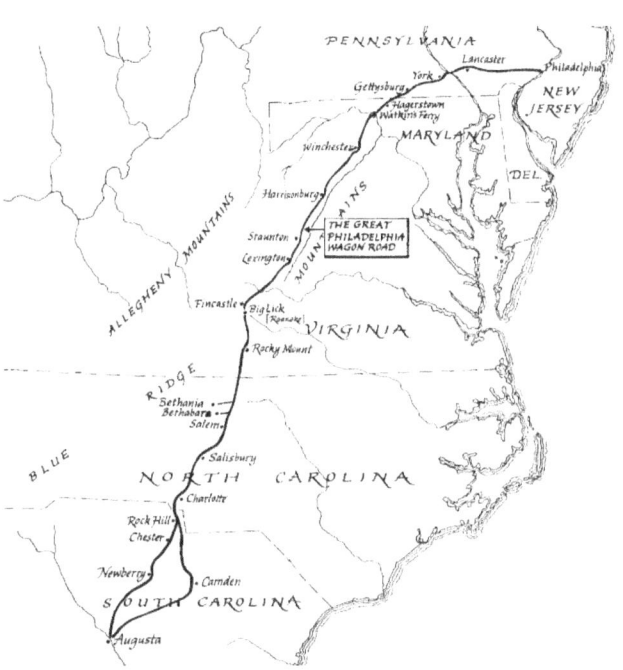

The couple had several challenges along the way. It was fall season and sometimes the nights were cold. There were rivers to cross and if food supplies ran low they had to hunt game to eat with their flint rifle or find a nut tree or berry bush.

There were many houses along the way and as the sun began to set they would search for a nearby house. After knocking on the door and introducing themselves the families would usually invite them into their home for a hot meal and a warm place to sleep. While fighting the dusty roads they would be in search for fresh water, after a long day of traveling down a dusty road a small stream of water was like finding gold. Their goal was to reach Townfork by early winter. They needed to settle in and cut firewood for winter. They also needed to make preparations to plant their garden and crops to feed their livestock.

A little over two months after their journey began the couple saw the iconic knob atop Pilot Mountain standing tall as the gateway to the abundant open lands of North Carolina. They would still have nearly a week of walking before they reached their new home. This new home for Benjamin and Zipporah was a small settlement in North Carolina called Townfork.

Once the couple arrived they quickly settled in and began their new life far away from their friends and family in Maryland. Benjamin did not own any land at the time and probably raised crops such as tobacco or cotton for a local land owner.

In early 1752 Zipporah had a special surprise for Benjamin. She was going to have the family's first child.

Benjamin and Zipporah decided it would be best if they had the child back in Baltimore. Traveling light they returned to Zipporah's parent's home in Maryland. Later that year they had their first child and named her Rebecca.

A couple of months later when Zipporah was able to travel the family of three returned to Townfork.

Judy Cardwell and Phyllis Hoots have spent countless hours researching Townfork and its first settlers. Through their research we have been able to piece together a timeline of Benjamin's family while living in Townfork. As early as 1751 Benjamin was on the tax list for Anson county paying one poll tax. At the time every male 18 years or older was required to pay a poll tax.

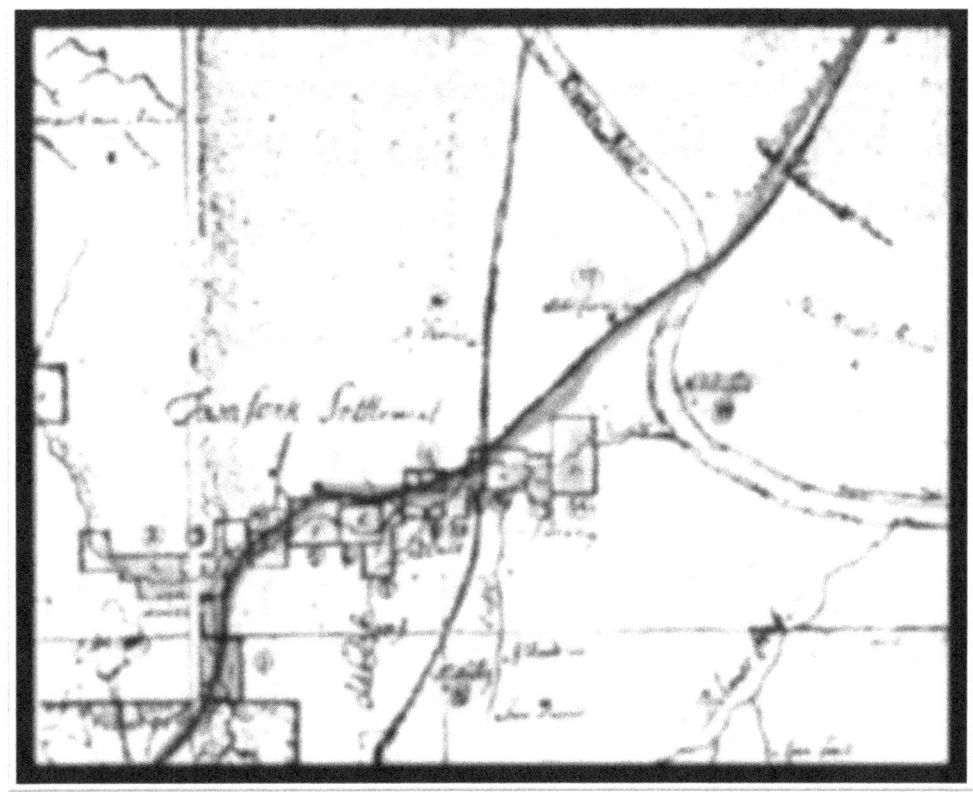

1771 Moravian Map showing the Townfork Settlement

Provided by: Judy Cardwell

The people of the community of Townfork had a good trading relationship with another community just to their south, the Moravians of Wachovia. Wachovia was located in what is now Winston-Salem, North Carolina. The Moravians had several technological advantages over Townfork; one of which was a water powered grist mill where Benjamin often took his wheat and corn to be ground. Adelaide Fries' book "Report of the Moravians in North Carolina" shows that on January 19, 1754 Benjamin visited Wachovia. This entry was found in the Wachovia Diary.

"In the evening Mr. Young and the younger guest(Nathaniel Gist) from Dan River arrived and spend the night with us."

In a later entry dated August 9, 1756 they wrote:

"Mr. Benjamin Young came to the mill, to have grain ground; Mr. Young spent one night here."

Another advantage of Wachovia was they had built a fortified wooden fort within their community around the town of Bethabara. The fort surrounded the entire town and was strong enough to repel Indian attacks and skirmishes between British and French soldiers who were often fighting over boundaries within the North Carolina colony.

There were several Indian massacres during this time because so much land had been stolen from the local tribes. One report showed where 18 settlers had been murdered by renegade Indians over a period of a few days. On occasions such as these Benjamin and his family would seek the safety of the fort at Bethabara until the trouble blew over. In 1755 Benjamin and Zipporah had another son. They named him Benjamin Young, Jr.

He would be the next ancestor in the direct line to Elias Young.

Times were good for the family as they began to establish themselves as true North Carolinians.

At this time all of the land in central North Carolina was owned by John Carteret, also known as the Second Earl Granville or Lord Granville. This land was given to Lord Granville by the King of England a few decades earlier.

This land mass was located just south of the Virginia border and stretched across Carolina from its western border to the Atlantic Ocean in the east and 60 miles south from the Virginia line. This tract of land became known as the Granville District.

In 1762 Lord Granville began allowing citizens of this area to apply for land grants.

Benjamin seized on this opportunity and on March 10, 1762 applied for a Granville Land Grant for 699 acres, which were located on both sides of the Townfork Creek.

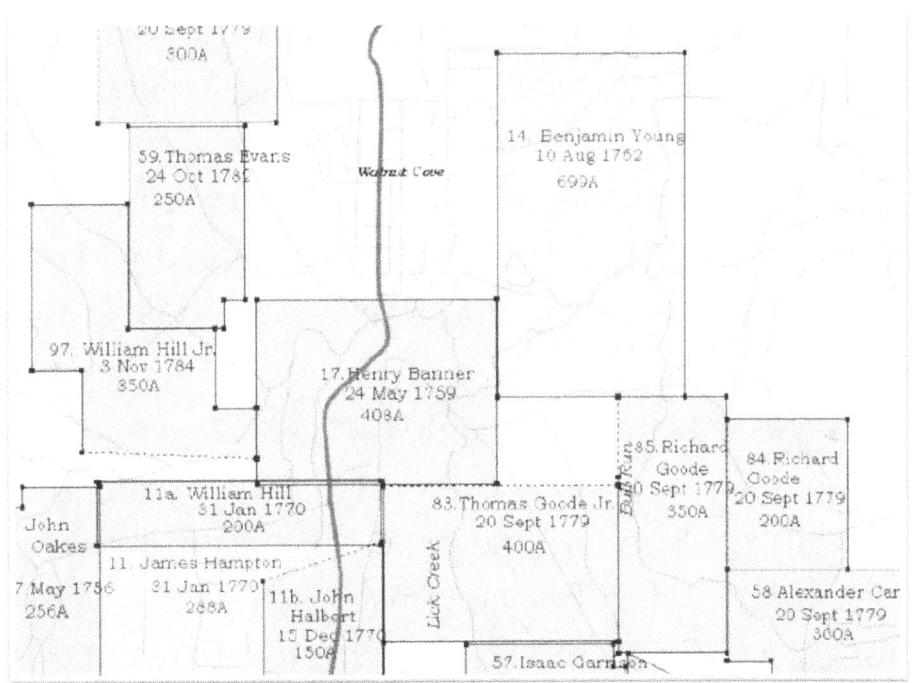

Map of Benjamin Young's land in the Townfork Settlement near present day Walnut Cove, NC. Provided by Judy Cardwell.

Three months later on May 10, 1762 Benjamin had 699 acres surveyed on both sides of the Townfork Creek. Chain carriers for his land were listed as Thomas Eson and Charles Angel. Chain carriers were men hired by the surveyor to help measure the land being surveyed. They would carry a chain of 100 links that was 66 feet long. One acre is equal to ten square chains.

Three months later on August 10, 1762 Benjamin received a Lord Granville Land Grant and was the owner of 699 acres in the Townfork settlement of North Carolina. He would be the first of our family of Young's to own land in America. Shortly afterward Benjamin moved his family to their new home on their own land and began farming. Benjamin was also a craftsman and practiced the art of wagon building. Records show that one of his grandsons, Christopher Young, was an apprentice to Benjamin in 1796 to learn the trade.

Although there is no written history of Benjamin Young, Jr. fighting in the Revolutionary War 1776-1782, it can be assumed since he was in his early 20's during this struggle he probably belonged to a North Carolina Militia. Almost all young men served with honor during this time to help the United States of America become a free and independent nation.

One story passed down through the generations of the Young family is that Bull Creek, near the Townfork settlement, got its name from one of Benjamin Sr.'s hunting trips. The origins of this story are unknown but the tale is that Benjamin went up the creek and stalked a large and ferocious buffalo and attacked him with his flint rifle. The buffalo was wounded and terribly mad at Benjamin. In the confusion and panic to save his life he lost his rifle and took to a tree. The buffalo stood at the base of the tree until the next day. When the buffalo left, Benjamin climbed down and went home empty handed.

In 1770 Surry County was formed from Rowan County, NC and the Townfork settlement fell in the jurisdiction of Surry County. Benjamin and his family are listed on many of the tax lists in the late 18th century. In 1782 Benjamin is shown owning 3 horses, 10 cows, and

699 acres.   Over the next 15 years there are many land transfers recorded, and his amount of property varies from 100 acres to 600 acres on the tax lists.

The first US Census from 1790 showing the Benjamin Young Family. There was 1 male over 18, 2 males under 18, and 3 females for a total of 6 in the Young household at the time the census was taken.

In 1800, when Benjamin was 67 years old he sold land to his son Benjamin Jr. In book 3, page 314 of the Stokes County Deeds it shows that on May 27, 1800 Benjamin Young Jr. paid $270 for 110 acres along Belews Creek and the Dan River that was owned by his father. There are also records indicating that sons Joshua, William, George, and Nathaniel Young purchased land from their father's farm.

Benjamin and Zipporah lived a happy and productive life after that eventually having a total of six children, three sons and three daughters. Benjamin Young, Sr. lived to the age of 76, passing away in 1809.

In 1782 Benjamin Young, Jr. met and married Jane Abbott. She was born in 1762 to Joseph and Elizabeth Priddy Abbott. Benjamin, Jr. was 27 years old and Jane was 20. Two years later in 1784 Benjamin,

Jr. and Jane had their first son, Robert. *Robert was next in the direct lineage to Elias Young and was Elias' great grandfather.* They would later have a second son named George.

Benjamin Jr. and Jane lived productive lives in the Walnut Cove area farming their land. Benjamin lived to the age of 66, passing away in 1818, while Jane survived him for 20 more years living until 1847 and passed away at the age of 86.

On December 20, 1804 Robert Young married Mary Aistrop, who was originally from Culpepper, Virginia. In the early years of their marriage they lived in Walnut Cove, North Carolina as farmers.

Soon after marrying, Robert became a member of the 1st Stokes Regiment of the North Carolina Militia commanded by Lt. Col. John Martin. The United Sates went to war with the British Empire in 1812 over trade restrictions and their desire for expansion into the Northwest Territory. This conflict became known as The War of 1812. Although the North Carolina Militia did not direct contact with the enemy they stayed trained and ready should they be needed during the two year conflict.

In 1818 Robert and Mary had a son named Robert Fletcher Young. He would go by his middle name and was known as Fletcher Young. *Fletcher Young was the next in the direct lineage to Elias Young and was Elias' grandfather.*

In the 1820's Robert Young became the overseer of Peter Hairston's Sauratown Hills Plantation on the banks of the Dan River near Sauratown Mountain.

The Hairston family owned nine plantations; most of these were in southern Virginia and northern portions of North Carolina. Peter Hairston bought the land he named Sauratown Hills in 1786 located in Stokes County, North Carolina. For the most part they raised livestock and grew tobacco on the 10,000 acre Plantation.

At one time there were 300 slaves listed as living on this particular plantation. In total the Hairston family's nine plantations owned 5,500 slaves, making them one of the largest slave owners in the South.

Robert, Mary, and their children lived in a large two story house on the Sauratown Hills Plantation. The house was located on the southern side of the Dan River. The house was split down the middle like a duplex would be built today. One side was the home of Robert and his family. The other side served as a guest house to the larger mansion that was built across the river for Peter Hairston and his family. The Hairston mansion burned down long ago but the guest house which was the home for Robert still stands today although it is in disrepair. The owner of this old house gave Allen Young the opportunity to visit the property and the following picture is of Robert and Mary's home as it looks today.

The Home still stands today where Robert Young and his family lived in the 1820's at the Sauratown Hills Plantation. The home was similar to a duplex today. Half was used by Robert's family and half was used by the plantation owner's guests to the plantation.

After 10 to 15 years as the overseer of Sauratown Hills, Robert decided he would like to own a farm of his own. On June 7, 1831 Robert purchased an unknown amount of land from Jacob Abbott for $332. Jacob was most likely related to Robert's wife's side of the family.

In 1838 Robert applied for and received a land grant from the State of North Carolina for 150 acres in Stokes County on the waters of Townfork Creek. He paid $10 per 100 acres for a total of $15 for this land.

Robert would live out the rest of his days there, passing away in 1855 when he was 71. Mary would live another nine years living with her daughter, passing away in 1864 at the age of 75.

Now, we will discuss the life of the next ancestor in the direct lineage of Elias Young, his grandfather, Fletcher Young.

Fletcher was married to Heptsey Starbuck on April 26, 1834. She died early in life and Fletcher later remarried. On August 6, 1948 Fletcher Young was married a second time to Millie Chandler. Fletcher and Millie bought a 400 acre farm in Forsyth County.

On July 1, 1857 Fletcher and Millie had a son they named Hester Young. *Hester Young was the next in the direct lineage to Elias Young and was Elias' father.*

Although it is believed Fletcher Young owned several slaves to help work the farm there is no record of that or of how many.

There is also no record of whether or not he fought in the Civil War, although he likely did. He would have been 42 when the war broke out. During the Civil War all of the slaves were freed by The Emancipation Proclamation, costing Fletcher Young much of his wealth. After the war massive taxes were levied on southern farm owners hitting Fletcher a second time.

Records show that in 1867 Fletcher had to put up for auction 300 acres of his 400 acre farm and a one horse wagon to pay back taxes on his farm. The losses were devastating to Fletcher and very demoralizing and would affect him for the rest of his life.

Fletcher Young passed away on March 21, 1871. He was 63 years old. Fletcher was buried on his farm on Goodwill Church Road near what is now the Goodwill Baptist Church near Walkertown, North Carolina.

Clyde Young, a Great Grandson of Fletcher Young tells us that a few years back a family friend, Eddie Parrish, took him to the property that Fletcher owned and showed him the general area where he was buried. The two began looking for grave stones and found them knocked over and thrown into a cluster of honeysuckle bushes. Fletcher's grave stone was broken in half but you could still read the engraved writing.

Fletcher
Young
March 21, 1871
Age 63

They also found a smaller grave stone that had the initials "F E Y" engraved across the top. It is not known who this belonged to. It is possible that it belonged to Fletcher and Millie's son, also named Fletcher Young but there are no records found that show his middle initial.

Fletcher's wife Millie lived on until January 21, 1891 and is buried at Goodwill Baptist Church in Forsyth County, NC.

This brings us to Elias Young's father, Hester Young.

In 1878 Hester young met and married Mary Jwanda Linville. The couple would settle down on Mary's parents, Emanuel and Eliza Linville's farm in the Belews Creek Community just east of Walkertown, North Carolina. They would live in this same community their entire lives.

This is Elias Young's grandparents on his mother's side, Emanuel & Eliza Linville. They gave birth to Elias' mother, Mary Linville Young in 1854.

Hester's main source of income was tobacco farming. The 1880 US Census was taken when Hester was 22 years old. He listed his occupation as farmer and his wife's as keeping house. Their first daughter Mary Annie was 8 months old at the time. Hester and Mary raised seven children over the years. Those children were Frank, John, Sally, Mary Annie, *Elias*, Jim and Rosie.

The picture above shows the old home place of Elias Young's grandparents, Emanuel and Eliza Linville. They are shown standing in front of the home, Emanuel with the white beard and Eliza to the far right. The old home place would also serve as Elias' parents, Fletcher and Mary Linville Young's home after they married in 1878 and was where Elias was born and raised during his early youth. This cabin stood near Hwy 158 on Goodwill Church Road in Kernersville, NC until it was torn down in the 1950's.

Above is a picture of the Hester Young Family in the late 1890's. From bottom left, Mary Young, Hester Young and their daughter, Rosie. On the top row from left are son, Jim, daughter, Mary Annie, and Elias Young.

This brings us to Elias Linville Young who was born on May 1, 1889 to Hester and Mary Young. He would live with his parents for the first 21 years of his life going to school in Walkertown, NC and helping them raise tobacco for a living

On June 13, 1910 Hester Young decided he wanted to own his own farm and bought 107 acres of farmland from a local farmer, Thomas Hammock for $900. On August 23, 1913 Hester purchased an additional 98 acres from his father-in-law Emanuel Linville for $1200. Hester Young remained a farmer his entire life.

STATE OF NORTH CAROLINA—FORSYTH COUNTY

THIS DEED, Made this 23 _____ day of August _____ A. D. 191.3.

by Emanuel Linville

of Forsyth _____ County, and State of North Carolina _____ of the first part

to Hester Young

of Forsyth _____ County, and State of North Carolina _____ of the second part,

WITNESSETH: That the said part___ of the first part in consideration of an agreement of lifetime maintenance and $1200 _____ _____ _____ Dollars,

to ___ paid by the said part__ of the second part, the receipt of which is hereby acknowledged ha___ bargained and sold, and by these presents do___ bargain, sell and convey to said part__ of the second part, and ___ his

heirs, all the right, title, interest and estate of the party of the first part in and to tract, lot or parcel of land in Forsyth _____ County, State of North Carolina, adjoining the lands of Gid Fulton, Shepherd Nelson, Isaac Haglip,

and others, bounded as follows, viz:—

[Handwritten metes and bounds description, partially legible]

Beginning at a stone on the west side of _____ _____, Shepherd Nelson corner running N 39° W 24 ch to a _____ Gid Fulton corner thence S 3° E 4.40 ch to _____ _____ N 58° W 11.50 ch, thence N 73° W, 9.25 ch _____ N 78° W 4.75 ch thence N 74° W 22.58 ch to Joseph Hester corner _____ on his line N 60° W 2.50 ch to Isaac Linville corner thence on his line N 53½° E 7 ch thence N 58½° E 11.50 ch to a stone Isaac Haglip corner thence on his line E 2 ch N 78½° E 5 ch S 80° E 6.10 ch S 65° E 21.25 ch to Nelson corner thence on his line S 43° E 4.80 ch E 7 ch N 83° E 4.94 ch S 73° E 9 ch S 10° W 4.74 ch S 85° W with branch S W S 49° W 2.75 ch S 75° W 5.40 ch S 5° E 11 ch to the place of beginning Containing 98 acres more or less.

Above is a copy of the deed to Hester Young from his Father-in-law Emanuel Linville for 98 acres of land in Forsyth County, North Carolina
Deed Book 128 Page 61 – August 23, 1913.

In February of 1929 Hester came down with Pneumonia. He suffered from this illness for eleven months and on January 23, 1930 Hester passed away.

On January 24th his funeral was held at Goodwill Baptist Church by Linville Funeral Home of Kernersville, NC. He was buried in the Goodwill Church Cemetery beside his mother Millie Young.

Nearly eight years later on January 5, 1938 his wife Mary Linville Young died and was buried alongside her husband, Hester at Goodwill Baptist Church.

With the birth of their son Elias Linville Young our small portion of the Young family was also born. Elias went on to marry his bride of 54 years, Grace Alma McGee. Together they raised their family of nine children through some of the hardest and trying times of our countries history. This book will take you through the lives of Grandpa and Grandma Young and their nine children.

Chapter Two

The Early Ancestry of
Grace Alma McGee Young

Chapter Two is devoted to Grace Alma McGee Young's early family ancestry. Alma's maiden name was McGee and that is the family line we will follow. The McGee name originates in Scotland in the 1100's. Our first direct recorded lineage of Alma's family ancestry begins with Robert McGhee, who was born in 1580 in Antrim County; a county in Northern Ireland. Robert later married Nancy Mary Smith, who was also born around 1580 in Ireland. They had a son named John McGhee on April 4, 1602.

John McGhee later moved to the United States and met Cynthia Campbell of Kentucky whom he later married. After their marriage they decided to move back to Ireland to spend the rest of their lives. They had a son, Alexander McGee *(notice he dropped the 'H' from his last name)* in Derry Ireland in 1634.

Alexander McGee would later marry Jane Milikin, also of Derry Ireland and they would spend the rest of their lives there.

They had a son named John Calvin McGee in Ireland in 1690. He is listed as a passenger of a ship that landed in Virginia in 1706 and was probably the first McGee in Grace Alma McGee's direct lineage to permanently live in the United States. He was listed as 15 years old on the ship's log. He would later marry Lydia Marsh of Virginia.

John and Lydia later had a son, Ralph McGee, in 1720 in Albemarle, Virginia. He would later marry Ann Clayton Wise, also of Albemarle, Virginia. They would have a son, Robert Magee, *(notice another name change here)* in 1738.

We are fortunate to have from this point forward a detailed family tree of Alma's early U.S. heritage dating back to Robert Magee, who was born in Sussex County, Virginia in 1738.

The first written history found of the McGee ancestry started with Harmon Magee who was born on July 7, 1760 in Sussex County, Virginia. He was the oldest son of Robert and Priscilla Magee.

In 1776 just after his 16th birthday Harmon was drafted into the Virginia Militia to help his fellow American countrymen fight for independence against the British monarchy. He served under Captain John Powell and marched to York, VA. Harmon served the Virginia Militia in three months tours on active duty and three months off active duty for a total of six tours of duty.

The Militia leaders realized their troops were farmers and were badly needed at home to help with crops and would not keep them for more than three months at a time. This greatly helped the morale of the troops.

Following the Revolutionary War, Harmon married Martha "Patty" Barham on December 27, 1781. The couple made their home in Sussex County, Virginia.

Patty Barham had a prestigious family heritage. Her direct ancestry can be traced back to Emperor Charlemagne, the monarchies of King Edward the First, Henry I, Henry II, Henry III, King John of England and William the Conqueror. This makes the Alma and Elias Young family decedents of royalty.

In 1792 Harmon moved his family from Virginia to Rockingham County, North Carolina. This was the first time one of Grace Alma McGee Young's direct ancestors moved to North Carolina.

After two years Harmon Magee moved to Guilford County, NC. Four years later he moved his family to Stokes County, North Carolina.

Soon after moving to Stokes County in 1798 Harmon and Martha had a son named Clemmons Magee.

In 1808 Harmon Magee bought his first tract of land in Stokes County and farmed that land for the rest of his life. He passed away in 1832.

In 1821 Harmon's son, Clemmons Magee married Delilah Robbins and they continued living in Stokes County. They had a son, Green McGee (*notice the name changed here*) later in 1821.

Green McGee would later marry Keziah Mecom in 1845 and they would have a son, John Clemmons McGee in 1846.
Green McGee lived a short life passing away in 1861 at the age of 40.

Green McGee's son, John Clemmons McGee, married Mary Elizabeth Taylor in 1870 and their youngest child was Grace Alma McGee

Alma's parents were John Clemmons and Mary Elizabeth Taylor McGee. John was born in 1846 and Mary was born in 1843. John and Mary met and married in 1870. When they married John was 24 and Mary was 27. You have to keep in mind this was only five years after the Civil War. Many men in the South married older women during this time because so many men were killed during the Civil War.

After marrying they purchased a farm about five miles west of Walkertown, North Carolina; about half way between Walkertown and The Smith Reynolds Airport in Winston-Salem, NC and made their living raising tobacco.

John and Mary had five children, Bob, Grover, Nan, a son, whose name cannot be found that died at age 21, and Alma.

Grace Alma McGee, whom this chapter is about, was the youngest of the siblings and was quite a surprise when she was born on July 13, 1893. Her Mother, Mary McGee, was 49 years old when Alma was born. Alma grew up going to school in Walkertown and helping her parents raise tobacco. She would meet and later marry Elias Linville Young on December 18, 1910 when she was 17 years old.

The rest of this book is about the lives of Alma and Elias Young and their nine children.

Above is a picture of Grace Alma McGee Young's parents, John Clemmons McGee and Mary Elizabeth Taylor McGee. This picture was probably taken in the mid-1870's.

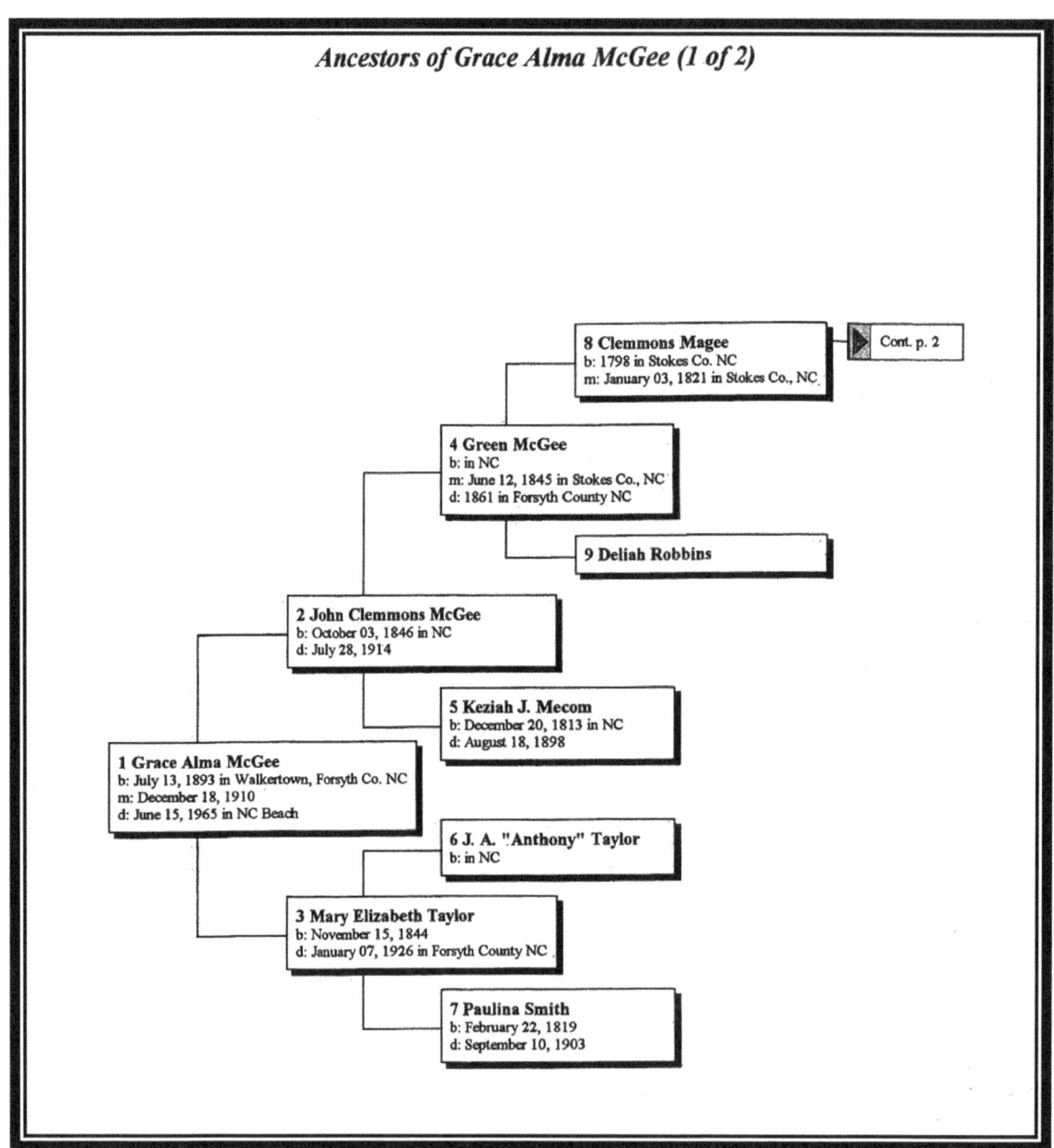

8 Clemmons Magee
b: 1798 in Stokes Co. NC
m: January 03, 1821 in Stokes Co., NC

Cont. p. 2

4 Green McGee
b: in NC
m: June 12, 1845 in Stokes Co., NC
d: 1861 in Forsyth County NC

9 Deliah Robbins

2 John Clemmons McGee
b: October 03, 1846 in NC
d: July 28, 1914

5 Keziah J. Mecom
b: December 20, 1813 in NC
d: August 18, 1898

1 Grace Alma McGee
b: July 13, 1893 in Walkertown, Forsyth Co. NC
m: December 18, 1910
d: June 15, 1965 in NC Beach

6 J. A. "Anthony" Taylor
b: in NC

3 Mary Elizabeth Taylor
b: November 15, 1844
d: January 07, 1926 in Forsyth County NC

7 Paulina Smith
b: February 22, 1819
d: September 10, 1903

Chart 0ne: This is the first of two family trees for Grace Alma McGee Young. It starts with Alma who was born July 13, 1893 and goes all the way back to Clemmons Magee who was born in 1798. Also notice the name spelling change between Green McGee and his father, Clemmons Magee.

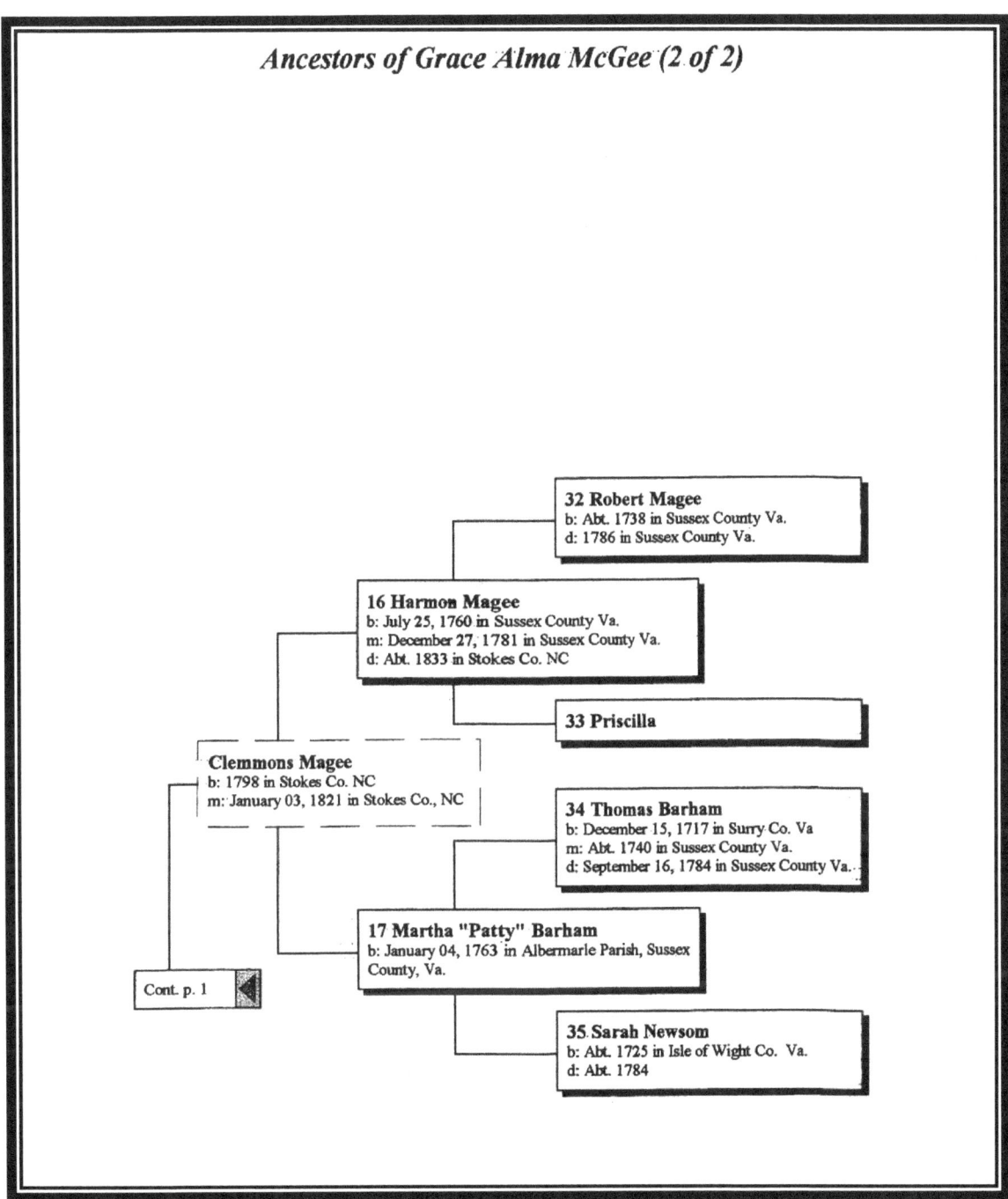

32 Robert Magee
b: Abt. 1738 in Sussex County Va.
d: 1786 in Sussex County Va.

16 Harmon Magee
b: July 25, 1760 in Sussex County Va.
m: December 27, 1781 in Sussex County Va.
d: Abt. 1833 in Stokes Co. NC

33 Priscilla

Clemmons Magee
b: 1798 in Stokes Co. NC
m: January 03, 1821 in Stokes Co., NC

34 Thomas Barham
b: December 15, 1717 in Surry Co. Va
m: Abt. 1740 in Sussex County Va.
d: September 16, 1784 in Sussex County Va.

17 Martha "Patty" Barham
b: January 04, 1763 in Albermarle Parish, Sussex County, Va.

Cont. p. 1

35 Sarah Newsom
b: Abt. 1725 in Isle of Wight Co. Va.
d: Abt. 1784

Chart Two: This is the second of two family trees for Grace Alma McGee Young. It starts with Clemmons Magee and goes back to Robert Magee, who was born in 1738. The two family trees span six generations of Grace Alma McGee's ancestry; all of whom lived in Virginia and North Carolina.

Chapter Three

The Marriage of Elias and Alma Young

The day was December 18, 1910 and it was a big day in Elias Young's and Alma McGee's life. They had made the decision to get married. Elias was up at sunrise that morning. He knew where he and Alma needed to go to say their vows and he had a full day planned.

He got a bright and early start that morning by eating his final breakfast with his dad, Hester and his mom, Mary. It would be his last day of living on the farm where he grew up in the Belews Creek, N.C.

While walking to the barn Elias' dad fulfilled the promise he had made long ago. He went to the second horse stall on the right and bridled the new beautiful jet black workhorse he had just purchased.

"This is Dan, Elias. He's a strong 2 year old workhorse and I just bought him for you. Over there is a new leather harness I also bought for you. I promised you if you waited until you were 21 years old to get married I would give you a workhorse. You did and well, here he is!" Hester grinned.

With that Elias and Hester put the new harness on Dan and proceeded to hitch him to Hester's one-horse buggy.

Elias didn't know it at the time, but Dan would be one of the greatest gifts he ever received. Dan would plow fields; pull wagons, tobacco sleds and any other chores needed for Elias for the next 40 years. Because of Dan, Elias never owned a tractor.

After saying his farewells to his father, Elias was off to pick up Alma. It was almost 10 miles to her house, which was east of Walkertown, but Dan drove at a trot and was there before Elias knew it.

When he drove up to Alma's home at the McGee home place", she was standing on the front porch with her mom and dad. She was wearing a new dress her parents had bought her and she looked beautiful.

"There's my bride to be!" Elias shouted. Get in and we'll go get this done."

With that, Alma quickly kissed her mom and dad goodbye and ran to the wagon.

"What a beautiful horse!" Alma said as she got on the wagon.

"My dad gave it to us as a wedding present." Elias grinned. With that Elias and Alma were off to Walkertown to tie the knot.

As they approached the town main street Elias said, "This is going to be easy."

Alma replied, "I get a little nervous having to go into a church I don't know. I'll be glad when this is over."

"You want have to get nervous this time, Honey." Elias grinned. "We don't have to go in!"

"What do you mean?" Alma inquired inquisitively.

With that Elias pulled up to the parsonage beside the church and out popped the minister, Bible in hand.

As soon as Elias pulled Dan to a stop the minister opened his Bible and began the wedding vows to Elias and his 17 year old bride to be. In less than five minutes Elias and Alma were Mr. and Mrs. Elias Young. Elias paid the minister $2.00 and they were on their way.

After a few days at a secret get-away for their honeymoon, Elias and Alma returned to their new home at the McGee home place. Whether they lived in the same house with Alma's mom and dad, John and Mary McGee or they had a small house on the farm of their own is not known for sure.

It was a situation that worked out well for all. Alma's parent were getting on in years. John was 64 at the time and was in failing health and Mary was 67.

Elias quickly pitched in chopping firewood, drawing water from the well, and making many of the repairs needed around the farm.

Within a couple of months he was preparing a tobacco plant bed and making preparations to plant the farm's eight acres of tobacco.

Things went well that first year and with Elias' ability to cure their tobacco to the desired golden yellow color the crop brought an excellent price.

In 1911 Alma brought Elias the great news she was with child and the days of the Elias and Alma Young family began.

It was with great joy on December 17, 1911 that their first child, Hubert was born. You could tell right from the start he was going to be long and lanky; just like his father.

In 1913 Alma had more great news for Elia and nine months later came Annie, their first daughter. In 1914 Alma's father, John, whose health had been failing for several years took a sudden turn for the worse. John passed away on July 29, 1914.

Elias and Alma continued living on the McGee farm raising tobacco after John passed away.

In 1917 Alma and Elias had their third child, Raymond. Raymond was a happy child and was always willing to help the family in any way he could.

In 1919 their fourth child, Hazel was born. Hazel too was a pretty little girl and would grow to become another of those beautiful Young girls. All four of Elias' and Alma's children were good children and willing to pitch in where needed on the farm.

In 1922 Elias started feeling the strains of such a large family and knew he needed more room for his children in the household and more tobacco allotment to allow him to earn more money for his family each year.

While visiting his father Elias discussed the possibility of renting the Whicker Farm which was next door to Hester's farm. In 1922 Elias and Alma moved themselves and their four children to the Whicker Farm. It was located in the Belews Creek Community near Goodwill Church east of Walkertown, North Carolina and right next to Elias' father, Hester Young's farm.

The house was a small log cabin and the acre allotment for growing tobacco was nine acres where they had eight acres on the McGee Farm. The improvements would make life better for the whole family.

Hubert, though only 10 years old was beginning to be a big help to Elias and the younger children were starting to help out, too.

In 1923 a fifth child Edna, was born and in 1925 a sixth child, Opal was born.

1926 would be a sad time for Alma. On January 7, 1926 Alma's mother Mary Taylor McGee passed away. She was 82 years old.

Later that year Elias and Alma purchased a brand new 1926 Model "T" Ford. The car would last them through the depression of the 1930's.

Speculation is the money to purchase the new car was from an inheritance from Alma's mother, Mary McGee's passing.

In 1927 Elias and Alma had their seventh child Elsie. Once again the household was beginning to get crowded.

In 1929 the stock market crashed. Elias and Alma didn't think anything of it; they didn't have any stocks. They overheard some of their relatives talking about it at a family get-together and they began talking about how bad times were going to be.

Elias on the way home told Alma, "How much worse could it be? We have so little money now."

They would soon find out. Instead of little money there would be no money. Instead of buying salt, pepper and sugar for cooking and kerosene for their lamps at the local country store; they would have to barter for them with a few dozen eggs and a chicken Alma had grown in her own back yard.

In 1930 Elias' father Hester Young passed away. It was really a sad time for Elias and after the funeral the Young family made the decision to put the farm up for sale.

Elias thought this would be the perfect opportunity for him and Alma to finally purchase a farm of their own.

When it came time to get down to business; old family wounds and jealousy quickly surfaced. Sibling rivalry kicked in and an agreement could never be made. A few months later the farm was sold to someone outside the family.

After the disagreement Elias and Alma decided it was time for them to move on. A couple of weeks later they found a farm available to rent in Oak Ridge, North Carolina and they made the move to "The Case Place".

This is the Hester and Mary Young House where they raised their son, Elias. The house was built in the early 1800's and the Young's moved here sometime before 1880. Elias lived here until he was 21 years old. This old house still stands today. It is located on Goodwill Church Road in Kernersville, NC.

Elias Young was 21 years old when he and Alma McGee got married. It was the best decision he would ever make in his lifetime. Alma turned out to be a loving wife and a wonderful mother to their nine children.

On December 10, 1910 Alma McGee to the right married Elias Young in Walkertown North Carolina, At the age of 17 she was already a beautiful woman and was very mature for her age. She and Elias would raise nine children over the coming years and they were proud of each and every one of them.

This is a picture of Elias Young holding his work-horse, Dan, on the right and his son-in-law Pete Flynt with another work horse on the left. This picture was taken in 1946 when Dan was 38 years old.

This is Elias Young in 1920. At the time he was 31 years old and had been married to Alma for nearly 10 years. He was also the father of their four children, Hubert, Annie, Raymond and Hazel.

Elias and Alma Young's first four children taken in 1923. Bottom row is Hazel; top row from left are Raymond, Annie and Hubert. This picture was taken on the Whicker Farm.

The Whicker Farm House where Elias and Alma moved their family in 1922 on Goodwill Church Road.   This picture was taken in the 1960's.

Chapter Four

"The Old Case Place Oak"

The Case Place

On the morning of Feb. 16, 1930 Elias and Alma Young were up at 5:00 A.M. getting ready for a full day. They were making the move from The Whicker Farm near Belews Creek to the Case Place in Oak Ridge, North Carolina. The plan was to get the move made in one day. The entire family would have to pitch in and work hard to accomplish this.

On this chilly morning Elias and Alma were working together as usual in the kitchen. While Elias started a fire in the cook stove Alma mixed up a big batch of homemade biscuits.

After starting the fire Elias began breaking some eggs to be scrambled and Alma prepared the percolator for a big pot of steaming hot coffee.

As aromas filled the home from the wood cook stove Elias called out, "Come children, time for breakfast!"

The children were quickly up and sitting on the benches at the kitchen table. They were all excited about the big move.

At the time of the move Elias had reached the age of 40 and Alma was 37. Hubert, who was already out of school, was 17. Four children were school age; Annie was 15, Raymond was 13, Hazel was 11 and Edna was 8. The two remaining children were Opal age 5, and baby Elsie was 2. Clyde and Junaita would come a little later.

The work ethics Elias and Alma had instilled in the children made them a great help in the home and around the farm. All of their hands would be needed today.

After breakfast Alma and the girls quickly washed and dried the dishes. After they were dry the wrapped them in newspaper and packed them in a wood barrel.

While this was going on, Elias began taking down the beds and Hubert and Raymond went to the barn to put the harnesses on their horse and mule and hitched them to the wagon.

Hubert and Raymond brought the wagon to the front of the house and loaded the bed frames and straw ticks that were used as a mattress onto the wagon along with Elsie's cradle. They covered everything with quilts to protect them during the journey to the Case Place.

Elias and Hubert began the trip with the horse and mule team pulling the wagon. Raymond, Alma, and the girls loaded the breakables into the family's 1926 Model T Ford.

Elias and Alma had purchased the Model T brand new in 1926 for the price of $350 from the Ford dealership in nearby Walnut Cove, NC. They were glad they had it. Trying to buy an automobile now would be next to impossible with the depression going on.

After loading the car everyone found a place to sit in the room left as Raymond went to the front of the Model T to crank it with the hand crank.

Raymond's head bobbed up and down as he turned the crank. Soon there was a chug, chug, chug and the engine fired.

Alma told everyone, "Bundle up and wear your hats over your ears all the way over. We don't want anyone catching a cold."

Then Alma turned to Raymond and said, "Do not drive fast."

Raymond replied, "I want do over 30 miles per hour, Mama."

Alma sternly replied, "Young Man, 20 miles per hour is fast enough!!"

When the Model T pulled into the driveway of the old Case homeplace the first thing they saw were huge oak trees all around the front yard. The trees were probably a hundred years old since they were most likely planted at the same time the old homeplace was built before the Civil War. One of these oak trees still survives today where the house once stood.

The house was a big two-story farm house with eight rooms. The windows were small and it had a large fireplace and chimney to the side of the house.

Elias already had a stack of firewood and some kindling on the front porch. Upon arrival Raymond quickly built a fire to warm his mother and his siblings.

Soon after, Elias and Hubert drove up and were glad to see smoke coming from the chimney. They got off the wagon and swiftly walked inside to get warm.

After a few warm minutes by the fire Elias and Hubert unloaded the cradle and put it near the fireplace. Then Elias and the brothers unloaded the beds and washstand from the wagon.

Elias and Hubert were in a hurry because they had to make one more trip today to get the rest of the family belongings from the Wicker Farm.

After driving the horse team at a steady pace Elias and Hubert arrived back at the Wicker Farm. The second load consisted of the wood cook stove, the kitchen, table, benches and chairs and a couple of chairs from the living room.

Also on the wagon was the family barn cat, Barney Google, and the family's two rabbit hounds, whose names were Drive and Lead.

Elias also had help from his brother, John Young, that day. John had the task of bringing the family's two milk cows and a crate of about a dozen roosters and laying hens.

Upon their return to The Case Place Elias and Hubert quickly unloaded the wagon and by 6:00 P.M. had the cook stove set up and hooked up to the outside stove pipe. Once the fire in the wood cook stove reached the right temperature Alma fixed a large iron frying pan of cornmeal mush. The family enjoyed the mush with brown sugar and cream. They all ate well after a hard day's work. After super while everyone was sitting around the fireplace Alma went over and opened a little chest where she kept her own special belongings. Inside was a little notebook with two pretty redbirds on the front. This was her personal diary where she kept notes of special events.

In it she wrote, "February 16, 1930, our family moved to The Case Place in Oak Ridge, North Carolina."

Afterward she looked around at her tired family and said, "It's been a hard day, but a successful one. Let's go to bed."

The following morning the Young family still had one more task to complete the move. That was to get Annie, Hazel, Raymond and

Edna started back to school at the new Oak Ridge School a few miles up the road. The brick school house was built in 1924. It was exciting for the Young children to attend the new modern school in Oak Ridge.

At their old school in Belews Creek the children had to walk to school. In Oak Ridge a school bus would come right by the house.

Alma had them ready bright and early. Opal wanted to go, too, but she was only five years old and couldn't.

Down the road came the bus and the children were in it in a flash and gone. Opal still remembers standing by the family hounds, Drive and Lead and watching the school bus drive up the road that day. After school Annie could not wait to get inside to tell her mother about their first day. Annie proudly explained, "You know how we have to draw all of our water from the well. They have this water fountain at school where you simply turn a knob and water flows up in the air for you to drink. They also have electric lights all over the school where all you do is turn a knob and the lights come on."

Alma replied, "Someday we'll have lights like that, but for now oil lamps will have to do."

Then Annie continued, "And they have toilets right inside the school. They don't have outhouses. The teacher said we were to call them restrooms." Alma was very pleased to hear of the much more modern school her children were going to attend.

Now that their move was complete it was time for the family to turn their attention to farming.

A Description Of The Case Place House, Buildings, and Land By Opal Young Flynt 81 Years Later

Opal Young Flynt told about the layout of the Case Farm where Elias and Alma lived from 1930 to 1942 in June of 2011. She was 86 at the time and the detail she told was amazing. This is how she described it.

The year was 1930 and Elias and Alma Young were looking for a new place to raise their family. They had seven children at the time ranging from 17 to two years old. Clyde would come a year later and Juanita three years later.

The Case Farm was just north of Oak Ridge, North Carolina and had over 200 acres of land. Elias and Alma liked what they saw and struck an agreement with Mr. Case and his wife to live in the old Case Family Home Place. The old home place had been built before the Civil War and although it had never seen a brush stroke of paint still was quite a sturdy house.

The Case's had recently built a new home and were getting on in years. The rent for the old home place would be half of the income from Elias and Alma growing nine acres of tobacco every year.

Included with the house Elias and Alma could raise all of the garden and animal feed they needed on the land of the farm. They also could cut any wood they needed for heating the home and cooking on their wood cook stove.

It was quite a time and place to live. They made their move as the Great Depression was beginning and Elias and Alma had to make everything they grew count. They did not have money to spend on extras and little to spend on necessities. They grew everything they ate. They even bartered chickens and eggs at a nearby country store for salt, pepper, sugar, kerosene, and a tube of Rose Snuff occasionally for Grandma Young.

The Old Case Home Place House

Now we will go back to a cold February in North Carolina and look at the old Case home place. It was a big two-story house. There were no screens on the windows, so if you wanted to open a window at night for a cool breeze to sleep you had to understand there may be a few bugs and every once in a while a squirrel or a raccoon may come into the house. The front yard was full of large oak trees.   One day Elias chose a sturdy straight limb and hung a rope swing for the children.

The house did not have running water or electricity and at night the family used oil lamps to see. There was a well house out back where you could draw all the water you wanted from a hand dug and rock lined hole 50 feet deep in the ground. There was a two gallon bucket attached to a hand crank and rope. Without running water there was not a bathroom in the house. The outside Johnny House served its purpose well.

As you approached the house the first thing you saw was a large rock shaped like a pillow that served as a step to the front porch. The front porch was quite small so the family seldom used it for sitting in the evening.

As you entered through the double doors on the front of the house the first room you saw was a hallway. The first room to the right in the hallway was the Parlor. It was the formal living room.

When you looked straight ahead and a little to the right there was a stairway to the three bedrooms upstairs. When you reached the top of the steps there was a small hallway and the first thing you saw was a large picture of Jesus Alma had hung on the wall. It remained there the entire 12 years they lived in the house.

While upstairs, to the right was the first bedroom. It was the girls' room where Annie, Hazel, Edna, Opal, Elsie, and Juanita slept. There were two large and very comfortable feather tick beds in the room and the girls made do with what they had.

To the left were the other two smaller bedrooms. One was Hubert's and the other was Raymond's. Raymond had a big double bed, so Clyde slept with him when he got old enough.

Downstairs in the entrance hallway to the left across from the Parlor was Elias' and Alma's bedroom. This room also served as a sitting room during the day and was the location of the only fireplace in the house.

Under the steps to the upstairs was a large open area big enough for a small bed. It was used as cousins and other family members came to stay frequently at the Young home. Straight ahead was the kitchen. Decades earlier the kitchen had been outside and you could still see the foundation rocks behind the house. This was common for homes built in the 1800's to prevent cooking fires from burning down the house.

In the Kitchen was a table for preparing food. To the side was a bench with a couple of two gallon white with red trim porcelain buckets filled with water from the outside well. One was for cooking and washing up at a nearby wash pan. The other bucket of water was for drinking. There was a porcelain dipper that hung on a nearby nail and everyone in the household used it.

At first Alma and Elias didn't have an ice box. That would come about five years later. For now they made do with a hole in the ground outside for keeping the milk and butter cool.

Alma had a great wood cook stove in the kitchen. It was bright blue and was used from 5:00 A.M. in the morning 'till suppertime seven days a week.

The wood stove consisted of a firebox on the lower left where small sticks of chopped firewood were used to heat the top cast iron cooking surface and the right side had a baking oven. Pine and poplar wood were used because they produced a quick hot fire.

The stove also had a water well for keeping hot water, but it had a leak and could never be used. Instead, Alma kept a large cast iron kettle of water on top of the stove at all times.

The rest of the top surface at breakfast was used for preparing food in Alma's big frying pan and making the morning coffee in their glass top percolator.

Later in the day the top surface was used for making soups, stews and other lunch and super meals.

The baking oven to the side was used for making biscuits at least twice a day and a pie or cobbler whenever fruit was available to make desert.

Alma was fortunate to have a full room size pantry above the kitchen. You see, when the Cases moved the kitchen inside the house they built a set of steps to a separate upstairs room to keep all those Mason Jars of canned green beans, corn, tomatoes, pickles, jellies and jams. They also had poles running across the top of the room to hang bunches of onions, dried peppers, herbs and other dried goods. Alma kept a whole winter supply of food in that room.

Downstairs the dining room was next to the kitchen. It was a small room that consisted mainly of a long narrow homemade dining table. At the far end were three chairs. Elias and Alma sat in two of the chairs during meals and Hubert sat in the other one. The rest of the children sat where they could find a place on the two benches; one on each side of the table. Opal remembers Raymond having his own special place at the far end of one of the benches near his mother and father and across from Hubert.

Back in the Kitchen Alma had a small table set up where she could look out the back window when she and the children were washing dishes. She had a small cupboard for storing the dishes.

There were many stories told and memories made over the years as the Young family called this house, Home.

The Barns, Out Buildings, and Sheds at the Old Case Home Place

Farms were not complete without barns, sheds, and other structures and the Case farm was no different.

About a hundred and fifty feet behind the house was a large feed barn. It consisted of a center open area, fours stalls for Elias's work horse Dan, a mule named Kit, and his two milk cows named Ella and Rose. There was a large hay loft over the stalls for storing loose hay. They would use a pitch fork with a long handle to place hay onto the top of the stack.   This was before the hay baler had been invented. There was also the family cat named Barney Google who lived in the barn. His job was to keep all the mice away. His reward was a big pan of milk fresh from Ella and Rose every morning.

Close to the barn was a large corn crib. It was a small wood building that set two feet off the ground to keep unwanted animals out of their crop of corn. Elias raised several acres of field corn every year to feed his work horse, mule, and two milk cows. Of course Elias would also take some of the corn to Mr. Hendrix's water powered grist mill that still stands today in Oak Ridge to grind the family a sack of cornmeal. When the Young's first moved to the Case farm State Highway 68 had not been built and a long overhead wood flume carried water from the dam to the mill. With this cornmeal Alma made a large pan of her famous cornbread.

A little closer to the house was the chicken coop. It was looked after by Alma. The coop consisted of a place for the chickens to roost and several covered boxes to provide a place for the chickens to lay their eggs. The chickens and eggs were a major food source for the family. Alma would continually allow one of the hens to sit on their nest until they hatched another eight or ten biddies. After all she had to replenish her own stock. And of course every Sunday dinner consisted of a couple of big fried chickens.

A little deeper in the woods were four wood fired tobacco barns. Elias would use them to cure the nine acres of tobacco he was required to raise each summer. All the wood had to be cut for firing each barn of tobacco to be cured.

In the winter these tobacco barns were also used to store the family's Irish potatoes and sweet potatoes. Elias would store both types of potatoes on wood planks raised off the ground and they would last without spoiling all winter.

There was one other building on the farm; an old multi-room school house that the community of Oak Ridge had discontinued using after they built the new Oak Ridge School. While a family rented part of the old school house as a place to live the other part was used by Elias and Alma as their pack house for storing their cured tobacco until it was prepared for sale at the Winston-Salem Tobacco Market. The old school house even had an old basement where Elias could put his tobacco to bring it into order. Bringing into order means adding moisture to the very dry cured tobacco leaves to make them soft and pliable before preparing them to sell at market.

Although the school house was old it had electric lights. It was the only electric power on the farm that the Young family could use.

There were no barbed wire fenced pastures on the Case Farm. Elias and the boys had to take the horses and milk cows from the feed barn to the well behind the house every day and draw several buckets for those animals to have water.

For the milk cows to graze Elias staked them to 50 foot cow chains for three or four hours every day. Elias also raised a couple of hogs every year. They were kept in an old split rail fenced in lot. The hogs were killed every Fall after a frost. It needed to be cold outside when the hogs were cut up to keep them from spoiling before the special curing processes were done. The hogs provided country ham, shoulder meat, sausage, bacon, fatback and the remaining hog fat was boiled in large wood fired iron pots to produce lard for cooking over the winter.

Each of these buildings on the farm were essential to providing food and money for the family throughout the year.

Working the Land at The Old Case Farm

The main crop grown by Elias and Alma Young on the Old Case Farm was tobacco. They had to raise nine acres every year and give half of the profit to the Cases to pay their rent.

You would have to plow all of the land into rows with your horse and mule. Then you would have to add fertilizer to each row. Next you planted each tobacco plant by hand and later kept the weeds hoed out. As the plants reach maturity each plant would need to be topped, which means the big flower at the top broken out. Next came suckering and removing those dreaded tobacco worms by hand.

Once the crop was ready to start pulling the leaves for curing, you had to pull three to four leaves from the bottom of the stalks once a week for about six weeks in a row. All the tobacco leaves had to be strung onto tobacco sticks at the barn and hung in the barn for curing. Elias spent many nights at the tobacco barns stoking the fires all night long to keep the temperature in the barns just right to produce those golden yellow tobacco leaves the market desired at auction time. This is something that Elias enjoyed and he continued to spend many evenings and nights sitting by the fire at the families tobacco barns.

After all that they had to take the cured tobacco off the tobacco sticks, sort it by color and tie the leaves into tobacco hands. The hands were then put on tobacco sticks and loaded into Elias' old 1926 T-Model Ford or a wagon pulled by a team of horses and driven to market.

It was quite a job raising nine acres of tobacco. The fruits of their labor were the big checks Elias and Alma got at the tobacco market. But then you have to keep in mind half the money went to Mr. Case for the Young family's annual rent. The rest of the money they made had to last the family an entire year. It wasn't enough to buy the families groceries at the local grocery store. It was only enough for bare necessities. That's why they had two large gardens and grew several more acres of corn, wheat and potatoes.

Elias and Alma grew two gardens every year during this time. In the summer they prepared their meals right off the vine. Later in the summer Alma with the help of her daughters canned hundreds of jars of corn, beans, tomatoes, peas, and other vegetables. They also canned several jars of jams and jellies.

The first of the two gardens was within a hundred feet of Alma's kitchen door. It had plenty of tomatoes, lettuce, onions, peppers, green beans, cucumbers and various other vegetables. Alma once bragged she had 14 different vegetables in the soup she was cooking on the stove that day.

The second garden was a couple of hundred yards away from the house. Where they grew potatoes, sweet corn, and a long row of popcorn. They also grew other vegetables they wanted to grow in large quantities. This garden was probably an acre in size.

Elias also grew several acres of field corn every year. The main purpose of this corn was to feed his work horse, mule, two milk cows and the two hogs he raised every year. Elias also had some of the corn ground into cracked corn at the local mill for Alma's chickens and a sack or two of corn mill for Alma to make cornbread.

Elias grew several acres of wheat that would be ground into flower for Alma's tasty biscuits and pies.

The Young family was also fortunate to have several other fruits, berries, and nuts that grew wild on the Case Farm. First there was the apple orchard. There were six large apple trees in the orchard. Four grew very sweet and tasty yellow apples. The other two grew what were known as horse apples. They were a green apple with lots of flavor. The farm also had four large cherry trees. Two were black heart cherries and two were red heart cherries. Alma used these to make jam and pie.

About a mile away from the house was a big blackberry patch. They grew wild and were plentiful every year. The family loved for Alma to uses these to make blackberry cobbler. When Elias would rotate crops from one field to another each year it seemed the idle fields found a way of producing a crop of dewberries. They simply came up and produced bountiful crops of berries. Deep in the woods there were also a couple of persimmon trees. They were good for making pies and persimmon pudding. Of course you'd better pick them ripe. Green persimmons were very bitter.

Elias had his own personal candy store in the back yard. He found a big fig bush back there when they moved to the Case Place. He couldn't wait for the figs to get ripe each summer. Each one was like eating a small candy bar.

And finally there were those wonderful hickory nut trees. At the end of summer the hickory nuts would fall to the ground and the Young children would pick them up by the buckets full and save them for eating during the winter. Times were hard during the depression, but the family of Elias and Alma Young took advantage of their surroundings and never saw a hungry day.

After they had moved in Elias and Hubert had as their top priority cutting and splitting enough firewood for the rest of the winter. It was mid-February and there were still two and a half months of cold weather ahead.

Elias searched the woods near the house and found a large maple tree blown over by the wind; probably last March. He checked the wood and it was dry. He knew that dry wood burned better in the fireplace. He also found a large oak limb that had fallen off one of the big oak trees in the front yard.

"I believe this will do us, Hubert." Elias said. "Let's get to work."

Elias and Hubert hitched Dan and Kit to the wagon, took the big two man crosscut saw, an ax, a maul, and a steel wedge and were off to work. The first thing they had to do was cut the wood with the crosscut saw into 18" lengths. That was a lot of hand sawing for the two. Once this was done; the large pieces had to be split with an ax into small enough pieces to fit into the fireplace. Some of the wood was a little harder to split and in those cases they had to use the maul and wedge.

Three days later Elias and Hubert had a tin covered shed full of wood behind the house. They felt sure it would last the rest of the winter.

Splitting the small pieces of pine and poplar needed for Alma's wood cook stove was Raymond's job. Raymond spent six or eight hours a week chopping cook stove wood all during the 1930's. He didn't mind. It was a necessity for the family and he knew that without it his momma wouldn't be able to make his favorite, cornbread.

A couple of days later Elias, Hubert, and Raymond got started on a new tobacco plant bed. They needed enough tobacco plants to plant a nine acre crop. They found a clearing in the woods and began plowing a 50 feet by 100 feet area to plant the tobacco seeds.

After getting the texture of the soil just right they planted the seeds. Tobacco seeds are really small. To be able to spread the seeds over the large plant bed area Elias thoroughly mixed them in a bucket of dry sand. He then broadcast the tobacco seeds over the entire plant bed area. After completing this task they covered the plant bed with cheese cloth. The cheese cloth protected the delicate tobacco sprouts and also partially shaded the plants from the harsh sun. Elias knew what he was doing. He had performed this task every year for the last 30 years.

Work is never done on the farm. After planting the tobacco plant bed Elias and Hubert planted five acres of corn and two acres of wheat. Then they planted Alma's garden near the house and they planted the big garden full of potatoes and several types of corn. All of these crops needed tending after planting and the work was hard. He had the entire family help and he knew a 10 or 15 minutes rest under a large shade tree every couple of hours could really help everyone's stamina. He even made sure his horse; Dan got a rest after every few rounds of plowing a field. Elias worked from the time the sun rose to sundown, but he knew the value of a break to himself, his help, and his animals.

A little later in the spring Alma came to Elias with some wonderful news.

"Elias", she grinned, "I'm going to have another baby!!"

Elias was so pleased; he and Alma loved children.

Work continued all during the summer. Every week there were two to three barns of tobacco to put in and there was the need for picking fruit, vegetables, and canning.

The family worked hard together and everyone pulled their weight. By late Fall Elias and Alma had sold their first crop of tobacco and it brought a good price. Alma and the girls had canned over 300 jars of vegetables, fruits, jellies, and jams. They were stocked well for winter.

On March 15, 1931 Elias and Alma's eighth child, Clyde was born. All the family was so proud of him. He would grow to have the Young good looks, would be a hard worker and in the late 1940's and early 1950's he would be one of the community's best baseball players.

In the fall of 1931 Opal finally got to start first grade. She was a big girl now and going to school every day with her brothers and sisters.

In 1932 Alma came to Elias with more good news. "Elias, I'm going to have another baby!"   Elias grinned from ear to ear.   On April 11, 1933 Juanita was born. She was the ninth child of the family and would be the last child they would have. The family rarely called her Juanita. They preferred to call her Wonnie and the name sticks to this day.

In the fall of 1934 Raymond did something no other family member had been able to do since the beginning of the Great Depression in 1929. He got a salaried job outside the home driving a school bus for Oak Ridge School every morning and every afternoon. He parked the bus right in the front yard of their family home at the Case Place.   No longer would the Young Children need to wait outside on cold mornings for the bus.

Raymond knew it was hard times for his family and shared his earnings to help the family in many ways. On Christmas Day of 1934 Raymond had a huge surprise for the family. When they got up that morning he was smiling one of those big Young smiles at the breakfast table.

"Why are you grinning so big?" Alma asked.

"You'll see after breakfast." Raymond replied. "I got the family something special."

After breakfast Alma and the girls washed and dried the dishes as fast as possible. They were dying to see what Raymond had for the family

"Lets all go to the parlor." Raymond grinned.

Elias, Alma and the rest of the children all rushed to see what Raymond had bought for them.

"There it is!! A brand new battery powered Philco radio and it's not one of those little ones. This cabinet stands four feet tall."

You got us this! Alma explained. "Turn it on; I want to hear it."

The entire family sat around the room as Raymond switched from channel to channel.

"We'll have the news right here inside our home, we'll get to listen to music and they have all kinds of weekly shows for us to listen to." Raymond said.

For the next two hours, the family did nothing but sit around and listen to the radio.

Raymond had bought the Young family a major advancement with this new technology inside their home. The whole outside world would now be at their fingertips. Before the only way they got news was when Elias went to the nearby country store and sat around and talked to the men neighbors.

Raymond didn't tell them at the time, but he had to pay $5.00 a month for the next eight months to purchase it. He didn't mind he knew he had made his family happy and proud.

In 1935 Annie met a young man named Clifton Crutchfield. Annie knew after only a short while this was going to be the love of her life. Both Elias and Alma liked Clifton. He seemed to have a good head on his shoulders and was a logical thinker.

By late September Clifton and Annie set their wedding date for November 23, 1935. Annie was looking forward to the big day, but one thing was lacking. She wanted so bad to have a beautiful wedding dress for her wedding. With money so short she did not want to ask her parents to buy it. Two weeks before the wedding on a Saturday morning Raymond asked Annie if she would go with him to talk to Elias. She thought this was unusual, but she followed him outside to the yard. "Papa," Raymond said, "I need to borrow the Model T this morning. My sister is getting married in two weeks and she doesn't have a wedding dress. They say they have some beautiful ones in Greensboro and I want to buy her one." Annie stood there stunned. A tear slowly trickled down her cheek.

Elias smiled and said, "Raymond take the car and don't worry about the gas. I'll pay for it. Now go on!"

With that Raymond and Annie were off to Greensboro. Annie tried on several dresses that morning. She wanted the perfect dress. Raymond patiently allowed her to take her time. He knew this was a special moment.

Finally she got the dress that met all her desires and Raymond with a big smile nodded his approval.

In November Annie and Clifton had a wedding and all of their families were there. The beautiful bride was so proud of her wedding dress.

Clifton and Annie would live in Oak Ridge for a couple of years and then Clifton got a job with a cotton mill in Greensboro called Cone Mills. They had a house to rent right beside the factory. Clifton rose through the ranks quickly and soon became a chemist specializing in colors and dies and over time became a great asset to the company.

The couple would become the first City Slickers of the family and they all did very well, but Annie never let them forget their family roots and values. The Biblical teachings from her mother would always lead Annie's and Clifton's decisions.

In 1936 the Young family did their usual plantings including nine acres of tobacco. The tobacco matured and appeared to be another good crop.

Then just as the tobacco started to bloom those big pink blossoms on top Elias noticed on some of the leaves a brownish dead area around the perimeter of some of the leaves.

In his more than 40 years of growing tobacco crops he had never seen this on his plants. Elias got in his Model T and drove down to the local country store to talk to some of the other local farmers.

One of the old timers said, "Elias, it sounds to me like you have a disease in your plants known as Ringfire. It's really rare. I only saw it once about 10 years ago. It could affect your whole crop. You see, the perimeter of every leaf dies. Wish I could tell you something different."

The man was right and the entire crop did as he said. Elias could only salvage what he could from the crop.

The family worked as hard as ever, but at the end of the season when Elias started selling his crop at auction some of the tobacco only brought ¼ cent per pound. The rest only went for a few pennies per pound. After paying Mr. Case half for rent the entire crop made his family a profit of $27.00.

The night of the final sale and after all the figures had been run Elias was so depressed he could hardly talk.

Alma saw how depressed the normally happy Elias was and sat down beside him and gave him a long hard talk.

"Don't you worry, Elias, we'll get by" Alma said trying to reassure him. "We have 40 bushels of sweet potatoes and 30 bushels of Irish potatoes in the tobacco barns and they will last all winter there. We have over 300 canned quart jars of tomatoes, green beans, corn, and pickles. We have several dozen jars of jellies and jams. We can buy a hundred pounds of flour for a dollar at the water powered mill right up the road here. There are chickens running around the yard we can eat and they provide us 7 or 8 fresh eggs per day. We have two hogs fattening in the pig pen and we have two milk cows in the barn. You know me and the children will work with you to get through this winter."

Elias began to smile. It was good to know the cupboard was full and the family was going to work together to get through the winter. But, Elias had no illusions. He knew it would be hard.

The main thing Elias had going for him this winter would be his wife, Alma. She was a survivor and she would make sure the family got through the winter.

Although it was going to be a hard year there was good news around the corner for the Young family. While in school in Oak Ridge Hazel and Edna became friends with a young lady named Annie Mae Rierson who lived across the road from the Young's. Often times after school Annie Mae would get off the bus with Hazel and Edna and spend the evening at their house. It was here that Annie Mae met their older brother, Hubert. Hubert took after his father with his tall slender build. Before long Annie Mae was visiting the Young house often, but not to see Hazel or Edna. She was there to spend time with Hubert. Within a few years everyone knew that Hubert and Annie Mae were a perfect match.

October 24, 1936 was the big day for the new couple. Early that morning both of their families gathered in the Young's front yard and wished them luck as Hubert, Annie Mae and two of their friends set out on a trip north to Danville, Virginia. 75 years later Annie Mae still remembers this day well. With a grin on her face she begins telling the story of that day. "This was before Clyde and Juanita had even started school. I was 17 and Hubert was 24. You had to be 18 to get married here in North Carolina so when I got to Danville I was 18". She laughs as she remembers pretending to be 18 that day so she could return home as Mrs. Hubert Young.

After returning to Oak Ridge as a married couple Hubert and Annie Mae entered the Young's house to find the entire family waiting for them around the dining room table. Alma and the girls had prepared a huge meal to celebrate their wedding. For the first 3 months of their marriage they lived upstairs in Hubert's bedroom while they saved their money and made plans to one day have a home of their own. In late February 1937 they had saved enough money to rent a small house across the road from the Young's. It was a perfect location for the new couple. Annie Mae was next door to her mother's house and Hubert was just across the road from the Young's farm.

It wasn't long before Hubert and Annie Mae shared exciting news with their families. They were expecting their first child. It was an exciting year for the Young's and on July 21, 1937 their first and only son, Carl Avery Young was born.

In 1938 two of Elias and Alma's children were married. First Raymond met Ruby Sizemore. Ruby lived with her parents across the road from the Young's. Raymond and Ruby's friends, John Lee and his wife, went with them to the home of Arthur Jones who was the Justice of the Peace and performed the ceremony. They came home as Mr. and Mrs. Raymond Young. Just like the other siblings they lived with Elias and Alma until they had saved enough money to rent a house nearby in Oak Ridge. It was not long before they rented the larger Lowery farm at the end of Union Grove Church Road in Oak Ridge. It was here that their first child Ken was born. Raymond and Ruby would make one more move and raise 3 more children in the coming years.

Soon after Raymond was married it was Hazel's turn. She met and fell in love with Marvin K. Moore. Since times were so hard for the first couple of years of marriage Hazel and Marvin lived with Elias and Alma at the Case Place.

During this time they had their first child Norma. In 1940 Marvin got a job with the Gibsonville Police department and soon after he and Hazel moved to Gibsonville, North Carolina. At the time Hazel was expecting their second child and a few months later MK was born.

In 1940 Edna met Raymond Goins. Edna knew this man was special and they were soon married. Raymond had one of the first motorcycles in the area and Edna loved to go for long rides with Raymond. Raymond was a welder by trade and had no trouble finding work. He could build mechanical machinery from the ground up. A few years later when World War II broke out in 1941 Raymond and Edna bought a camper they could pull behind their car and moved to Norfolk, Virginia where Raymond worked as a welder throughout the war. Edna was a master of making do with what she had and they got along just fine in the small camper. If they wanted to go back home to visit Elias and Alma they simply hooked the camper to the back of the car and came back to Oak Ridge.

On December 7, 1941 the whole world changed. The Japanese had attacked Pearl Harbor in the Pacific and there was talk of World War II. Who in the family would go to war? What changes would be made to the Young's way of life? Only the future would tell.

Even with all of this going on Elias heard of a farm for sale on Bowman Road in Oak Ridge, North Carolina about five miles from where they lived. Elias and Alma jumped in their car and rode over to look the farm over and they liked what they saw. Elias had lost the chance to buy a farm 12 years earlier and he wasn't going to let this opportunity pass him by. A firm handshake with the owner and a deal was struck. Elias and Alma were finally going to own a farm.

They Thought…

Elias and Alma Young in
the 1930's.

Opal Young when she was 7 years
old and Clyde Young when he
was One year old. In the background is one of the many big 100
year old oak trees in The Case
Place front yard. This picture is
from 1932.

Hubert and Annie Mae Young when they first got married in 1936.

This is a picture of four of the Young sisters. Top from left are Edna and Hazel. Bottom from left are Opal and Elsie. This picture was taken in 1934.

The picture above is of the (Oak Ridge School) school bus Raymond Young drove during the mid-1930's. It was the first salaried job by a Young household member since the beginning of the Great Depression, which started in 1929. In the picture are Elias and Alma's children, top from left Edna and Annie and bottom from left Clyde and Hazel. This picture is from 1934.

TAYLOR'S WAREHOUSE

For the Sale of — Leaf Tobacco

Insurance and Storage Free — All Errors Promptly Corrected

TAYLOR WAREHOUSE COMPANY, Proprietors

Winston-Salem, N. C., ~~OCT 4 1934~~ 193.......

Sale Made for *C F Young & Cose*

NO.	POUNDS	PRICE	TOTAL
	296	9½	28 1
411329	10	36	3 60
	100	26	26
	136	18	24 8
	5 42		8 2 0
LESS WAREHOUSE CHARGES		60	3 5
AUCTION FEES		90	
COMMISSION 2½ PER CENT		2 0	78 65
ADVANCES			
FREIGHT AND DRAYAGE			
NET PROCEEDS		$	

This is a receipt from a portion of their tobacco crop that was sold at Taylor's Warehouse in Winston Salem, NC. At this sale on October 4, 1934 they sold 542 pounds of tobacco and made $78.65. A week later on October 10th they sold another 320 pounds for $80.49. That season they brought home nearly $160.

Chapter Five

Living on the Lowery Farm

It was 1942 and everything was changing around the family of Elias and Alma Young. First and foremost was the fact that the Japanese had attacked Pearl Harbor, Hawaii a few months earlier bringing the United States of America into World War II. With this event everything changed.

For the family of Elias and Alma Young, who had endured over a decade of the Great Depression it meant many opportunities would open up for the entire family. Hubert, the oldest son of the Young family had put it well a few years earlier, "During the depression you couldn't buy a job!" How things had changed. Suddenly jobs and opportunities were everywhere.

As for the Young family children many were adults now and leading solid lives of their own. Hubert, the oldest son had married Annie Mae Rierson and they had decided farming would be their way of life. Hubert raised mainly tobacco for a living and he and Annie Mae were so proud of their three young children, Carl, Loretta, and Brenda, who would come in 1944.

Annie, the Young's second oldest daughter had married Clifton Crutchfield and after farming for a while, Clifton was hired by Cone Mills in Greensboro, North Carolina.

Clifton proved to be a very smart individual and was chosen to be one of Cone Mills first chemists. Clifton was self taught in this field, but his abilities to innovate and maintain strong documentation of his findings made him a very valuable employee to the company.

Cone Mills made sure Clifton was well looked after, providing he and Annie a home in downtown Greensboro, NC, which was within walking distance of Clifton's job. Clifton and Annie were also proud to be the parents of three beautiful daughters at the time, Jo-Anne, Wilma and Phyllis.

Raymond had married Ruby Sizemore and he decided at the time to make a career working for a local silk mill as well as farming tobacco. Raymond and Ruby were also the proud parents of two fine young boys, Ken and Gary.

Hazel had married Marvin K. Moore Sr. and they had recently moved to Stokesdale, North Carolina. They decided to make their living by starting a country store in Stokesdale and would run it there for the next decade. Hazel and Marvin were also very proud to be the parents of their two young children Norma Jean and MK Jr.

The next daughter in line, Edna had recently married a young man by the name of Raymond Goins. Raymond was a welder by trade and could build almost anything. When World War II broke out he and Edna bought a mobile home, which they could pull behind their car and they moved to Newport News, Virginia. Raymond would spend the rest of the war building ships for the war effort, both transport and battle ships. Although Edna and Raymond both loved children, they never would never have any of their own.

As for Elias and Alma, they were on the verge of a major move themselves. They had rented the Case Place for the past twelve years and wanted to buy their own farm.

Finally in the spring of 1942 Elias struck a deal to purchase the 200 acre Lowery Farm, which was located about five miles from the Case Place. The farm was in the Oak Ridge community on Bowman Road, *(now known as Pepper Road)* and none of his remaining children at home would have to switch schools.

Elias had a simple plan to pay for the farm. He would use the profits from his nine acre allotment of tobacco to pay down the farm each fall. A firm handshake with the Lowery Farm owner and the deal was struck. Within a matter of a few days Elias, Alma, and their four remaining children still at home; Opal, Elsie, Clyde and Wonnie moved their belongings to the new farm.

Opal still remembers her and Elsie skipping and hopping through the house singing, "We're going to own our own home!" The big white 2-story house had five rooms downstairs and two large bedrooms upstairs. For the first time in any of their lives the Young family would have electric power.

Elias remembered well going to the power company to get the power turned on for the big white house. "Mr. Young, we won't be able to get out today to turn on your power. It will have to be tomorrow. Can you wait?"

Elias grinned and replied, "Mam, I've not had electric power in my home for over 50 years. I think I can wait one more day."

At the time of the move Elias was 52 years old and Alma was 49. The ages of their four remaining children living at home were; Opal, 17, Elsie, 15, Clyde 10 and Wonnie was 8.

The 200 acre Lowry Farm was really a beautiful place and it had everything needed to make a smooth transition from the Case Place and continue their normal farm life.

Besides the big white house there was another large building right behind the house. The family used it for storage and the gasoline powered washing machine Alma would soon purchase. Elias also had a large pork meat box in this building for storing salted down pork meat over the winter. Elias kept his cured shoulders and hams hanging from the rafters in the well house.

Across Bowman Road from the big white house were a whole complex of farm structures necessary for running a farm.

First there was the feed barn. It was a strong structure consisting of two hay lofts, a second storage area on the ground floor for hay and two large work horse stalls. One was for Elias's black work horse, Dan, who was now 32 years old and the other was for his golden colored mare, Puss Goldie.

Beside the barn was a hog pen where Elias and Alma raised two hogs every year. The hogs would be killed and dressed every winter after first frost, providing meat and cooking lard for the next year. Every year this would be repeated.

Also located in this complex was a large wood shed, enclosed on three sides. This building kept the firewood and wood cook stove wood dry. There was a carport with a room for the work horses' harnesses and other equipment. To the back of this structure was a stall where the family milk cow stayed.

There was a large corn crib close to the barn where a year round supply of field corn ears were stored to feed the two work horses, the milk cow, and the two hogs Elias raised each year.

About 200 feet behind the feed barn were three wood fired tobacco barns. Two of the barns were large barns capable of holding over 400 sticks of tobacco each. The third tobacco barn was what Elias called the half-barn. It was much smaller capable of holding about 250 sticks of tobacco.

All three tobacco barns were needed back then for the nine acres of tobacco they grew. You could see the family up at daylight removing 400 sticks of cured tobacco and by 7:30 A.M. be in the field pulling another barn of green tobacco.

Behind the tobacco barns were the remaining 180 or so acres of farm fields and timberland. At least 50 acres of land had been cleared for farming over the years. The farmland was cleared in 5 to 10 acre plots all connected by a long dirt road down through the woods. The remaining timberland was filled with pine trees, oak trees, maple trees and poplars.

Elias was a wise farmer and planned on using the farm fields properly. He would make sure he rotated his crops every year making certain not to deplete the soil of its necessary nutrients.

In all Elias planned on planting nine acres of tobacco, 12 acres of field corn for the animals, four acres of corn for the family to eat, five acres of wheat, an acre of Irish potatoes, an acre of sweet potatoes, an acre of watermelons and muskmelons, and across the road behind the big white house about two acres of vegetable gardens.

The fruit and nut trees were another major source of food on the Lowery Farm. The fruit and nut trees. Deep in the woods, right between two of the main tobacco growing fields was a huge persimmon tree. Not only did it provide lots of persimmons for Alma's wonderful pies, it would also be one of Elias's favorite shady spots to rest his work horses on hot summer days.

To the back of the big white house was an orchard consisting of five apple trees and two peach trees. These would provide fresh fruit in summer and jellies and preserves for the long winter months. There was a pecan tree right across the road from the big white house. It would provide thousands of pecans every year. Saving the sweetest for last there were two huge cherry trees; one a black heart cherry tree inside the hog pen and a pink cherry tree right outside the hog pen. Many of Elias and Alma's grandchildren would climb those trees in summer over the years and eat their fill of the sweet fruits. To Elias and Alma this farm was nearly perfect. It was everything they wanted for themselves and to continue raising their family.

In the spring of 1942 Elias did what he had done every year as far back as he could remember. First he prepared a tobacco plant bed to grow the young plants for his nine acre tobacco crop. Next he planted corn, wheat, Irish potatoes, sweet potatoes and two acres of gardens near the big white house. On many occasions you may see Hubert or Raymond driving up to give a hand. With Alma, Opal, Elsie, Clyde, and Wonnie always willing to pitch in wherever needed Elias always found a way to get the work done. The planting went well that spring of 1942 and even though there was a World War going on in Europe and the Pacific Elias and Alma had so much to be thankful for.

Then one evening there was a knock on Elias and Alma's door. It was the owner of the Lowery Place with some very bad news.

He asked Elias and Alma to come out and sit on the porch, because they needed to talk.

"Elias, I've decided to sell the Lowery Place to a nephew," the man said.

You could see the fire in Elias's eyes as the information sunk in.

"We shook hands and had a deal! A man's word is his bond in this day and age! You can't do that to me!" Elias shouted as his voice rose with every additional word.

"Well, legally I can," the man replied. "You see, you didn't put any money down on the farm and my nephew got a lawyer and he did. It's all legal."

"My nephew said you can live here as long as you want," the man continued. "You will pay him the rent of half the profits of your nine acres of tobacco."

Elias was so angry he wanted to wring the man's neck, but wisely he held his temper. Then Elias replied, "I think you'd better leave now. I have a strong urge to kick your…." With that, the man scampered off the porch and ran to his car.

Opal, who had been listening from inside the house through a window still remembers this moment. "I was so angry I went and tried to kick the back screen door off the hinges!" she sighed. "For the second time in his life my Papa had lost the opportunity to buy his own farm."

The next day Elias went to town to hire his own lawyer. This could not stand he thought to himself. A man's word is supposed to be his bond. When Elias sat down with the lawyer the first question he asked was, "How much earnest money did you put down to buy the farm, Mr. Young?" "Actually, I didn't put down any," Elias replied. "We shook hands." Then the lawyer gave Elias the sad news, "Elias if you had given the man $10 dollars he couldn't have done what he did. As sad as it sounds, what he did is legal and quite honestly I can't help you." After a couple of days of total anger and frustration Alma decided it was time for the family to sit down and talk about this situation. Alma had a way of putting things into perspective, even in the worst of times.

Elias, Alma, Opal, Elsie, Clyde and Wonnie all went out and sat on the front porch where they could at least enjoy the evening cool air. "Family, this is one of the toughest things we have ever faced." Alma said. "It's as though someone has stolen something from us and we can't do anything about it. Now, we can live in anger and frustration for the next month, year, or decade and it won't change anything. I for one refuse to let these horses hind ends ruin another day of my life. I'm going to go inside after a while put my head on my pillow and get a good night's sleep. Tomorrow morning I'm going to wake up a happy person and get on with my life. And if each of you knows what's good for your own hearts you will do the same thing." The rest of the family sat there silently and let the words slowly sink in as to what Alma had said. Not much was said after that. Then, as darkness set in on the porch Elias grinned that special grin he had and said, "Well, Mama, let's go get a good night's sleep."

The next morning Alma and Elias were up at 5:00 A.M. cooking breakfast for the family. And at Alma's suggestion they decided to sing a few happy tunes. It was a hard thing to take what had happened to them, but they knew the best thing they could do would be to simply move on and be happy in their hearts.

In late 1943 Opal and Elsie were starting to go out and meet some of the young gentlemen of the community. One night they planned on going on a double date with two young men, one from Oak Ridge and one from nearby Kernersville, NC. Elsie thought she would be going with Pete Flynt. Opal would be going with the other gentleman from Oak Ridge. As they walked out to the car somehow the two sisters switched dates. Such a simple thing they thought. As it turned out Opal began dating Pete on a regular basis and soon Opal knew she had met the love of her life.

Keep in mind there was a war going on and things could change suddenly. And as luck would have it they did for Opal and Pete.

One evening Pete came to see Opal and told her the bad news. I got a draft notice and I have to go into the Army next week. They knew this would be a hard time for both of them. With all the lives being lost in the horrendous battles in Europe there was even an unspoken concern he may not come back, but they never talked about that. Pete was going to miss Opal so much.

"Honey, I'll write you every day!" Pete promised.

"And I'll do the same!!" Opal replied.

Then before they knew it Pete was taking nine weeks of basic training at Fort Bragg, North Carolina. After a short stay at a base in Maryland he was transferred to Fort McClellan Army Base in Anniston, Alabama.

Opal and Pete both knew this would be the last stop before Pete was shipped overseas. Pete did not want to wait until he got back from overseas to marry Opal and she did not want to wait either.

A formal proposal and a couple of passionate love letters later the final decision was made. Opal was going to Alabama to marry Pete. Opal packed her suitcase and quickly made plans to go. Her first stop was to spend the night in Greensboro, NC with her sister, Annie's family. After a good night's sleep Clifton drove Opal to the train station where she bought her ticket to Anniston, Alabama. Opal still remembers the train traveling the back woods areas of South Carolina and Alabama and seeing how rundown the old depression era houses looked. It gave her a new appreciation for the quality of life her Mama and Papa had given her.

When Opal got to Anniston Pete was beaming from ear to ear. All of the plans had been made. Opal would spend the night at a nearby boarding house and the next day they would be married. Everything worked as planned and Pete's Army buddies made sure the couple had some privacy the next couple of days at a nearby bungalow.

Sadly, it was short and sweet and then Opal was on her way back to North Carolina. Pete got his orders a week later and was on his way to Europe on a Navy ship. When he got there he was immediately sent to Belgium. There the Allied forces were in a major battle with the German forces known as The Battle of the Bulge.

Pete, whose job was to carry a bazooka, recalled the fierce fighting on the battle fields during that time. He once had a large fir tree right beside him blown to tiny bits by an enemy mortar shell. One night while attempting to get some sleep in a freshly dug fox hole, Pete's unit was overrun by the Germans. He and eight other members of his platoon were captured. During the confusion Pete raised his hands and a German soldier shot him in his left hand.

Pete and his fellow captors were taken to a nearby make shift basement prison where they waited to see if they would live or die.

Only brave heroics by Pete and some of the other soldiers saved some of the men's lives.

Back home Opal received word from the Army that Pete was missing in action, but that's all she knew. She didn't even know if he was dead or alive. It would be six weeks before she would hear about Pete's condition. Then one day she got a letter in the mail. It was from Pete! "Hi Honey, I'm in an allied hospital in France. I got captured by the Germans and I got shot in the hand. I'm OK and they say in a couple more weeks they're going to let me come home. It was the spring of 1945. Opal was so glad to hear the news. Pete was finally coming home."

Within three more months the Allied Forces of The United States, Great Brittian and France, from the east and Russia from the west finally battled the German's into submission. The war would cost millions of lives, but to the people of the United States of America it was worth it. Freedom meant that much to them.

All that was left now was the battle in the Pacific. The Japanese had promised they would battle hand to hand to the last man. Some U.S. military planners projected as many as two million more American lives may be lost to defeat the Japanese in this manner.

When the U.S. dropped the first atomic weapon on the Japanese city of Hiroshima the Japanese people thought it was a fluke. Nothing in the world of war was that powerful.

When the U.S. dropped the second atomic bomb on Nagasaki, Japan they knew the United States could literally wipe them off the face of the earth. Within a few days the Japanese surrendered totally ending World War II. It was finally over and now all of our boys across the United States were coming home.

In 1946 Elias and Alma had established in their hearts that the Lowery Farm was going to be their home for years to come. The land grew good crops and it was a wonderful place to raise their children.

There had been a few changes since the war ended. Their daughter, Opal, who had married Pete Flynt during the war, had moved to Sandy Ridge, North Carolina where she and Pete farmed tobacco.

The children still living at home were Elsie, who was 16 years old, Clyde who was 13 and Wonnie who was 11.

The biggest change however was the fact that the Lowery Farm big white house had become the hub of all of Elias's and Alma's extended family.

Every Sunday afternoon Elias and Alma's children and their grandchildren would come back home for a few hours to eat and visit with family. While the men folk talked outside under a shade tree the women would be gossiping and telling of their week inside. In the yard you could see a dozen or more grandchildren running and playing games like tag and baseball. It was a fun place for the entire family. On many of those Sundays someone would bring a camera and take a few pictures. The famous family line-up pictures would become a standard for the Young family for years to come.

The biggest Sunday event of the year for the family was always on Mother's Day. After everyone had gone to church the family gathered for lunch. Each family prepared and brought their favorite meats, casseroles and vegetables there were also cakes and pies for dessert. This event was always held outside with either a big flat bed farm trailer or saw bucks and boards with table cloths spread over the top used to hold all the food. And believe me; no one went home hungry that day.

Several other traditions were started during this time as well. All of the grandchildren loved to come and spend the night at Grandma and Grandpa Young's house. During the school year they may spend a night or two on weekends. During the summer they may spend a whole week at a time. Every grandchild will still tell that Grandma Young had the best hugs and each grandchild felt they were her favorite. When the grandchildren stayed, their main directions from their parents were to mind and to help in any way you could. There was a lot of work to be done on the farm and your job while there was to pitch in and help.

There were a lot of perks to going to Grandma and Grandpa's house. On May 1st everybody got to go barefooted.

Then there were those big cherry trees over at the hog pen. Shimmy up one of those trees and you could get the sweetest treat on earth. There was always plenty of work to do and Grandma and Grandpa made it seem more like fun than work.

For the boys, they may need to help feed hay or corn to the animals. They may get to help put the harnesses on the work horses and ride those horses to the field.

Some of the work was hard, like suckering tobacco or getting those nasty looking green horn worms off the leaves of the tobacco. But Grandpa Young took frequent breaks and had a half gallon mason jar of water resting under a shade tree if you got thirsty. As for the granddaughters, they helped Grandma do all kinds of things around the house. They may be learning how to make homemade biscuits at breakfast, then going to the garden with a big bucket and picking a mess of green beans for lunch. There was always some kind of vegetable to be canned and many of the granddaughters still use Grandma Young's methods to this day.

When it came to putting in a barn of tobacco, everybody helped. The boys would go to the field and pull sled loads of tobacco while the girls helped string the tobacco onto sticks at the tobacco barn. After that was done everybody helped carry and hang those 400 or more sticks of tobacco in the barn. Grandpa Young still cured tobacco with wood back then and the boys enjoyed spending the night with Grandpa and listening to old tales of ghosts.

The grandchildren were not always working on their visits. The boys enjoyed playing and climbing in the barn and everybody loved playing in the vast woods. Grandma always had one of those 500 word puzzles to work on and there were Rook cards and a checker board if you wanted to play a game.

Grandma Young also introduced most of her grandchildren to the board game, Monopoly. On any given Saturday you could see her on the floor playing this game with three or four of her grandchildren.

These were great times and the Young grandchildren would carry on these visits for years to come. Each grandchild will tell you the things they learned at Grandma and Grandpa Young's. They taught them a strong work ethic and how to spend each day enjoying their work.

Also during this time Alma had a neighbor a couple of hundred yards up the road who started to work for Adam-Millis, a local sock and hosiery manufacturer located in nearby Kernersville, North Carolina. The factory was only about five miles up the road.

One day Alma's neighbor came to Alma and told her Adam-Millis was hiring and recommended that she would be a great employee. Alma at first laughed at the idea even though it made her feel pretty good she was recommended. After more consideration and a long talk with Elias, Alma went and applied. She was excited and nervous when they told her she got the job. Alma did not have a car, but the neighbor let Alma ride with her.

During this time Adam-Millis had a special savings program where you could buy a savings bond every month. Alma quietly joined the plan and began saving money. She had a secret reason for saving this money.

There were a few changes in schooling in the late 1940's for the Young family. Elsie and Clyde had to change schools when they went to high school from Oak Ridge School to Colfax High School. It was a longer bus ride but there were also some good things that happened because of this.

For Elsie, that is where she met a boy in her class named Reavis Marshall. At the time he was one of the top high school baseball prospects around. After graduating high school he was quickly signed by the Boston Braves minor league organization, and was off to show his skills. While Elsie and Reavis did begin dating some at the time, it was not meant to be for them to commit their lives to each other quite yet. Elsie would go on to graduate from Colfax High School in June of 1948.

Clyde also enjoyed going to Colfax High School. In addition to his studies he was also a great high school baseball player. All those chores he did around the farm made him a strong young man. He played first base and he could field with the best of them. During his senior year the whole area took notice of his skills. He was so good he made the Guilford All-County Baseball Team. For a country boy from Oak Ridge competing with young men from both the cities of Greensboro and High Point that was quite a feat. Clyde proudly graduated from Colfax High School in 1950.

Wonnie was also coming of age during this time to start dating and soon met a fine young man she liked named Rufus McCormick. Wonnie had to make a hard decision at the time. Did she want to continue on going to high school or did she want to marry Rufus. She knew Rufus was the love of her life and decided to go ahead and get married. In 1950 the couple tied the knot and later settled in Greensboro, North Carolina. There, both Rufus and Wonnie got jobs with J.P. Stevens where they made the still famous Wrangler jeans.

Their marriage was a good decision and as of this writing the two have been married for 62 years and counting.

Wonnie never forgot her decision not to finish high school and vowed some day she would. In the mid-1980's she went back to high school at Guilford Technical Community College and in 1986 she got her High School diploma. It was one of her proudest moments.

There were several more grandchildren born into the Young family between 1946 and 1956. Hubert and Annie Mae Young added a daughter, Barbara. Clifton and Annie Crutchfield added a son, Cliff, and a daughter, Maggie. Raymond and Ruby Young added a son, Ronnie and daughter, Linda. Pete and Opal Flynt added three children, Shirley, Jimmy, and Gracie. Juanita and Rufus had a daughter, Lynn, and a son named Gordon. This was a happy time for the extended Young family. They were all spreading their wings.

In the early 1950's the size of the family still living at home was getting smaller and smaller. With Wonnie marrying Rufus McCormick and moving to Greensboro, that only left Elsie and Clyde at home. Both of them had graduated from high school and Elias and Alma both knew it was just a matter of time before they would be on to a life of their own.

Alma and Elias did not really discuss this much, but they both knew it would be a lonely time for them without any children to raise. It is all they had done for nearly 40 years. They were wonderful parents teaching their children strong moral values, a faith in God, and a strong work ethic. The family would come in on weekends and they knew there would be grandchildren in summer spending two or three days with them all summer long. Maybe they wouldn't get too lonely.

Elsie continued living at home during the early 1950's working for a while at Sears Mail Order in Greensboro, NC and then later for Southern Silk Mill in Kernersville, NC.

Because of the Korean War her boyfriend, Reavis Marshall had joined the U.S. Navy in 1950 and after basic training was stationed in the war zone off the coast of South Korea.

Reavis finished his four years of service with the Navy in 1954 and was honorably discharged. He and Elsie were married in January of 1955.

Clyde also continued to live at home during the early 1950's and helped his father, Elias, raise tobacco.

In the spring of 1954 Hazel and her husband, Marvin Moore, decided to go their separate ways.

When Alma and Elias heard the news they would have it no other way than for Hazel, Norma and M.K. to come and live with them in the big white house on Pepper Road.

This made the transition much easier for Hazel. Soon after moving Hazel got a job with Adams-Millis Hosiery Mill in Kernersville, NC and she would work there the next several years.

Later in 1954 Clyde was drafted into the U.S. Army. He spent a year stateside going through basic training and other forms of special training and then his final year was spent in Germany. Clyde finished his two years of service and was honorably discharged in 1956.

When he returned to Oak Ridge, NC Clyde got a job with Lorillard Tobacco Company in their Research and Product Development Department. He would work there for the next decade.

Also in 1956 Clyde met a beautiful young woman named Shirley Smith. The two started dating and were married later in 1956.

The 15 years on the Lowery Farm had been good years for Elias, Alma, and their family. So many good things had happened during this time. With 1957 approaching both Elias and Alma were starting to think about retiring. They had worked long and hard for so many years. For the first time in their life they were thinking about resting for a while and simply enjoying life.

This is of Elias and Alma and all of their children in 1945. Bottom row from left are Elias and Alma. On the top row from left are Clyde, Hazel, Raymond, Edna, Opal, Hubert, Elsie and Wonnie. The little boy in the window of the car to the right is Hazel's son, MK Moore and the little boy on the running board of the car is Raymond's son, Gary Young.

Above is a picture of Elias and Alma in their front yard when they lived at the Lowery Farm. This picture was probably taken in 1945.

The picture above was taken on the front steps of The Big White House on the Lowery Farm. From left are Elias and Alma's three sons, Clyde, Hubert and Raymond. This picture is from 1947 or 1948.

This picture is of is of all of Elias and Alma's daughters. From left are Annie, Hazel, Edna, Opal, Elsie and Juanita. This picture was taken in April of 1956 at The Lowery Farm.

Elsie and MK in 1953 at the well house drawing water for Elias's work horses Dan, the black horse on the left and Puss Daisy, the golden mare on the right.

This is a great picture from 1946 of the grandchildren on a Sunday afternoon on the front porch steps of The Big White House at The Lowery Farm. From left top row are Carl, Norma, Kay and Ken. From left bottom row are Wilma, JoAnn, Phyllis, Gary Wayne, MK and Shirley.

This is one of those famous Mother's Day Get-togethers at Alma's and Elias's. Top from left are Annie Mae, Ruby, Alma, JoAnne, Ila Mae, Juanita, Lizzie, Annie, Opal, Elsie, Edna, Elias, Hubert, Raymond, Clyde, Pete Flynt, and Raymond Goins. In the front row from left are Brenda, Maggie, Barbara, Shelby, Cliff, Phyllis, Wilma, Faye, Kay, Loretta, Carl, Ken, Billy Hester and Gary. This picture is from 1946.

Elias's tobacco barns he used to cure tobacco from 1942 until 1958 on the Lowery farm. These barns and a third tobacco barn behind them still stand today. This picture was taken in 2011.

This is Alma sprinkling top dressing fertilizer on her green beans in the garden behind the Big White House on the Lowery farm.

Elias and Alma's first great grandchild of the family, Cynthia. In the picture above are Great Grandma Alma, Grandma Annie, Mother JoAnne and Great Granddaughter Cynthia. This picture was taken in 1956 or 1957.

Elias teaching MK how to plow a field with a two-horse team. This picture was taken in 1955.

Elias and Alma's children in the late 1950's. From left are Juanita, Clyde, Elsie, Opal, Edna, Hazel, Raymond, Annie and Hubert.

Chapter Six

1957-1970

The Little Green House

The year was 1957 and Elias and Alma had been living on the Lowery Place for 15 years. During this time Elias had farmed the land growing nine acres of tobacco each year and since the late 1940's Alma had worked at Adams-Millis Hosiery Mill in Kernersville, North Carolina.

Elias was 67 years old now and was feeling his age. The family had worked hard the last few years to help him grow his tobacco crop.

Depending on their work schedules, Elias's son, Hubert and his children would help for a while, then son, Raymond and his family would help as well as Clyde. Hazel, MK, and Norma who lived with Elias and Alma also helped. Elias had to continue farming to pay the rent on the Lowery Farm.

Quietly in the background Alma was working away and she just kept putting those U.S. Savings Bonds back every month for nearly a decade now. Alma was 64 and could soon retire and draw Social Security. If they did not have rent to pay a lot of things could change for her and Elias.

For once in their life things appeared to be falling into place for the couple. For you see right next door to their house was a little green house for sale.

On Sundays after church it was common practice for Elias and Alma's children to bring their families and visit.

Quietly, on one of those Sunday afternoons, while Elias and the men talked under a shade tree outside, and the children played games in the yard, Alma and her daughters went to Alma's little metal box in the corner of the living room. She opened the small box and counted her savings bonds.

You should have seen the smile on Alma's face when the total was finally calculated.

"I have just enough!" Alma grinned. "I have just enough to buy the little house next door. Elias and I will finally own our own home and Elias and I both can retire."

Everything continued to fall into place. Hazel, who was living with Elias and Alma at the time, had just bought a mobile home for herself, MK, and Norma. She could move it behind the Green House and they could live there. Norma and MK were just finishing high school and would soon be moving on themselves.

Elias and Alma both could draw Social Security and they knew they would keep growing a big garden for food.

Alma and Elias struck a deal and the purchase was made. Finally, for the first time in their lives Elias and Alma owned their own home.

Shortly after the move Hazel met a nice gentleman, who lived up Pepper Road from the Young's, named Conrad Morris. Conrad was a carpenter by trade and could build almost anything. Hazel was so glad to meet such a good person. They soon fell in love and in 1958 they were married.

One of the luxuries the little green house did not have when Alma and Elias bought it was an indoor bathroom. Money was so tight after purchasing their new home and Elias and Alma thought they may never have a bathroom inside. They could deal with it. After all, they had never had one before.

Then Hazel's new husband, Conrad had an idea. If each of Elias's and Alma's children would contribute just a little money, he could install the new bathroom himself.

There was just one small problem. Alma would never accept charity from anyone, not even her own children. The bathroom would just have to wait. She taught all of her children you always earn what you get. That's the way it had always been.

Even during the Great Depression when the Federal Government gave away hoop cheese to families for free, Alma would not take it. She loved the taste of this cheese and found that if a neighbor got some she would go to them and barter eggs and garden vegetables for the cheese.

The family got together and tried to figure out a solution. After all, Elias and Alma needed a bathroom inside. Finally Alma found a way that she could live with it. If the children would let her will the money they gave when she passed away, then she would accept the money for the new bathroom.

At last with a deal struck Conrad could get on with the job. He got Opal's husband, Pete Flynt, to help him and soon afterward Elias and Alma had a brand new bathroom.

Alma had worked hard all her life and seldom had free time to do what she wanted to do. Now she did and she took full advantage of it.

Sometimes she would take a few days and go to the North Carolina coast with one of her children and their family and would walk the beach or spend a day pier fishing. She loved catching a mess of fish and having a fish fry afterword.

At other times Alma may take the bus to Greensboro to visit her oldest daughter, Annie, and her family. Annie's daughter, Maggie, still remembers seeing Grandma Young walking down the street to their house.

"We all knew we were going to have a good time when Grandma Young came to visit".

In early 1960 Alma got a chance to go to Washington D.C. Hubert's daughter, Loretta, had recently graduated from high school in 1959 and got a job with the FBI in Washington. When she moved there she didn't take her car because she didn't know her way around. When Loretta came back home to get her car to take back with her she asked her mother, Annie Mae and Grandma Alma, to ride back to Washington with her.

Alma enjoyed the trip so much. She got to see all the sites in Washington and on the way home she and Annie Mae got to take their first passenger train ride home.

Elias also enjoyed the free time of his retirement years. His favorite pastime was going to the beach with family and getting to spend a day pier fishing. Just give him a rod and reel, a mess of shrimp for bait, a bucket of ice for his catch and a 12 ounce Pepsi Cola, and he was ready for a morning of fishing.

In December of 1960 Elias and Alma had a very special celebration. On December 18th they celebrated their 50th Wedding Anniversary. And what a celebration it was. All of the children and their families came on that special Sunday to enjoy cake and punch. Dozens of other friends and neighbors came to visit from miles around.

Elias and Alma could be proud of their accomplishments over the years. At the time they had raised nine wonderful children. They also had 25 grandchildren and four great grandchildren and you can bet they were proud of each and every one of them.

Over the next few years Elias and Alma were blessed with many visits on a weekly basis from the family. In the summer Grandma and Grandpa Young's was the place for the grandchildren to spend a few days or a week. Every grandchild loved the way Grandma Young made each of them feel special and there was always something new to learn.

The granddaughters may be learning how to prepare a stew in the kitchen or Grandpa Young may be giving tips on growing a garden to the grandsons. There was always a cherry tree or an apple tree to climb to get a special treat.

In the summer of 1965 Alma got the opportunity to go on another trip to the North Carolina Coast with her son, Raymond and his wife, Ruby. She was so excited about going.

They had the plans all made. The mornings would be spent pier fishing and every night they had a special dinner planned. When they got to the coast and settled into their room they all went out for a hotdog supper. That night Alma did not feel well and could not get her stomach to settle down. She did not think much of it and thought that after a good night's sleep she would feel better.

The next morning Raymond and Ruby were up early. They were going to fix bacon, eggs, and biscuits for breakfast. They knew Alma would want to do her fair share so they went to wake her so she could help. Raymond called to Alma, but she didn't answer. Then he went closer. Alma had always been easy to wake before. "Mama, get up. I know you want to help me and Ruby fix breakfast this morning." Raymond said. As Raymond got beside her he noticed she did not appear to be breathing. Panic struck Raymond as he realized the situation.

"Mama, Mama, are you OK?" Raymond yelled. Raymond knew in his heart his Mama was gone, but his mind raced and told him to go get help right away. Since they didn't have a phone in the house he quickly jumped in his truck and went to a fire department down the road. They sent a paramedic team back with him to help Alma.

When they arrived and examined Alma they gave Raymond the sad news. She passed away one month before her 72nd birthday.

Tears filled Raymond and Ruby's eyes as the news sunk in. Now Raymond had the sad task of telling the rest of the family. He went to a nearby telephone and started making calls. Every member of the family was saddened by the news. The children had lost their Mama and the grandchildren had lost Grandma Young.

It would take quite a while for the family to adjust to the loss. Alma had always been there. Elias had lost his wife of 55 years and the love of his life. It was truly a sad time for him and the rest of the family.

The family still continued to get together and many times they would tell a funny story or special memory about Alma. As time went by they decided they were fortunate to have her for as long as they did and blessed to be the children and grandchildren of such a great woman. To this day the family still tells stories of Alma McGee Young and every story ends with a smile.

After Alma passed away Elias settled into a life without his partner, but he did his best to move on. His children and their families continued to visit on Sunday afternoons after church and Elias was always glad to see them.

Elias was now in his late 70's and had given up driving a long time ago. One of his children worked with him each month to make sure his bills were paid on time and if he needed some groceries someone was always dropping by to take him.

Elias' favorite pastime during his later years was rocking in his rocking chairs. He had one on the front porch of the little green house and another favorite in his living room.

On many occasions during the week an older grandson would drop by and sit and share some old memories. Sometimes if Elias was thirsty they would go up to "Cannonball" Wilson's country store and get a big 12 ounce Pepsi.

Grandpa Young's younger grandsons also loved spending time at the little green house back then. Clyde Young Jr., Moochie McCormick, R.D. Marshall and great grandson, Kelly Young were all in their preteens during this time and really enjoyed visiting and playing together at Grandpa's. The last grandchildren were born in the late 1950's through the 1960's. Clyde Young Jr. and Lisa Marshall were born in 1957. RD Marshall Jr.

was born in 1960 and Clyde's two daughters, Rhonda and Gina were born in 1959 and 1969.

In 1969 Elias' health took a turn for the worse and over time he was unable to take care of himself. The family held a meeting to decide what to do for their family's patriarch. Each of the children volunteered their time to help look after Elias. They set up a schedule where one could stay in the morning, another in the afternoon, and someone else would stay at night.

Elias was well attended to those last few months.

On August 28, 1970 Elias Young passed away ending a cherished era of the Young Family. He was buried beside his loving wife, Alma, at Union Groove Baptist Church in Oak Ridge, NC.

You may think this is the end of the story. Well it's not, for the rest of the book we will tell the stories of each of Elias and Alma's nine children and 26 grandchildren. There are stories of overcoming hardships, achieving educational goals, solid working careers, and happy family lives.

Turn the page and lets enjoy the stories of their lives.

Will Celebrate Today

Mr. and Mrs. Elias L. Young of Kernersville, Rt. 2, will celebrate their 50th wedding anniversary at an open house today from 2 to 5 p.m. Mrs. Young is the former Alma McGee of Walkertown. The children of the couple are: Raymond Young, Clyde Young, Mrs. Conrad Morris and Mrs. Raymond Goins, all of Oak Ridge; Mrs. James Flynt of Kernersville; Mrs. Reavis Marshall of Colfax; and Mrs. Rufus McCormick and Mrs. Clifton Crutchfield both of Greensboro. They have 25 grandchildren and four great-grandchildren.

On December 18, 1960 Elias and Alma Young celebrated their 50th Wedding Anniversary. Family and friends from miles around came to celebrate this special milestone in their lives.

This is a portrait of Elias and Alma Young in 1960 when they celebrated their 50th Wedding Anniversary.

This is a classic picture from 1958 of from left, Elias, Alma and their son Raymond Young. Alma always wore high heels to church, but they hurt her feet. They came off as soon as she got in the car. And of course Elias had to have a cigarette afterward, too.

This is a picture of Alma and Elias' daughters standing in front of the green house. From left are Elsie, Wonnie, Edna, Annie, Hazel and Opal. This picture was taken in 1958.

Above is a picture of Edna, and Hazel building a snowman in the front yard of the little green house that Grandpa Young lived in in the late 1960's.

To the left is a picture of Elias Young pier fishing on the North Carolina Coast. Notice he had some shrimp, a bucket for his catch and an ice cold 12 ounce Pepsi. This picture is from the early 1960's.

Above is probably the last picture of Elias, Alma, and their children taken together. Alma would pass away on a fishing trip to the North Carolina Coast a few months later in 1965.

This is a picture of Elias Young sitting in his rocker on the front porch of the green house. This picture is circa 1967.

Elias Young's grandchildren and great grandchildren loved to come and play at his house when they were in their preteens. In the picture to the left are Hubert, Kelly, Grandpa Young, R.D., Carl, Moochie and Clyde, Jr. This picture is from the late 1960's.

In the last months of his life Elias Young had several family members stay with him day and night at his house. In the picture above are his grand-daughter, Norma Moore Campbell and his son Raymond Young taking their turns.

Chapter Seven

The Hubert Young Family

It was only one day shy of Elias and Alma Young's first wedding anniversary on December 17, 1911 that their first child, John Hubert Young was born on The McGee Home Place in Walkertown, North Carolina. Hubert was born into a simple and hard life of farming. Hubert was a long and lanky young child and it was easy to see he was going to have a physic just like his father, Elias.

As a child, Hubert developed a close relationship with his grandmother, Mary McGee. Mary was in her late 60's when Hubert was born and her husband, John McGee, died in 1914 when Hubert was only two years old. He always fondly recalled his grandmother and the times he spent with her. Over the next few years as Hubert grew into a young boy he followed his father, Elias, almost everywhere he went. He wanted to be a farmer like his father and Elias would let Hubert help by carrying water from the well or wood to the stoves.

In 1922 when Hubert was 10, Elias and Alma along with Hubert's younger brother, Raymond and younger sisters, Annie and Hazel moved to the Whicker Farm in the Belews Creek community near Goodwill Church east of Walkertown, North Carolina. The house was next to Elias' father, Hester Young's farm.

By now Hubert was in school and during the summer months he was doing a full day's work helping his father on the farm. Yes Hubert was quickly becoming a strong young man. In 1930 Elias and Alma moved the family again. This time Hubert was 19 years old and helped move the family to the Case Place in Oak Ridge, North Carolina. They lived about two miles north of the Oak Ridge Military Academy on the current Highway 68.

The Rierson family had a small farm house across the road from the Young's. One of their children, Annie Mae Rierson, attended school in Oak Ridge and became friends with Hubert's younger sisters Hazel and Edna. Annie Mae would often get off the school bus with Hazel and Edna and spend the afternoon at the Young's house.

There Hubert and Annie Mae met and became friends. Over time that friendship grew into a boyfriend – girlfriend relationship and in 1936 they decided it was time they became husband and wife. In a recent interview Annie Mae still remembers that special time. "We had decided to get married on October 24, 1936 in Danville, Virginia," Annie Mae stated. "This was before Wonnie and Clyde had even started to school. I was 17 and Hubert was 24. You see, you had to be 18 up there to get married so when I got up there I was 18". Annie Mae was still laughing as she finished the story.

After they were married money was tight as the Great Depression still lingered. Hubert and Annie Mae moved in with Elias and Alma for two or three months until they could save enough money to rent a house of their own.

After that they rented a small house right across the road from Elias and Alma and began raising tobacco of their own.

Annie still remembers those early days of marriage. Annie from the start was a good manager of her household and already knew how to cook. One thing she liked to do in those early days was learn new recipes from Alma.

Alma gladly shared her recipes with her new daughter-in-law. One of Annie Mae's favorites was – "Alma McGee Young's Ice Box Fruit Cake". Alma taught Annie Mae how to make this their first Christmas after they were married and she has continued to

---

Alma McGee Young's Ice Box Fruit Cake

1 box dark raisins

1 - 16 oz. container candied mixed fruit

1 - 8 oz. container candied red cherries, cut in half

2 cups pecan, chopped

2 cups English walnuts, chopped

1 cup black walnuts, chopped

1 box Nabisco Graham Crackers, finely crushed

1 - 16 oz. package large marshmallows

1 - 14 oz. can Pet evaporated milk

Thoroughly mix all ingredients (except marshmallows and evaporated milk) in a large mixing bowl. Melt the marshmallows in the evaporated milk over low heat. Pour the milk mixture over the fruit and graham cracker mix and combine thoroughly. Your hands work best in this step. Cut three sides of the top off the graham cracker box and line the inside with wax paper. Firmly press the mixture into the container. Keep the cake stored in the refrigerator and cake may be cut one week later.

make it every Christmas since.

It was in this early house that Hubert's and Annie Mae's first child, Carl Avery Young was born on July 21, 1937. He would be their first of four children. Carl would grow to be a sturdy youngster, long and lanky like his father and grandfather, Elias.

In October of 1937 Annie Mae's mother, Etta Rierson, and sister, Jenny, came to live with Hubert and Annie Mae. They were a welcome addition to the family willing to help in any way they could. Annie Mae's father, Frank Rierson, passed away in February 1923 due to burns suffered in a fire. Frank rode his mule to the store to buy kerosene and on the way back home some of the kerosene splashed on his wool pants. After arriving home, he came into the house to warm in front of the fire-place and his clothes caught fire and he was gravely injured. He died at home seven days later.

Times were still hard during the first couple of years of Hubert's and Annie Mae's marriage and they were not yet able to buy a car of their own. If they really needed to go somewhere they could always go across the road and Hubert's brother, Raymond would let them borrow his car.

After selling his tobacco crop in the fall of 1938 Hubert finally had enough money to buy his first car. He bought a 1936 Ford from the Ford dealership in nearby Kernersville, North Carolina. Yes, that was a proud moment for Hubert and Annie Mae.

In 1939 a great opportunity opened up for Annie Mae. Adam-Millis, a sock and hosiery mill in nearby Kernersville was hiring women to work at their factory. This was a major shift in hiring during this era. For the most part only men worked in local factories back then. The slogan – "A Woman's Place Is In The Home" would never be the same.

Because Annie Mae's mother, Etta was living with her and Hubert and could babysit Carl, and they had just purchased a 1936 Ford, Annie Mae was able to apply.

Annie Mae was hired on the spot.

While she was in training Annie Mae was paid 10 cents an hour, working seven hours a day. She was paid every two weeks and she remembers when she got her first check it was for $7.00.

After training, she worked in the looper room. In this area she was paid by how many dozen socks she could make in a day. Annie Mae continued to advance and soon got a much better job being an inspector. With this job she checked the quality of other people's work instead of being on a production line. Annie would go on to work in the textile industry, mostly at Adam-Millis, for the next 42 and one half years greatly helping her family's quality of life.

Over the next several years Hubert and his family made several moves to different farms in Oak Ridge looking for larger farms to grow tobacco own. A few years after Carl was born they moved to the old Peagram farm in Oak Ridge.

Then they rented a small farm house on Hwy 150 on the Williams farm. Then they moved to the Honeycutt farm on Bunch road for a short time before renting a large farmhouse on Beeson road that was the old Beeson Farm.

During these moves Hubert and Annie Mae had their first daughter, Evelyn Loretta Young on October 9th, 1940. Four years later Brenda Mae Young was born on December 8th, 1944.
Their fourth and last child, Barbara Ann Young was born on December 19th, 1946.

In 1957 after Hubert's mother, Alma retired from a working at Adam-Millis, Elias and Alma moved from The Big White House on Pepper Road to a smaller Green House next door. This gave Hubert and Annie Mae the opportunity to rent The Big White House. Hubert was happy to get the bigger nine acre tobacco allotment. They wouldn't live there for long however; for in 1958 Hubert began building his family a brand new brick home. The project would be a labor of love and would be the first home his family didn't have to rent.

Hubert never thought of a home rented as being in any way his. Only if you owned it would it become your home. The day Hubert, Annie Mae and family moved in Hubert was beaming with joy. Carl still remembers his father walking through the front door when they moved in and said "Hubert you're finally home."

Hubert was a quiet and mild mannered man who cared deeply for his family. He lived a peaceful life and provided well for his family. Sadly he passed away on April 8, 1996 and was buried at Oak Ridge Methodist Church.   Annie Mae continues to live in the house they built together more than 50 years ago.   Hubert always enjoyed his children and grandchildren when they came home to visit and always welcomed each one with a smile.

Hubert and Annie Mae Young right after they got married in 1936.

This is a great picture of Hubert's and Annie Mae's son Carl in 1938 riding his tricycle. At the time they lived right across the road from Elias and Alma on Highway 68 Just north of Oak Ridge, North Carolina.

Hubert was a farmer all his life. Here is a picture of him helping his father, Elias at corn picking time in the fall of 1955. Families helped families back then. There was no extra money for hiring people to do farm work.

This is a picture of Hubert and Annie Mae Young and all their children. From bottom left are Hubert and Annie Mae. From top left are Carl, Loretta, Brenda and Barbara. This picture is probably from the early 1960's.

This is a four generation picture of Elias Young with his oldest grandson. From left are Great Grandpa Elias, Grandpa Hubert, Great Grandson Kelly and Father Carl. This picture is from the early 1960's.

Above is a picture of Hubert and Annie Mae Young's daughter, Brenda at the family tobacco barn in the 1950's.

Hubert and Annie Mae built this house for their family in 1958 and Annie Mae still lives there today.

Hubert and Annie Mae Young with their children, Carl, Loretta, Brenda, and Barbara.

Carl Avery Young

Carl Avery Young was born on July 21, 1937 and is the oldest son of Hubert and Annie Mae Rierson Young. He makes his home in Summerfield, North Carolina today.

Carl remembers from an early age he was the lucky child that had his own room since he was the only boy in the family. His room was upstairs and was cold in the winter and hot in the summer; even with the windows open. There was no central heating or cooling back then.

As far back as he could remember Carl enjoyed following his father, Hubert on the farm. He was constantly learning something new and was always ready to take on more responsibility.

By the time he was six years old, Carl was responsible for bringing in firewood from the woodshed behind the house. It was quite a job since not only did the family heat the house with firewood, but they used it for all the cooking on the wood cook stove as well.

By the time Carl was eight, he was in charge of feeding the family's work horses, mule, cows and hogs.

It was also about this time Carl remembers Hubert started taking him to the Old Mill in Oak Ridge to have their wheat and corn ground into flour and cornmeal from the grain they had grown on the farm.

Lee Hedrix owned and operated the mill at the time. While the grain was being ground Carl enjoyed fishing in the creek behind the mill.

Carl spent his early life attending Oak Ridge Elementary School through the seventh grade. In the first grade Carl took the bus to school. The following year he and a friend, James Tuttle decided they would rather walk the ¾ mile distance instead. Carl still remembers walking by Frank Linville's hog farm along the way.

When Carl was about 9 years old he got a goat and a cart. His family couldn't afford a pony. He trained the goat to pull a cart and sled and yes, they had a lot of fun.

When he turned 10 for one of the few times in his life he got very sick. The doctor said he had come down with the mumps. Carl would spend the next 10 days in bed before he was well enough to go back to school.

By the time Carl turned 12 he was old enough to help his daddy with the farm. Carl always loved working mules and horses with farm equipment with his daddy.

"You didn't have to ask me twice!" Carl grinned.

While he and Hubert worked the farm Carl remembers his mother, Annie Mae and Grandma Rierson canning vegetables out of the garden and cooking three meals a day.

Carl remembers seeing nearly 500 cans of food stored up for the winter on a yearly basis. They had pork once or twice a day and chickens out of the barn yard once a week or when they were needed.

Although they did most of the cooking, Carl remembers Hubert making very good gravy and sweet tea with lemons sometimes on Sundays.

Also, during these early teenage years, Carl enjoyed rabbit hunting with his friends and playing baseball. On hot summer days he and his friends enjoyed going to the creek off Bunch Road in Oak Ridge where the state pumped sand. The hole made a great swimming pond.

One of Carl's proudest moments was when he was 14 and Hubert gave him his own crop of tobacco. He had a half acre of land to plant his own crop on.

When Carl reached the 8th grade he switched over and went to Summerfield High School. He would continue there until he graduated high school.

Right after he graduated from Summerfield High School Carl joined the Army for 6 months of active duty and then served 5-1/2 years in the Army Reserve.

When he turned 19 he got his first job at Southern Bell Telephone and Telegraph Company and continued working there his entire career.

In 1958, Carl met and fell in love with the love of his life, Frances Kiger. On March 15, 1959 they were married in South Carolina.

As for children, Frances already had a son, Bruce from a previous marriage who was born in 1956.

They would also have two more children of their own, Kelly, who was born in 1961 and Jill, who was born in 1966.

In 1960, Carl and Frances bought their first house, which included five acres of land. It was a four room block house on Scoggins Road in Oak Ridge.

For a short time after that they rented the Roy Nelson farm also in Oak Ridge.

In 1966, Carl and Frances built their own home at 1731 Oak Ridge Road and lived there for 29 years.

In 1995, they built a home in Summerfield, NC and they still proudly live there today.

Carl is a strong historian on the art of farming and in a future chapter will tell us the story of a complete year in farming as he and his father, Hubert used to do.

This chapter will reveal a history of farming in the 1940's thru the 1960's that has been all but lost. We are so thankful for his sharing this knowledge with us.

Hubert with his son Carl at their home on Hwy 68 across the road from Elias and Alma's house around 1940.

The Carl Young Family at Jill's graduation. From Left to right are Bruce, Francis, Jill, Kelly, and Carl.

Evelyn Loretta Young Hauser

Late in the afternoon of October 9, 1940 Annie Mae Young started her labor pains and knew she was going to have hers and Hubert's second child that night.

Hubert quickly went to a neighbor's house and made a telephone call to Dr. Whitaker in Kernersville. "Annie Mae needs your help right away Dr. Whitaker! We're on Highway 68 about a mile north of Oak Ridge. I'll leave a lantern at the end of our road so you'll know where to turn."

This was still the age when children were born at home instead of at the local hospital.

That night Annie Mae and Hubert became the proud parents of their first daughter, Evelyn Loretta Young. Loretta was a beautiful baby and Mother and Father couldn't be prouder.

Over the next several years while growing up, Loretta remembered always being surrounded by a close family. Her grandparents Elias and Alma Young lived right across the road at the Case Place along with several other aunts and uncles.

At home there were of course Hubert and Annie Mae and her brother, Carl. Also living in their home were her grandmother, Mary Etta Rierson along with Mary Etta's sister, Jenny Rierson. Loretta has said many times over the years we were blessed to have them both.

Since Annie Mae worked at Adams Millis Hosiery while the children were young, Grandma Rierson and her sister, Jenny were always at home cooking meals and helping to raise the children.

Loretta never remembers a time when there wasn't an abundance of food in her house.

"Daddy and Mama planted large gardens and we gathered by the bushels." Loretta explained in a recent interview. "We canned the extra vegetables for use in the winter."

Another fond memory Loretta has is of her daddy having bee hives for years and she remembers honey always being on their table. She didn't remember having to buy much at the store except for the essentials that couldn't be grown or raised on the farm.

Loretta remembers that they never knew how many people would be at their house come dinner time. If more people showed up she remembers Mama putting in another pan of biscuits. If they ran out of chairs at the dinner table the men would eat first and then the women and children would eat when they were finished.

Loretta spent her grade school years at Oak Ridge School. Her high school years were spent at Summerfield High School where she graduated in 1959.

Shortly after graduating high school Loretta got a job at Piedmont Jewelry Store on Lawndale Drive in Greensboro, North Carolina.

She only worked there for a short while as a major opportunity came her way with a job working at the Federal Bureau of Investigation in Washington D.C.

Loretta remembers when she moved to Washington to work for the FBI she didn't take her car because she didn't know the city that well. After a couple of months of riding the bus from her apartment to work she decided to go back home and get her car.

Loretta's Grandma Alma Young and her mother, Annie Mae rode back to Washington with her to see where she lived and worked. It turned out to be a fun several day trip for all.

Loretta suggested to Alma and Annie Mae that on the way back home they should take the train rather than ride the bus. Loretta had ridden the bus home once before and remembered all the stops they had to make and how crowded and hot the buses were.

Grandma Young said more than once the bus would be OK with her. Loretta insisted the train would be better and the following morning took them to the train station and put them on a direct train to Greensboro. Grandma Young did not protest.

A couple of days later Annie Mae and Grandma Young called and told Loretta how much they enjoyed their first experience of riding a train. This made Loretta feel a lot better.

A little later Annie called Loretta and told her the real reason Grandma Young wanted to take the bus home. She had noticed all the high train trestles on the way up and she was feeling a little afraid to ride the train, but in the end she did enjoy the train ride.

Loretta stayed in Washington D.C. for about a year and decided to come back home.

Upon her return in 1961 she got a job with Liberty Mutual Insurance Company in Greensboro, NC.

In 1963 she met a very nice young man named Bill Hauser.

Bill's profession was that of an accountant and he was a rising star for the Hanes Corporation; the same company that make the famous Hanes t-shirts and under wear. Over the years Bill would become one of their top executives.

Loretta and Bill both knew each was the person they wanted to spend the rest of their life with and were soon engaged to be married.

Bill and Loretta were married June 20, 1964 at the Oak Ridge Methodist Church at 5:30 PM, and it turned out to be the hottest day of the year.

After Bill and Loretta were married, Loretta worked at Jones & Gilbert Insurance Agency in Winston- Salem until their daughter; Amy Elizabeth Hauser was born on October 21, 1966.

Loretta was a stay at home Mom until Amy started school.

Then in 1972 Loretta started working for the Winston-Salem School System as a secretary in the Guidance Department and worked there for the next 18 years.

From the time Bill and Loretta got married in 1964 until today the couple has lived in Winston-Salem, North Carolina.

There was a short period of a year from 1990 until 1991 the couple did move to Greenville, South Carolina because Bill's management talents were needed there.

The couple transferred back to Winston-Salem in November 1991 and bought a home on Guinevere Lane, where they still live today.

Bill and Loretta are so proud of their daughter, Amy who graduated from UNC- Chapel Hill with a nursing degree in 1988.

She would later continue her education and in 2001 received her MBA and Masters in Health degrees from Georgia State University in Atlanta.

She is currently the Service Line Administrator for Transplant Services at Children's Hospital in Atlanta, Georgia.

Today Loretta and Bill both enjoy retirement and traveling is one of their favorite hobbies.

Loretta and her older brother Carl in the mid 1940's.

This is a picture of Bill and Loretta Hauser and their daughter, Amy.

Brenda Young Coble

In early February of 1944 Annie Mae came to Hubert with more great news. They were going to have another addition to their family before the end of the year. Then on December 8, 1944 their third child, Brenda was born.

Brenda was a cute little girl who always seemed to have a smile on her face. She remembers growing up in big farm houses where they had lots of room to run and play.

In the winter time when it was cold there were always lots of warm homemade quilts to stay warm in the cold North Carolina winters.

Brenda still recalls the houses were heated with wood. She remembers back then having both a wood stove and an electric stove in the kitchen.

Like her other siblings, Brenda's memories of her mother and Grandma Rierson were of them cooking and canning.

Brenda and her younger sister, Barbara were told from an early age they had the smallest hands, thus they had the duty of washing the canning jars and washing the cucumbers before canning.

Brenda also remembers her daddy had many more responsibilities than just tending the fields farming. He had cows for milk and butter, horses for farm work, and hogs for meat.

The family also had two pets; a cocker spaniel named Blacky and a parakeet named Pete.

Annie Mae taught Brenda how to sew at a young age and she never remembers a time when she didn't know how.

One time she thought her doll needed some warm clothes so she raided the sock drawer and cut them up to make doll clothes. She's sure she got in trouble for it when her Mamma found out.

Every summer the entire family would work together in the tobacco fields. Before the crop would come in Hubert would buy all of the kids a new straw hat at the general store to help protect them from the hot summer sun.

After coming in from a long day's work of putting in a barn of tobacco they would wash off with homemade lye soap to help remove the tobacco gum from their hands and the stains from their clothes.

Brenda loved visiting with Grandma Alma and Grandpa Elias Young. Grandma Young kept board games for all of her grandchildren to play when they would visit. Brenda learned to play monopoly while sitting in the floor with Grandma Young.

Brenda still grins when she tells this story. In the mid-1950's she remembers one Christmas Raymond Goins brother, Arthur, gave all of the kids a box of candy. Brenda was so excited and wanted to make her candy last as long as possible so she saved her favorite pieces with nuts inside for last. Before she had a chance to eat them her cousins, MK and Gary found the candy and ate it all!

Brenda attended Northwest High School near Oak Ridge, North Carolina and was in the first graduating class in 1963.

It was about this same time she met a handsome young man named Donald Coble. They fell in love and were later married at the same church where sister, Loretta was married; Oak Ridge Methodist Church.

Donald had a great job for the era. He was an airline pilot for Eastern Airlines.

For a while the couple lived in Greensboro, North Carolina, but later moved to Homestead, Florida.

After moving to Homestead Brenda recalls, "I thought when I grew up and moved on I would not farm anymore. Alas, I talked my husband into buying land in Homestead, Florida where we planted avocado trees and I bought a tractor and got to play in the dirt a lot!"

Donald would continue flying for the Eastern Airlines until he retired in 1998.

Donald and Brenda have two children, Terri and Don Jr. and one grandchild, Ronald.

The couple still lives in Florida today.

On the left is Brenda Young Coble with her friend Lynda Meadows playing tennis together in the late 1950's

Brenda and Donald Coble with their children Don Jr. and Terri and their grandson Ronald.

Barbara Ann Young Williams

On December 19, 1946 Hubert and Annie Mae had their fourth and final child, Barbara Ann Young. She like the others was born at home in Oak Ridge, North Carolina.

When she was young one of her favorite things to do was visiting with Grandma and Grandpa Young and playing with all of her cousins.

"Grandma always greeted you at the door with a big smile on her face; she was always glad to see you" Barbra said of her grandmother, Alma Young.

She moved with the family when she was young but she remembers growing up in the brick house Hubert and Annie Mae built. She shared a bedroom with her two sisters and didn't have a bed of her own until she was in high school.

Because she was the youngest child she was often playing while the others worked in the tobacco fields. She would ride on the tobacco sleds from the field to the tobacco barn and play in the dirt around the barn while the older children worked.

"I had a great time, so my siblings say"

Barbara can remember running out to the mailbox when Aunt Hazel Young would bring the mail. Hazel was the mail carrier for Oak Ridge at this time.

She remembers her daddy loving Christmas time. Hubert would go out and cut a big tree for the house and they always had a great Christmas morning. Then they would have lunch with the entire family. She remembers getting dolls and tea sets when she was young and she always got a box full of goodies.

Although her mother, Annie Mae's cakes were the best Hubert would take Barbara to the store on her birthday and let her pick out a cake wrapped in paper. She thought this was very special.

Barbara described herself as an outdoor girl. She said there was always a lot to do especially a lot of playing, but as she got older you'd better believe she did her share of the work.

As for Barbara's schooling she spent grades 1-8 at Oak Ridge Elementary School, her ninth grade at Summerfield School and grades 10-12 at Northwest Guilford. Barbara graduated in 1965.

She will never forget all of her classmates she graduated from school with that went to the Vietnam War and that several of them did not come back.

On October 24, 1965 Barbara married Gerald (Jerry) Wayne Williams. They were married at Hubert and Annie Mae's house in Oak Ridge.

Jerry was a computer operator at IBM and would spend his entire career working there. Barbara started her career with the US Postal Service in 1971. She would work there for 37 years in various departments.

After they were married they lived in an apartment for 6 months before buying a farm on Scoggins road in Oak Ridge. On the farm they raised Black Angus cows and had a variety of other pets and animals as well.

Jerry and Barbara had four children over the years. Jerry Ann was born in 1966, Jennifer Leigh in 1969, Mandy Joan in 1977 and Matthew Thomas was born in 1980. All of Barbara and Jerry's kids were involved in sports from a young age. Mandy clogged and made the Clogging Hall of Fame in 1992.

Jerry and Barbara later built a new house on the same farm and live there today

Barbara's favorite slogan is –

"Love your family, all the rest will take care of itself."

Barbara and Jerry with their children, Jerry Ann, Jennifer, Mandy, and Matt.

Barbara proudly poses with her four grandchildren, Cody, Carrie Ann, Catie Beth, and Caleb.

Chapter Eight

The Annie Mae Young Crutchfield Family

The date was October 24, 1914 and it was a very proud day for Alma and Elias Young. On this day their second child and first daughter, Annie Mae Young was born. Annie was a beautiful baby and was such a joy for Alma.

Annie would spend the first eight years of her childhood growing up on the McGee Farm, which was Alma's parents' farm just west of Walkertown, North Carolina.

In 1922 Elias and Alma moved the family to the Wicker Farm. It was located in the Belews Creek Community near Goodwill Church east of Walkertown, North Carolina and right next to Elias' father, Hester Young's farm.

Annie was a very smart child and as she grew she pitched in to help in any way she could around the home. She quickly learned how to cook, assist in raising and tending the garden, and could can any fruit or vegetable brought into the house. She was Alma's chief assistant.

Annie wanted to help her father, Elias in the fields to grow the tobacco and other crops, but she found out early long periods in the sun gave her severe headaches and she was unable to do so. This did not bother Elias and Alma. Helping Alma run the household was a full time job and her help made everything run smoothly.

In 1930 when Annie was 15 Elias and Alma moved their family to the Case Place farm, located about two miles north of the community of Oak Ridge, North Carolina just off NC Highway 68.

Even though the 1930's were hard times for much of our nation due to the Great Depression Annie's parents made the best of the situation renting their home and raising nine acres of tobacco on the Case Farm. The farm was 200 acres and the Young family could raise and grow anything they needed for the survival of the family.

By the spring of 1935 Annie had turned 20 years old and had become a truly beautiful woman. One day she heard a knock at the door and a stranger was standing there with his hat in hand. He had run out of gas on the nearby highway and needed to know if he could borrow a gallon of gasoline.

"My name is Clifton Crutchfield from a town called Ether several miles east of here and I just ran out of gas on the highway. I need to know if it would be possible for me to borrow a gallon of gasoline if you have any on hand. I'll bring your can right back full gas once I get it filled at the service station." Clifton said.

Annie was glad to help the young man in need. She directed him to a shed behind the house where Elias kept a can filled with gasoline for their car.

As Clifton started toward the shed he thought to himself, "That's the most beautiful woman I've ever seen!! Thank you Lord for letting me run out of gas today."

After putting the gas in the tank Clifton was able to start his car. Then he was off to the nearby country store to refill the can with gasoline. He was so glad he needed to return the can because he would be able to see the beautiful young woman again.

When Clifton returned he came right out and told Annie she was the most beautiful woman he had ever seen and asked her for a date. Annie really liked the young man and gladly accepted.

To both it was love at first site and as they dated through the summer. Each knew this was the person they wanted to spend the rest of their life with.

Clifton's father, Webster (Webb) Crutchfield was born on May 17, 1884 and his mother, Melvina (Vine) Rayle Crutchfield was born on May 12, 1886. They were married in 1907 and owned a tobacco farm in Ether, North Carolina.

Clifton was born on April 11, 1911 and was 24 years old when he and Annie met. Clifton was a hard worker and was known for having a very sharp mind.

In the fall of 1935 on one very special evening Clifton got down on one knee and asked, "Annie, will you marry me?"

This moment made Annie so happy and of course she said yes.

Times were hard and Annie knew she and Clifton would not be able to afford a fancy church wedding with all the trimmings. They instead would go Danville, Virginia and be married by a Justice Of The Peace.

Annie had always dreamed of getting married in a beautiful wedding dress, but with times so hard she did not want to impose on Elias and Alma for such an expensive purchase.

At breakfast on the Saturday morning a week before her wedding Annie's brother, Raymond asked Elias if he could borrow the keys to the family's Model 'A' Ford.

"Why?" asked Elias.

"Because I want to buy my sister a wedding dress for her wedding." Raymond replied.

Annie could hardly believe her ears. Tears of joy streamed down her face as she heard what her brother was saying.

The two spent the day in nearby Greensboro picking out just the right dress.

On the morning of November 23, 1935 Clifton and Annie along with Clifton's older sister, Hallie and her husband, Eck Jones made the drive up to Danville, Virginia for the big event.

It was a beautiful wedding and Annie was so proud of her wedding dress.

After their honeymoon Clifton and Annie decided because money was so tight to live with Clifton's parents in Ether, North Carolina for a while. Annie pitched in there just as she had at home and was a great help to Clifton's mother, Vine.

Since it was winter time Clifton, who was really good with a rifle and a shotgun, spent a lot of time hunting for food for the family. Anything Clifton brought home Annie was able to cook for a tasty meal the following day.

In the spring of 1936 Clifton was able to find a farmer back in Oak Ridge who needed someone to grow his crop of tobacco. Along with the agreement to grow the tobacco came a house in which he and Annie would live.

Clifton proved to be a great farmer and a good provider for his family. Annie was glad to be back in Oak Ridge close to her family.

On October 1, 1936 Annie and Clifton had their first child, Joel Annette Crutchfield. The family would call her Jo Anne.

Jo Anne was a beautiful baby and was the first grandchild in the family for Elias and Alma. And you'd better believe Grandma Alma was proud of this child.

A little over a year later on December 31, 1937 Annie's and Clifton's second child, Katherine Marie Crutchfield was born. To the family she would be known as Kay.

Three years later on February 26, 1940 Annie and Clifton had their third child and third daughter, Wilma Lee Crutchfield, and on October 12, 1942 Clifton and Annie had their fourth daughter, Phyllis Ann Crutchfield. After Phyllis was born the family moved to Brown Summit, NC and then to Edgeville, NC for a short while.

In 1943 Clifton got a job with Cone Mills at their Print Works Plant in Greensboro, North Carolina. Clifton was so proud of this job. Not only would he be working with one of the nation's top textile manufacturers, but he and Annie would get a house to live in as well. 1603 Upland Drive, Greensboro, North Carolina would be the family's address for many years to come.

The house had three bedrooms, a living room, a kitchen with a pantry, one bathroom, and a front and a back porch. Clifton and Annie were so proud of the bathroom. It was the first one they had with indoor plumbing. The house had three fireplaces to keep the house warm. Clifton purchased both coal and wood from local suppliers. They no longer had to cut and chop their own wood.

There was also a garage behind the house that had an entrance from an alley running behind the house. Another advantage to the location of the Upland Drive residence was that it was within walking distance of Clifton's job. During his entire 35 years of working at Cone Mills he never had to drive a car to work.

Clifton started out as a factory worker, but he learned the inner workings of the huge factory quickly. His hard work ethic and his strong ability to remember details did not go unnoticed by Cone Mill's top management.

A short time after he was hired the Cone Mills Print Works Plant started a new chemistry department and asked Clifton to be a member of the new team. Clifton gladly said yes and got a promotion to Chemist. The chemistry department was responsible for bleaching large bolts of cloth before color was added in the printing department. It was important to get the bleaching process just right.   Clifton was a master at keeping strong documentation and soon was able to set standards for the bleaching processes throughout the plant. These standards would be used for years to come. Because of these standards Cone's products had consistent color from batch to batch and the quality of their cloth was superior to many other textile manufacturers in the industry.

The move to Upland Drive was a good one for Clifton and Annie. From this point forward the Crutchfields would be affectionately known as the Young family's 'City Slickers'.

There were so many advantages to living here. Good quality schools within walking distance from home and all types of opportunities for the children of the family to learn and grow.

July 12, 1944 was a happy day for them when their first and only son, Clifton Daniel Crutchfield, Jr. was born. He would be known to the family as Cliff.

Clifton and Annie now had five children and Clifton was so proud to finally have a son.

As time went by the Crutchfields adjusted well to life in the city of Greensboro. There was so much to do. There was a nearby YMCA swimming pool and the family enjoyed The Guilford Courthouse National Park, that was also only a few miles away.

On Sundays after church Clifton and Annie enjoyed loading up their children in their 1938 Buick and traveling down Highway 220 to Elias and Alma's house. The country setting and wide open spaces of the Lowery Farm where Elias and Alma lived allowed the children to run and play around the house and in the nearby fields and woods all afternoon. Clifton and Annie also enjoyed the visits because it gave them a chance to catch up on the latest from other family members.

On June 26, 1946 Annie and Clifton had their sixth child, Margaret Maurene Crutchfield. She would be known to the family as Maggie. Maggie was a happy baby and to this day carries one of the warmest smiles you have ever seen.

After Maggie grew into a young child she started sleeping with her older sisters. The sleeping arrangements were tight for a while. The way the bedrooms were set up, Clifton and Annie slept in the front bedroom, Cliff slept in a single bed in the middle bedroom and the five sisters slept in two double beds in the back bedroom. Maggie, being the youngest and smallest usually slept at the foot of one of the beds so everyone would have plenty of room.

In 1947 Clifton and Annie were able to replace their old ice box with a new electric refrigerator-freezer. It was much more convenient and no longer would large blocks of ice need to be brought into the house. Annie loved it and kept it stocked full of food. She also enjoyed the fact she could now make homemade ice cream any time she wanted in the new freezer.

A couple of years after Maggie was born Annie got a job at the Cone Mills Revolution Rayon Plant in Greensboro. She would work 2nd shift in the spinning department.

This was a major departure from the way Annie was brought up. Most women during this era stayed at home and looked after the household.

Annie saw many advantages to this. It would bring much needed money into the household and would allow the children to have a better quality of life. The children all pitched in at home and helped as needed to make the household run smoothly. Jo Anne, who was the oldest, took charge of the younger children. The rest had their own chores as well.

While the rest of the girls helped with the cleaning, washing, ironing and cooking, Cliff made sure the lawn was mowed each week. Cliff still remembers that old reel push mower quite well.

During this time Clifton worked 3rd shift. JoAnne would often cook breakfast for him when he arrived home from a hard night's work.

In 1950 Cone Mills made two major upgrades to Clifton and Annie's house. First, they installed an oil circulator stove in the living room which could heat the entire house. No longer would the family have to carry in coal and wood from the outside and maintain fires in the fireplaces.

The other major upgrade was to the bathroom. A brand new wash tub complete with showerhead was added. This greatly improved the efficiency of the six children getting ready for school in the mornings.

Jo Anne was babysitting by the time she was 12 and the other sisters found work in downtown fashion clothing stores by the time they were 16.

Cliff in his younger days joined the Boy Scouts and learned a lot of lifes lessons during the process. He still remembers for one of his merit badges walking all the way from his home in Greensboro to Grandpa and Grandma Young's home in Oak Ridge. The hike was 25 miles and Cliff made it just fine.

As Cliff got older he found odd jobs to do to earn extra spending money. When he was in the eleventh grade his father, Clifton got him a job at the Cone Mills Print Works Plant. Cliff remembers at the time his salary was $1.28 per hour. His father's salary was $1.80 per hour. Annie and Clifton would continue working at Cone Mills until they retired in the late 1970's.

All during those year the bond of the Crutchfield family remained strong. The children's careers would spread them all across the country from Washington D.C. to Tucson, Arizona.

After Clifton and Annie retired they wanted to get away from the city and get back to a country setting similar to the way they grew up many years before. They found a place in the mountains of North Carolina. It was located on Glade Valley Road about half way between Galax, Virginia and Sparta, North Carolina. It was a beautiful place with great view of the mountain ranges.

Clifton planted a manageable garden behind their house and he was always proud of his harvests.

Clifton bought a pick-up truck and had a camper installed on the back. The camper had all the comforts of home. Clifton and Annie would pack up and off they would go to visit family and friends or they may decide to take an extended vacation. It was a good time in their life.

Yes Clifton and Annie have passed on now, but their memories will stay in their family's hearts forever.

This is a picture circa 1947 of Annie and each of her six children. On the top row is Jo Anne. On the middle row are from left, Kay, Annie, Maggie in Annie's lap and Wilma. On the bottom row are from left Phyllis and Cliff.

This picture is of Clifton and Annie's children visiting Elias and Alma Young's farm in Oak Ridge, North Carolina. This was a Sunday tradition during their childhood. The children on the top row from left are Jo Anne and Kay. The children on the bottom row from left are Phyllis, Wilma and Cliff. This picture is circa 1945.

Clifton with his catch from the local pond in Greensboro, NC

The Crutchfield Family in front of their home on Upland Drive. On the bottom row from left are Maggie, Cliff, Second Row are Phyllis, Wilma, and the top row are Clifton, Kay, Jo Anne, and Annie

Annie Mae in 1948 when she and Clifton took a vacation down to White Lake, North Carolina. Annie and Clifton rarely got to go without the children. This time Clifton's parents, Webb and Vine Crutchfield looked after the children for them. Behind Annie Mae is their family car, a 1938 Buick.

This is a picture of Clifton and Cliff from the early 1950's.

Joel Annette Crutchfield

The date was October 1, 1936 and it was a happy time at the Annie and Clifton Crutchfield household. On this day their first child, Joel Annette Crutchfield was born. From that time forward the family would call her Jo Anne.

Not only were Clifton and Annie proud to have their first child, Alma and Elias were excited because Jo Anne was their first grandchild.

During Jo Anne's early years her family lived in Oak Ridge, North Carolina. The house they lived in was typical of the time. It did not have electricity or indoor plumbing and the heat came from wood fireplaces.

When Jo Anne was six she started the first grade at Oak Ridge School. She would spend her first two years of schooling there.

In 1943 Jo Anne's family made three moves. Two were only for a few months to Brown Summit, NC and Edgeville, NC.

The third was a major advancement for the entire family. This was when Clifton got a job at the Cone Mills Print Works Plant in Greensboro, North Carolina.

The move gave the family electricity, indoor plumbing and for the first time an indoor bathroom.

Jo Anne attended Proximity School for grades 3 – 9. It was within easy walking distance from home. She could even come home to eat lunch. There was a YMCA swimming pool close by and there were many other activities that she enjoyed including Girl Scouts.

By the time Jo Anne was 12 she started earning her own spending money by babysitting for nearby neighbors.

By the time she was 14 Jo Anne was working at downtown Greensboro dress shops earning $4.00 a day plus commissions. During the Easter season when women bought special outfits to wear to church on Easter Sunday Jo Anne would earn $10.00 per day for two weeks. At the end of the two weeks Jo Anne thought she was rich.

Jo Anne spent grades 10 – 12 at Greensboro Senior High School. After graduating she continued her education for one more year in business school.

After graduating business school, Jo Anne went to work at Western Car Loading Company in Greensboro. She would work there for the next 10 years.

Shortly after settling into the new job a friend introduced Jo Anne to a young gentleman named Lester Sapp in 1955.

Lester worked in textiles and was a supervisor at the time they met. The two dated for the next year and on December 8, 1956 Lester picked Jo Anne up after work with ring in hand and they drove to York, South Carolina and were married. They were both working and had no time off they had to postpone the honeymoon until later.

After renting an apartment for a short while, Jo Anne and Lester purchased their first home in 1960. In 1962 they purchased a home in the Guilford College area of Greensboro.

It was also during this time that Jo Anne and Lester had their two children Cynthia and Jann.

In 1965 Lester got an opportunity for a promotion from supervisor to department head at the textile firm where he worked. To do so the family would have to move to Sumter, South Carolina and Jo Anne would have to give up her job at Western Car Loading Company. The family quickly made the decision to move. Jo Anne began looking for work as soon as they got there and quickly found a job at Campbell's Soup Company in their transportation department.

They both worked hard and saved their money to buy a summer lake house in Santee, South Carolina. This was a dream of theirs for many years. Jo Anne and Lester liked the lake house so much they decided to make it their permanent residence in 1977 and continued living there until 1989.

Jo Anne and Lester then moved back to Sumter to finish out their careers. Jo Anne retired from Campbell's Soup Company in 1992 and Lester retired in 1995.

After retiring Jo Anne and Lester made the decision to go their separate ways.

Jo Anne enjoyed her retirement years traveling and visiting family and friends. For a while she lived near Charleston, South Carolina and later moved back to North Carolina to the town of Clemmons.

She has recently moved to Durham, North Carolina to be close to her children and grandchildren.

Jo Anne was the oldest of the six Crutchfield children and would be a great help to Annie around the house as the children grew. From left to right are Jo Anne, Kay, Wilma, Phyllis, Cliff, and Maggie.

The family of Jo Anne and Lester Sapp.

Katherine Marie Crutchfield

On December 31, 1937 Clifton and Annie Crutchfield had their second child, Katherine Marie Crutchfield. She would be called Kay by the family.

Kay's earliest memories date back to the late 1930's. The Great Depression was still going on and times were hard. Fortunately Clifton and Annie lived on a farm during this time and could grow the family's food.

In 1941 World War II broke out and it seemed everything changed. Many necessities were in short supply and had to be rationed. Kay remembers sugar was hard to come by and her family had to use lots of Karo Syrup. Gas was also in short supply and had to be purchased with ration stamps. Another basic food necessity butter was replaced with margarine. Kay still recalls the large plastic bags of margarine they would get. They had a little dot of red dye in the bag which would be mixed into the white margarine to make it look like butter.

In 1943 Kay's family moved to 1603 Upland Drive in Greensboro, North Carolina when Clifton worked at the Cone Mills Print Works Plant. Kay had just turned six and would soon start first grade at the nearby Proximity School. The school was close enough for she and her sister to walk to school and they could even come home for lunch if they wished. Kay would continue going to Proximity School through the ninth grade.

Another fond memory Kay recalls was when she was about seven years old, Clifton and Annie would pile all the children in their old 1938 Buick and they would head up Highway 220 to Summerfield and then on to Oak Ridge. They were headed to Grandpa and Grandma Young's farm. When they arrived cousins, Ken Young, Carl Young, and Norma Jean Moore would join Kay and Jo Anne for an afternoon of fun.

Kay recalls, "We would go over to the tobacco barns where there were these giant vine swings and we would swing on them for hours every time we visited. I also enjoyed going to the vegetable garden with Grandma Young to pick vegetables for our family to bring back home to Greensboro. All the kids would go to the hog pin and climb a big cherry tree whose limbs were out over the hog pin. Mother and Daddy would always warn us to be careful we didn't fall into the hog pin and get our clothes dirty."

When Kay turned 13 she started getting part time jobs in downtown Greensboro. Her first job was with a little dress shop called Bellas Hess.

When she turned 14 Kay got a job at Woolworths where she had the task of demonstrating the nation's first walking doll right after they came on the market.

At 15 Kay went to work at Belk Department Store. She first worked on Friday afternoons after school until closing time at 9:00 P.M. Later she got to work full time there during the summers of her high school years.

Kay spent grades 10 – 12 at Greensboro Senior High School. At the time the school had over 1500 students and was the only high school in Greensboro.

After graduating Kay got a full time job with J.P. Stevens Trucking Company in Greensboro.

She also started taking night classes at nearby Guilford College to improve her secretarial skills.

After working at J.P. Stevens for a couple of years Kay's friend and co-worker, Dessie Lamonds wanted Kay to meet her brother, Bob Ivey. Bob had recently got out of the military. Kay and Bob started dating and soon fell in love.

On June 27, 1959 the two were married at a beautiful church wedding with over 100 friends and family in attendance. After their honeymoon the couple settled down in Greensboro. Bob and Kay had many decisions to make about their future. Bob wanted to be a good provider, but knew he would need more education to do so. Bob's dream was to become an electrical engineer. He knew with industry booming the demand for this skill would be high.

After discussing their options at length they decided Bob needed to go to school full time until he got his degree in Electrical Engineering. Kay would work full time during these years to support the family. For the first two years of his education Bob attended High Point College in nearby High Point, North Carolina. Then the couple moved to Raleigh, North Carolina where Bob spent his junior and senior years studying at North Carolina State University.

The hard work and sacrifice paid off. Bob graduated with honors and was qualified to become an Electrical Engineer.

To get the best jobs and needed experience Bob and Kay would need to move several times over the next few years.

Bob's first job was in Silver Springs, Maryland. That is also where Kay and Bob's first daughter, Karen was born in 1965.

Two years later after a move back to Greensboro Kay and Bob's second child, Robert Christopher was born. Both children were a joy to Kay.

Bob and Kay continued moving to where Bob's skills were needed. The family would move several places across the country and even had to move twice overseas during these early years.

Then, with all the experience Bob had gained he was able to find a position in Brentwood, Tennessee that would require no more moving. This would be the family's permanent home.

Kay was so glad to finally settle down and really enjoyed living there. Her children, Karen and Chris were in elementary school at the time and this would be where they called home.

Their neighborhood had a swim and tennis club right down the street and all the family spent many hours there over the years. Later during Karen and Chris' high school years both were on the school tennis team.

Kay worked off and on during these years. She kept her skill levels up by continuing to take classes as needed at nearby Vanderbilt

University. Later in 1985 after the children graduated from high school Kay and Bob decided to go their separate ways.

Two year later tragedy struck Kay's family. Her son, Chris was killed in an automobile accident on February 7, 1987. Chris was only 19 years old. It was a very sad time in her life.

Kay continued living in Brentwood and found a new career interest in real estate. She attended several classes in nearby Nashville and got her real estate license.

Kay became a top sales person and received several awards over the years.

Kay's sales abilities and good looks did not go unnoticed by the owner of a local real estate agency, Harold Gordon Weaver. The two started dating and for the second time in her life, Kay fell in love.

The couple was married on October 28, 1994 and after a beautiful honeymoon in San Francisco settled down in Brentwood.

Kay and Gordon spent seven wonderful years together before his passing in 2001.

Kay has lived in Brentwood, Tennessee for over 40 years. She still enjoys living there because her daughter, Karen, son-in-law, Scott and her four grandchildren live close by.

Bob and Kay Ivey with their children, from left Karen and Chris. This picture was taken in 1968.

This is a picture of Kay and her second husband, Harold Gordon Weaver. This picture was taken shortly after their marriage in 1994.

Wilma Lee Crutchfield

On February 26, 1940 Clifton and Annie Crutchfield had their third child, Wilma Lee Crutchfield. She was a cheerful little baby and a joy to Clifton and Annie. Wilma was born in Oak Ridge, North Carolina, however her first memories of childhood were in 1943 when she and her family moved to 1603 Upland Drive in Greensboro, North Carolina. That is when Clifton got his job at the Cone Mills Print Works Plant.

Upland drive was still a dirt road back then and Wilma and her siblings enjoyed gathering with other children in the neighborhood and playing softball in the street. They occasionally had to stop for a car, but not very often. Other games they enjoyed playing were hopscotch and Red Rover, Red Rover.

Swimming was also a frequent activity during the summer months. Battle Ground Park was a great place to go and the nearby YMCA had swimming three times a week. She remembers there being separate girls days and boys days back then.

Wilma did her fair share helping around the house as she grew up. She helped with the dishes, kept her room clean, and had her turn hanging clothes out on the clothesline.

Wilma started first grade in 1946 at Proximity School and would continue going there through the ninth grade. Wilma still remembers walking with her sisters, Jo Anne and Kay two short blocks to school and being able to return home for a quick lunch. She would later attend Greensboro Senior High School.

Although Wilma's parents worked very hard they always took time out for vacations. Wilma remembers every July they would go to White Lake, North Carolina for a week for swimming and relaxation.

Another favorite destination for the family was Hanging Rock State Park in Stokes County, North Carolina. They enjoyed packing a big picnic lunch and when they got to the park, taking the hiking trail all the way to the top of the mountain. The views were spectacular up there.

On Saturdays they went to Grandma and Grandpa Young's house where all the cousins were. They all had great times playing in the woods and around the tobacco barns. Annie and Clifton would stay until 5:00 P.M. and then head home.

Wilma and her family were members of nearby Grace Baptist Church. They attended church there on Sunday mornings, Sunday evenings and Wednesday evenings.

One Sunday evening in 1955 after the services at Grace Baptist Church Wilma went home with a friend named Louise Carter. Louise was dating a young man named C.J. Majors at the time. When C.J. came over that evening his cousin, Van Bolin came with him.

Wilma described Van as being very charming. They went out that same evening for ice cream and their romance began. Wilma had no doubts Van was going to be the love of her life and a few months later they drove to Chesterfield, South Carolina and were married.

In 1956 they had their first child, Diane. In 1958 they had their second child, Debbie and in 1966 they had their third child, Neal. Wilma and Van enjoyed being together and raising their children over the years.

Van worked in construction and hung drywall. While his first jobs were just he as an individual doing work for local contractors, Van later started his own business called Bolin Drywall. Years later after Van and Wilma's son, Neal graduated high school, he also joined the family business and they changed the name of the company to Bolin and Son Drywall.

Wilma had plenty to do staying at home raising their three children and helping as she could with Van's drywall business.

In 1970 Wilma and Van decided to go their separate ways, however they remained friends as they raised their children and were solid grandparents to their grandchildren.

After their marriage ended Wilma went to work full time with the Greensboro Credit Bureau for several years. She later became employed with a mortgage firm as a loan originator. From there Wilma went to work at Piedmont Triad International Airport as their volunteer manager and coordinator. Wilma and Van remained close friends over the years and when Van passed away in 1999 Wilma and all three of their children were there at his bedside.

Today Wilma lives in Stokesdale, North Carolina and continues to work at the Greensboro Triad International Airport part time in their Parking Services Division.

A lot of Wilma's time these days is spent taking care of her oldest daughter, Diane, who has MS.

Wilma loves to swim still and is a very active participant at the YMCA in Greensboro.

Wilma has also kept a strong bond with her siblings over the years and they all try to get together at least twice a year.

Van and Wilma with
their children, Dianne,
Debbie, and Neal.

Wilma and her entire family pose for a picture while visiting at Wilma's house.

Phyllis Ann Crutchfield

On October 12, 1942 Clifton and Annie Crutchfield had their fourth child, Phyllis Ann Crutchfield. Phyllis was born in Oak Ridge, North Carolina, but her earliest memories come after the family had moved to 1603 Upland Drive in Greensboro, North Carolina in 1943.

As with her other siblings, some of Phyllis' fondest memories were of visiting Grandpa and Grandma Young. By the time she was five she enjoyed spending the night with her grandparents. Grandma Young had one of those big smiles and such warm wonderful hugs and Grandpa was always doing something around the farm.

One of Phyllis' funniest memories while spending time with them was one day when Grandpa went out to feed the hogs. When Grandpa returned Phyllis asked if he got the hogs slopped.

His answer was, "Yeah, what didn't slop me!"

As a young child, Phyllis' chores included washing dishes, hanging laundry on the back yard clothes line and keeping her room clean. Later as a teen she was responsible for waxing the linoleum floors.

When she was young her mother was a good seamstress and would sew play suits for her to wear. She also remembers how frugal her family had to be back then. If a pair of shoes had a tear or a worn heel you did not throw them away. You took them to Morrison's Shoe Shop to repair them so they would last another year.

One of Phyllis' favorite deserts was prune cake. Annie made sure she always made her one for her birthday.

As she grew older Phyllis did odd jobs for family and neighbors. She remembers once earning 10 cents from a neighbor and afterward running over to Pegram's Candy Store for a quarter pound Baby Ruth candy bar for her dime. She ate the whole thing on the way home.

Phyllis attended Proximity School through the ninth grade. It was so nice to have her school just two short blocks away from home.

A special treat for Phyllis and her family was when Grandma Young would catch a bus from Oak Ridge and go to Greensboro for a surprise visit. The visits were filled with fun and laughter and

Grandma would always bring a bag of orange slice candy when she visited.

At the age of 16 Phyllis got a job in the credit department at Montgomery Ward in downtown Greensboro. It was her first job and she was excited to be making her own money.

Her mother and father always worked hard and she remembers every 4th of July week when Cone Mills closed they spent the week at White Lake, North Carolina.

Phyllis' brother, Cliff remembers those vacations too. He especially remembers there was a motor boat that took passengers around the perimeter of the big lake for a fee of $2.00 per person.

Well, not everyone had to pay the fee. Anytime Phyllis and sister Kay went for a ride he let them ride for free. They were so pretty he considered them good advertising and his demand for rides increased.

In 1959 Phyllis began dating a boy she had met a couple of years earlier at the Greensboro Municipal Swimming Pool. His name was Ron Alberty and he had just got out of the Navy.

At Christmas Ron proposed marriage and Phyllis happily said yes. Their wedding date was set for late June 1960 after Phyllis' graduation.

Phyllis attended Greensboro's new Page High School and graduated in 1960. As a special treat the graduating class got to take a senior trip to Washington, DC after graduating.

After returning home Phyllis began making plans for her wedding. On June 26, 1960 Ron and Phyllis were married at a beautiful Church wedding in front of lots of family members and friends.

They spent the next week in Daytona Beach, Florida on their honeymoon.

After returning home it was time for the newlyweds to settle down and start their careers.

Ron had already applied for and accepted employment before their wedding in Alexandria, Virginia. Their first step was to move to Virginia. Ron's expertise was in the new field of electronics and specializing in the design of microcircuits. Ron and Phyllis made the move and quickly settled in to their new home.

Phyllis wanted to start her own career and since they were close to Washington DC she took the Federal Government Civil Service Exam. Within a few weeks she was working for the Federal Government in downtown Washington.

In 1961 Ron changed jobs and moved the family to Silver Spring, Maryland.

When the couple moved Phyllis was expecting their first child. In February of 1961 their son, Kerry Dean Alberty was born. Both Phyllis and Ron were so proud of him.

Then, in late 1962 Ron got an offer to go to work with the Harris Corporation in Palm Bay, Florida. Ron gladly accepted and the move was made.

Harris Corporation was a major supplier to the U.S. Military in communications. The job turned out to be very rewarding and fulfilling for Ron and was where he would spend the rest of his career.

In March of 1963 Phyllis and Ron had their second child, Rhonda Lynn Alberty. She was a beautiful little girl and a joy to her parents. Phyllis still recalls how smart she was. By age six she was writing her own poetry.

After Phyllis' children got a little older she decided to go back to work. She found a job with Patrick Air Force Base, which was only a few miles from where they lived.

Life was good along the Florida east coast for the family. There was always plenty to do with the warm sunshine and the ocean nearby. On the weekends they enjoyed water skiing on the inland waterways.

The family would live in Florida for the next two decades. Then on October 24, 1979 tragedy struck the family. Their son Kerry was unexpectedly killed in a car crash. Phyllis remembers it being a hard time for the family. "Kerry was a good student and a good natured child. His favorite hobby was surfing. He grew to be a delightful young man and we really wish he could have known more of his extended family."

Later in 1979 Phyllis and Ron decided to go their separate ways.

Afterward Phyllis applied for and accepted a civilian position at Vandenberg Air Force Base located on the coast of central California. The Base was a ballistic missile launch sight and an unmanned satellite launch site.

Phyllis' daughter, Rhonda, made the cross-country move with her. Rhonda still had a year of high school left at the time and graduated in June of 1981.

Phyllis loved this part of the country and hoped to buy a home there, however the California prices were so high she decided against it.

In the summer of 1981 Phyllis accepted a position at Lockheed Martin Aerospace Corporation in Denver, Colorado.

The new position was a major career advancement for Phyllis. Now she was a Senior Financial Analyst working on cost proposals for military missile systems contracts. Some of the proposals were for hundreds of millions of dollars of equipment.

Phyllis settled in nearby Littleton, Colorado and lived there for the next 10 years. Phyllis spent her leisure time gardening in the summer and downhill skiing in the winter.

In 1990 Phyllis met a man named Hank Esser, and they soon started dating. Hank was a Subcontract Manager at Lockheed Martin at the same facility where Phyllis worked.

Hank and Phyllis were married on March 24, 1991. In attendance at the wedding were Phyllis' daughter, Rhonda, her husband and children, and Hank's family and friends.

Afterward the couple spent their honeymoon in Kauai, Hawaii. When Phyllis and Hank returned to Colorado Phyllis moved to Hank's home in Englewood, Colorado.

A few months later Phyllis told Hank of a dream she had had for several years, but was never able to pursue it. She wanted to go into the field of psychology and help people with their psychological problems. Many people needed professional assistance to get through the troubled times of their lives and Phyllis felt it would be very rewarding to help them.

Hank was supportive and a few months later Phyllis started night school at Metropolitan State College of Denver. She studied hard and in May of 1994 she graduated with a Bachelor of Arts Degree in Psychology.

Immediately following Phyllis became a psychotherapist for Samaritan Counseling Center of Denver. She worked there from 1994 through 1999. She liked it better than any other job she had ever had.

After Hank and Phyllis retired they took time to relax and enjoy life. They enjoyed traveling and were involved in many St. Andrew UMC church activities.

Sadly Phyllis lost hank in 2009. It had been a wonderful happy marriage.

Today Phyllis' hobbies include antique doll collecting, gardening, Sudoku and reading. She also enjoys keeping in touch with family.

Phyllis still lives in Englewood, Colorado.

This is a picture of Phyllis and her first husband, Ron Alberty. Behind them is their son, Kerry and in front is their daughter, Rhonda. This picture is from the mid-1960's.

Phyllis with her second husband, Hank Esser. This picture is from the mid-1990's.

Clifton Daniel Crutchfield, Jr.

On July 12, 1944 Clifton and Annie Crutchfield had their fifth child, Clifton Daniel Crutchfield, Jr. He was Annie and Clifton's first and only son. Clifton was so proud to finally have a son in the family.

Cliff was born with the family living at 1603 Upland drive, Greensboro, North Carolina and would spend his entire childhood there.

Cliff was born into a family with four older sisters and a fifth, Maggie would come two years later.

From an early age Cliff helped out around the house doing his share of the chores. He was responsible for taking out the garbage, getting in wood from the wood pile, and mowing the yard with a manual reel push mower. He even helped with the dishes when it came his turn.

When Cliff was six years old he started at Proximity Elementary School and would spend his first six years there. He would continue and spend grades 7 – 9 in Proximity Jr. High School. The school was only two blocks away, a block if he took a shortcut through the woods.

Cliff really enjoyed doing things with his father. By age three he was going on hunting trips and to local lakes fishing with his father.

Just like his older sisters, Cliff really enjoyed going to Grandpa and Grandma Young's house for a Sunday afternoon or to spend a few nights when he was growing up.

Cliff recalls as a young child, "I loved to sleep out at Grandpa Young's wood fired tobacco barn during curing season. Grandpa would scare the bejeesus out of me with ghost stories and tales of bears, accompanied by strange noises I did not think were imaginary.

Grandpa would pull ears of corn from the field and throw them over the coals in one of the tobacco barn fire boxes to roast. They were probably old ears of corn, but my memory tells me they tasted great. I seem to recall that Grandpa got up every two hours to stoke the fire during the night. He had to be a great tobacco curer because I remember that he went to Canada several times to help them cure tobacco."

In true boy form, Cliff enjoyed listening to New York Yankees baseball games on the radio and later played little league baseball for several years.

When he was 12 Cliff joined the Boy Scouts and really enjoyed it. He learned many lessons of life there.

One of the merit badges Cliff needed to earn while in scouting was the hiking merit badge. He and a friend, Don Pearce decided their hike would be a 25 mile hike from Cliff's house in Greensboro to Grandma and Grandpa Young's house in Oak Ridge. The hike took a little over eight hours.

When Cliff and Don made the turn onto Pepper Road about a half mile from Grandma and Grandpa Young's house, Don collapsed to the ground and said he could go no further. Just let me die right here. With Cliff's urging and sometimes assistance by letting Don put his arm around his shoulder, Don survived the rest of the journey.

When they got to the Young household they found that Cliff's cousin, Brenda Young, was spending the week with Grandma and Grandpa Young. Don instantly made a miraculous recovery from his exhaustion and never mentioned being tired the rest of the visit.

After finishing his sophomore year Cliff, with the help of his father started that summer at Cone Mill's Print Works Plant full time on 2nd shift. He then scheduled his junior classes to end at 2:00 P.M. so he could continue working 2nd shift full time during the school year.

A real turning point in Cliff's life occurred while he was working at the mill. He was working with one of his neighbors, who was a year older than him. He told Cliff about a U.S. Air Force program that would pay you to go to one of 15 top colleges in the country, and then commission you as an Air Force Officer. You only needed to take a qualifying test, and have completed one year of college on your own to qualify for the program.

Cliff thought if you are going to dream, dream big and decided he wanted to go to Harvard University. The decision was made and Cliff made this his new plan of action.

In his senior year Cliff got a job with the Sears Mail Order Warehouse full time on 2nd shift which was also near his home in Greensboro and continued his plan of saving money.

After graduating from Page High School in 1962, Cliff continued to work at Sears.

He also started his freshman year of college taking a full load at nearby Guilford College.

After completing his first full year of college Cliff was ready to enlist in the Air Force in September of 1963. His plan was to go to San Antonio, Texas, complete his basic training and then be off to Harvard. At least that is what the Air Force recruiter told him.

The story changed a bit after he finished his second phase of Air Force basic training in Biloxi, Mississippi. That is when Cliff was informed that most of the airmen being accepted in the AECP program had already completed 60 – 90 hours of college credit.

So then it was forget Harvard and get to work serving four years of Air Force enlistment.

Things worked out well when he managed to latch on to an in service nomination to the Air Force Academy. In 1965, that morphed into a Congressional appointment to the Academy, and that proved to be another big turning point in his life.

Cliff came home to Greensboro on leave to visit and to prepare for the four years he would spend in Colorado at the academy.

Sadly while he was home Grandma Young unexpectedly passed away. Cliff went and stayed with Grandpa Young for two nights right after it happened and still remembers how sad Grandpa was over the loss. Cliff had to leave for Colorado the next day and was unable to stay for the funeral.

A couple of weeks before Christmas in 1965 the academy held a Christmas Formal and one of Cliff's classmates set him up on a blind date.

The girl's name was Penelope Leigh (Pen) Pearson. Pen was a beautiful young woman who was attending nearby Colorado University studying business finance. She and Cliff were both freshmen at the time.

The two really hit it off and soon fell in love. The two would date for their next four years of college. In 1969 Cliff proudly graduated from the U.S. Air Force Academy. After graduating Cliff still had four more years of active duty to serve in the Air Force. He had hoped to become a jet fighter pilot, but his eyesight was not good enough to do so. He decided then to become a navigator. Jet fighters required a two man crew. The navigator was responsible for the weapons systems on the plane. Cliff's next move was to Sacramento, California where he spent a year in Navigation School. As luck would have it, Pen had also graduated in 1969 and afterward accepted a position with Wells Fargo Bank in San Francisco. This meant the two lived close enough together to continue dating.

On Christmas Eve of 1969 at The Top of the Mark in San Francisco Cliff asked Pen to marry him. The couple was married on July 5, 1970 in Pen's hometown of Oxnard California. In attendance were many of Pen's family and friends and two very special guest from Cliff's side of the family. Maggie was a bridesmaid and Jo Anne did her part to represent the rest of the family.

After the wedding Cliff received more special training and then got the call to go to Vietnam.

His responsibility there was to be part of a two man crew flying F-101 VooDoo and F-4 Phantom jet fighters. While the pilot flew the plane, Cliff's responsibility was to be the weapons systems officer.

Cliff still recalls his first flight mission into enemy territory. He said he looked down and said to himself, "Hey, they're shooting real bullets at us!"

The tour in Vietnam was long and rigorous. In all Cliff flew 107 combat missions while there and his crew brought their plane back safe every time.

Finally in 1974 Cliff's tour of duty with the Air Force was up. He left the Air Force as a captain. He was glad he and Pen could finally settle down to a normal life.

After getting out of the Air Force Cliff had to decide what type of career he wanted to have to support Pen and hopefully the children they were planning on having.

A short time later, while visiting Pen's parents in California one of Pen's uncles suggested to Cliff go into the field of Environmental Science. The field was new and had so much potential. To pursue this field Cliff would need to go back to school for two more years to get a masters degree. Cliff decided to go to the University of North Carolina at Chapel Hill. The school was only about 50 miles from where Cliff grew up in Greensboro. He would be back home close to family while he got his education.

Cliff and Pen made the move across country and settled into an apartment near the university. At the time of the move Pen was expecting their first child. A few weeks after arriving in Chapel Hill, Pen had their first child, Amy. Sadly the infant passed away six weeks later. It was a sad time for Cliff and Pen and taught them just how precious life is.

Cliff finished his two years and got his masters degree. Hee had an opportunity to teach some classes while taking these courses and found he enjoyed teaching more than anything he had ever done. With two more years and a PHD in Environmental Science Cliff could become a college professor. While continuing his education, Cliff and Pen had two more children, Jeremy in 1976 and Jeff in 1977. Over the years the two were great students and great athletes. Cliff and Pen spent a lot of time as they grew up watching them play baseball, soccer and volleyball.

After graduating from UNC in 1978 Cliff joined the faculty at the University of Arizona in Tucson as a professor in Environmental Science.

It was also about this time Pen got to fulfill one of her lifelong dreams. She went back to college and studied hard to become a Certified Public Accountant. Pen also went to work for the University of Arizona in their accounting department.

A few years later while Cliff was teaching at the University of Arizona, an Air Force Engineer from Davis-Monthan AFB there in Tucson took a ventilation course from Cliff. During the semester he asked Cliff if he would be interested in an Air Force slot at his office at the base.

Cliff's reserve duty would involve working with his office one day per month and he would also need to spend two weeks on active duty during the summer. It was a deal too good to pass up. After several years of service Cliff retired from the Air Force Reserve in 1999 as a Colonel.

For 25 years both Cliff and Pen had exciting and fulfilling jobs at the University. Both Cliff and Pen retired in 2004 and they still live in Tucson today.

Cliff graduating from the U.S. Air Force Academy in 1969.

This is a picture of Cliff, Pen, and their two children, Jeremy and Jeff.

Margaret Maurene Crutchfield

On June 27, 1946 Clifton and Annie Crutchfield had their sixth and final child, Margaret Maurene Crutchfield. She was a cute little baby with a wonderful smile. She would be called "Maggie" by the family.

Maggie was born with the family living at 1603 Upland Drive, Greensboro, North Carolina and she would spend her entire childhood there.

From the time Maggie was old enough to sleep with her five older sisters she remembers having to fit in wherever she could. For a few years she slept at the foot of the bed with two of her sisters so all could have plenty of room.

Maggie remembers in those earlier years even though they had an oil circulator and a fireplace for heat, the bedrooms were not heated. They used a lot of quilts, and in the mornings they ran to the oil heater to get warm.

Maggie really enjoyed living Upland Drive when she was growing up. There were trees to climb in the back yard and lots of children her age to play with in their neighborhood. They enjoyed playing games like red rover and kick the can.

There was a playground at the end of the street. Maggie's brother told her that was Texas and for years she believed him.

Maggie really felt blessed by the closeness of her family while growing up. They enjoyed playing games like checkers and Rook together or putting together a large puzzle.

There was a piano in the living room and many times the family gathered around it, and while Kay played they sang gospel songs.

The family went to church on Sunday mornings, Sunday nights and Wednesday nights. They did not eat out a lot back then, but they would get a cone of ice cream after church from Yum Yum Ice Cream Shop. Mom would get butter pecan and Dad would get vanilla. Maggie liked butter pecan.

On Fridays the family enjoyed a big box of Libby Hill fish, which could be purchased for $2.00 for a family box.

Clifton received the Greensboro morning and evening newspapers. He read them cover to cover every day.

Another happy part of growing up for Maggie was her fond memories of visiting Grandma and Grandpa Young's farm.

In Maggie's own words, "I got to go to the farm and spend weeks at a time in the summer. I remember helping in tobacco and spending the night at the tobacco barn with Grandpa, helping to put wood in the fire boxes to cure the tobacco. I helped milk his cow when I got older. I helped Grandma Young churn butter. Grandma Young always played cards with us and made us feel special. I remember sleeping upstairs and hearing the rain on the tin roof. We caught fireflies and played Ain't No Bears Out Tonight. I remember making ice cream in a hand churn freezer and my cousins and I would eat it so fast it would make our heads ache. We would go swimming at the swimming hole and go out into the watermelon patch with the salt shaker. I learned about hard work, being happy with what you had, respect of others, love of family and so many values not written down. I also learned the value of prayer from my Grandma Young."

Maggie went to school at Proximity Elementary School for grades 1 – 6 and Proximity Junior High School for grades 7 – 9. The schools were only two blocks away and she was able to walk to school the whole nine years. Maggie spent grades 10 – 12 at Page High School.

Maggie made the high school basketball team at Page and turned out to be a really good player.

While in high school Maggie and Cliff were very close. By then all of their siblings had moved on and they each had their own bedroom at home. Cliff drove them to high school in the family's pink Pontiac.

Also during this time Cliff's best friend, David Barbour, became Maggie's boyfriend. Maggie and David would continue dating through high school.

During this time that Maggie's Aunt Edna Young Goins decided to go back to school and become a Licensed Practical Nurse. This action by Aunt Edna had a strong influence on Maggie's desire to become a nurse as well.

At age 14 Maggie had her first association with nursing when she became a Junior Grey Lady at Wesley Long Memorial Hospital in Greensboro.

At age 16 Maggie went to work as a nurse's aide at Moses Cone Hospital in Greensboro. Maggie continued working there for the rest of high school.

Maggie graduated from Page High School in 1964.
After graduating Maggie and David Barbour got engaged to be married. They were married on October 17, 1964. Maggie tried to make the marriage work, but David developed some habits Maggie just could not accept. The couple went their separate ways three years later.

In 1967 Maggie enrolled in Nursing School at Charlotte Memorial Hospital in Charlotte, North Carolina. The course was a two year work-study program where she could earn an Associates Degree in Nursing.

Over the next two years Maggie worked very hard. She graduated in 1969, and after passing the state board exam became a Registered Nurse in the state of North Carolina.

Maggie would continue working at Charlotte Memorial Hospital for three more years.

In 1970 Maggie man named Chris Breden. He lived in the same apartment complex where Maggie lived. The two started dating and soon fell in love. The couple was married later that year on August 19, 1970.

Maggie and Chris had three children over the next five years, Mathew Jurgen in 1971, Molly Hope in 1974 and Micah Daniel in 1975. Chris also brought two children of his own into the marriage, Rosie and CJ.

Maggie's hard work really paid off. After getting experience on the hospital floor as a nurse, her next step was to become a nursing supervisor. A couple of years later she was promoted to Director of Nursing when she accepted a position at a hospital in Scotland Neck, North Carolina. Two years after that she accepted a nursing position at Weyerhaeuser Corporation in Jacksonville, NC and later became their personnel manager.

Maggie's marriage to Chris lasted for seven years and then they decided to go their separate ways.

In 1977 Maggie got an extraordinary opportunity to advance her education. There was a Martin Luther King full scholarship available for a two year course to study Nursing Administration at Duke University. To Maggie's amazement, she was awarded the scholarship. She had to continue working full time as a nurse, raise five children; and take a full course load at the university.

She had a great moral supporter at the time, her brother, Cliff. Cliff was going to the Air Force Academy at the time and wrote Maggie several times a week. The encouragement did a lot to pull Maggie through the two years. Maggie graduated in 1979 and was so proud of herself. After graduating Maggie moved to Taylorsville, North Carolina. For ten years she worked in post-op surgical nursing and supervision at Iredell Memorial Hospital in Statesville, NC.

In 1984 Maggie and ex-husband Chris Breden decided to give marriage another try. Chris brought with him another son, Jacob from his recent marriage. The marriage lasted four years and he was gone once again. When he left Maggie this time she had six children to raise on her own. Fortunately each of these children were very smart and helped Maggie keep the house in order. They would all go on to do well in life.

In 1989 Maggie accepted a position at Frye Regional Hospital in Hickory, North Carolina where she works as the charge nurse of youth services. She has worked there for 22 years now and counting.

In 2009 Maggie was attacked by a patient at Frye Regional and was beaten severely. The incident left her in critical condition. It would take a shoulder replacement and nine months to recover.

In 2010 Maggie met a gentleman named Alan Paul Taylor and soon after they started dating. Alan was both an Engineer and a Baptist Minister and had a wonderful personally.   On August 25, 2010 Maggie and Alan were married and have lived happily together ever since.

This is a picture of all of Maggie's children. They are Mathew, Molly, Micah, Rosie, CJ, and Jacob. This picture was taken in December of 2008.

Alan and Maggie Taylor on their wedding day, August 25, 2010. Maggie has proclaimed Alan the love of her life.

Chapter Nine

The Raymond Young Family

The date was June 12, 1917 and it was a proud day for Alma and Elias Young. It was on this day their third child, Raymond Lee Young was born. Raymond would grow to be a caring and giving man, who liked to make people smile and laugh. Raymond spent the first five years of his childhood growing up on the McGee Farm, which was Alma's parent's farm west of Walkertown, North Carolina.

In 1922 Elias and Alma moved the family to the Wicker Farm. It was located in the Belews Creek Community near Goodwill Church east of Walkertown, North Carolina and next to Elias' father, Hester Young's farm.

About a year later Raymond started first grade in nearby Walnut Cove, North Carolina and spent his first seven years of school there.

By age seven Raymond was helping his father, Elias and his older brother, Hubert in the farm fields raising their eight acre tobacco crop, field corn for the animals and two large gardens for the Young family's food.

There was a wide creek that ran through the middle of the Wicker Farm and when Raymond had free time he would go fishing there. On many occasions he caught enough fish for Alma to have them as a meal for supper.

Raymond had his own secret spot where the fish were always plentiful. Even years later after Raymond was married he came back here if he wanted to have a great day of fishing.

By age ten, Raymond was plowing the fields with the family work horse, Dan and could chop cook stove wood and firewood as well as Elias or Hubert.

In 1930 when Raymond was 12 Elias and Alma moved their family to the Case Place Farm on Highway 68 in Oak Ridge.

Raymond was mature for his age and while Elias and Hubert drove a two horse wagon to move the family's furniture, Raymond drove Alma and the rest of the children to their new home in the family's Model "T" Ford.

Raymond continued his education at nearby Oak Ridge School and would go there through the eighth grade. At the time Oak Ridge's school only went through the eight grade, but he had the option to attend school in Summerfield.

In 1932 Raymond decided to stop in the eighth grade and work on the farm with his father and Hubert.

At the time there were no public jobs. The Great depression had slowed industry across America to a screeching halt. Raymond helped Elias and Hubert raise the nine acres of tobacco on the Case Place.

In the spring of 1933 Elias wanted to show his appreciation for all the hard work Raymond was doing around the farm and decided to let Raymond have an acre of his own tobacco this year. Raymond was so proud to have his own crop and meticulously tended his acre while continuing to do his normal chores around the farm.

Raymond would always remember that special day in October of 1933 when he took his crop of flue cured tobacco to Taylor's Warehouse in Winston-Salem, North Carolina and sold his poundage. He walked away with $50.30 for his summers efforts. It was the first money he had ever earned.

In the fall of 1934 Raymond applied for and got a job with nearby Oak Ridge School to drive one of their school buses. The job required Raymond to pick up children from around the area each morning and carry them to school and then each afternoon go back to the school and take those same students home. The job took about four hours a day and allowed Raymond to do his work on the farm.

Raymond's younger sisters all loved the fact that Raymond was driving the Oak Ridge school bus. Hazel, Edna, Opal and Elsie were all going to school at Oak Ridge and it was great having their school bus parked in their front yard every morning.

During the 1930's news from the outside world was hard to come by for the Young family. The family did not get a newspaper, and they did not have electricity. Usually news was brought to the Young household when Elias went to the local country store and talked to some of the other farmers there.

All that changed on Christmas day in 1934 when Raymond presented the family with their own battery powered Philco cabinet style radio. The radio stood four feet tall and had two large batteries the size of car batteries inside to power the unit since the Young's still did not have electricity.

For the first time the family could get the latest news of the world and listen to their favorite radio shows in their living room. Raymond's radio was a major advance for the Young family.

Raymond spent the next eight months paying $5 a month from his bus driving paycheck to pay for the radio. It was well worth it to Raymond. He was finally able to give something back to his family.

Raymond made another major purchase with his earnings from driving the school bus. In 1936 Raymond's older sister, Annie was getting ready to get married to her fiancé, Clifton Crutchfield. Annie knew the times were hard and did not even think of asking Elias and Alma to buy her a new wedding dress.

Two weeks before the wedding Raymond went to Annie and told her, "Annie, you and I need to take the car to Greensboro today."

"Why?" asked Annie.

"Because I'm going to buy you a new wedding dress for your wedding!" Raymond grinned.

Annie was so happy that day. She and Raymond spent the whole day in Greensboro picking out that special dress.

Over the years the Young family would recall this moment time and again. It was one of their true bright spots during the Great Depression.

Around this time Raymond heard about job openings at Mock Judson Hosiery Mill in Greensboro, North Carolina. Raymond went to Greensboro and stood outside the factory hoping to get a chance to go inside for an interview. There were also 200 other men standing outside with him that day. To Raymond's amazement he and another man were the only two men chosen from the entire crowd.

At the time Mock Judson employed over 1300 people and made silk and nylon hosiery. The name was shortened to MoJud by the locals. Raymond met two of his coworkers that lived in nearby Summerfield, Willie Jones and John Lee. Willie would drive his Model A Ford and pick John and Raymond up on his way to the mill. They would become close friends over the years.

Raymond worked in the throwing department where they made the thread for the hosiery. Raymond dyed the thread to a specific color and then sent the spools to the factory floor to be manufactured into socks and womens hose.

Raymond and John Lee had another favorite pastime during the mid and late 1930's. They both were members of the Oak Ridge semi-pro baseball team.

Raymond was left handed and was one of the best pitchers in the league. He had a curve ball other batters could not hit. The team gave Raymond a new nickname while on the team. He was known as "Lefty" Young.

In 1936 Raymond began to notice one of his neighbors, Ruby Sizemore. She lived less than a mile down Hwy 68 from the Case Place on the opposite side of the road from the Young's.

Ruby was a beautiful young woman and was about a year younger than Raymond. Raymond liked Ruby from the start and soon they started dating. Before long Raymond knew he had found the love of his life.

Ruby was born on April 1, 1917. Her father was Thomas Lafayette Sizemore. He was born on July 3, 1873 in North Carolina. Ruby's mother was Nancy Elizabeth Johnson Sizemore. She was born in 1880 in Sauratown, North Carolina. Sadly Nancy had passed away in 1931 when Ruby was 13 years old. After her mother died her sisters helped to take care of Ruby and the younger children.

Thomas was a farmer and ran a sawmill. He had a team of horses that would pull his sawmill to each piece of land he was hired to cut.

In January 1938 Raymond and Ruby decided it was time for them to get married. After sharing the news with their families Raymond called his friend, John Lee and told him the good news. John and his wife rode with Raymond and Ruby to Arthur Jones' house. He was a justice of the peace who lived between Oak Ridge and Stokesdale. They were married in the Jones' living room.

For the first year of their marriage Raymond and Ruby lived with his parents for a few months.

On November 15, 1938 Ruby and Raymond had their first child, Kenneth Ray Young. This was such a proud day for the couple.

A couple of months later Raymond and Ruby moved from Ruby's father, Thomas' house to an apartment. They found a house with an upstairs apartment for rent on Salisbury Street in Kernersville.

Raymond had the only car in the Young extended family at the time and would kindly allow other members of his family to borrow the car if they needed transportation.

They did not stay in Kernersville for long. In 1941 they moved back to Oak Ridge and rented a small house on Bunch Road from the Cline family. They both enjoyed living closer to their families and being able to raise a small garden of their own.

Around this time Raymond got a new job at Southern Silk Mill in Kernersville, North Carolina. The mill was located at the intersection of Highway 66 and E. Mountain Street, which is right across the street from where Parks Chevrolet is in Kernersville today.

A few months later on December 7, 1941 the Japanese attacked Pearl Harbor. The following day President Franklin D. Roosevelt declared war on Japan and Germany. Over the next five years any man born before 1927 in the United States was eligible for the draft. The family knew that it was just a matter of time before Raymond was called.

On April 12, 1942 Ruby and Raymond had their second child, Gary Wayne Young. Raymond now had two young sons and a wife to support.

During this time Raymond continued working for Southern Silk Mill in Kernersville. Like most factories during World War II a major portion of their work was for the war effort. There was a shortage of nylon and silk so the factories began using rayon to make hosiery.

Southern Silk Mill was contracted by the U.S. Military to make parachutes out of rayon for their troops. Raymond was needed at the silk mill and because of this he was never drafted by the military.

In the fall of 1942 Raymond and Ruby rented a two story farmhouse at the end of Union Grove Road in Oak Ridge and they lived there for the next three years.

On July 12, 1945 Raymond and Ruby bought their first home. It was a small farmhouse at 5412 Union Grove Church Road, just up the road from the house they were renting. They paid $3000 for the house and land.   Raymond put down $500 and would make payments each year until it was paid for.   This is where all the children would call home.

It was a small three room farmhouse with a front and back porch. There was a living room on one side and a bedroom on the other with a fireplace that was shared between the two rooms. Behind the living room was the kitchen with a wood burning cook stove.

There was an attic upstairs that was used for storage and sometimes was used as a bedroom for some of the children or Raymond. Ken remembers sleeping in the attic as a young child. One cold winter night he started a small fire in the attic to keep his dog warm.

Ken recalls, "When Daddy found out what I had done he whipped my rear end all the way down the stairs!"

Just behind the house was a well to draw water. The house didn't have running water at the time. About 150 feet behind the house was the outhouse. On one side of the family house was a big garden and on the other side of the house was pasture. The front yard had a large tree with a tire swing hanging from it and every spring Ruby planted beautiful flowers all around the house.   Behind the house were two barns.   One had a carport, and inside the other barn was a stall where the milk cow was kept along with a loft for storing hay. There was also a small corn crib built up off the ground to keep animals out of their feed corn. The back half of the property was filled with trees. Gary still remembers Raymond paying him and Ken a nickel for every tree they cut down and split up for firewood for the winter.

During wartime there was a shortage of men to work at the local factories so they started hiring women. In 1945 Ruby was hired at

Vance Hosiery Mill on Main Street in downtown Kernersville. The extra money helped to pay for Ruby and Raymond's new home.

Ruby never got her drivers license and during this time she rode to work with her friend, Ila Parker. Ruby worked at Vance Hosiery until 1949.

On October 4, 1949 Ruby and Raymond's third child, Ronald Lee Young was born.

Two years later they had their fourth and final child, Linda Gail Young.

During the early 1950's Raymond continued to work at Southern Silk Mill in Kernersville and also raised a crop of three and a half to four acres of tobacco every year.

The entire family pitched in to raise the crop of tobacco. The boys would even miss two or three days of school in the fall to put in the final barns of tobacco.

In 1953 Raymond added a new oil circulator to heat the house in the living room. This meant a lot less wood chopping for Ken and Gary.

In 1954 Raymond built Ruby a brand new kitchen on the back of the house. The new kitchen was a major upgrade adding a new electric stove and refrigerator and plenty of counter space for Ruby to make her famous buttermilk biscuits. This allowed them to turn the old kitchen into a bedroom.

In 1955 Raymond made another addition to the home. This time he added a new bathroom with a commode, sink and bathtub, although the bathtub was not completely new to the family. The tub had been sitting in the pasture and was used as a water trough for their horse. No more trips to the outhouse for the Young family. Raymond also built a new screened in back porch encircling the old well.

Raymond enjoyed bird hunting and in 1957 had one of the best bird dogs around. Raymond's brother-in-law, Pete Flynt, worked at R.J. Reynolds Tobacco Company in plant security at the time and had a supervisor that also enjoyed bird hunting.

One Saturday the supervisor went hunting with Raymond and declared Raymond's hound the best bird dog he had ever seen. Raymond told the supervisor to take the dog home with him and keep him for a couple of weeks. Of course this thrilled the supervisor.

After returning the dog the supervisor told Raymond there was an opening at Reynolds in his plant security department and he would put in a good word for him if he applied. The next day Raymond applied for the job and found you could be no older than 38 to be hired in this position. Raymond was 40 at the time and assumed he would not get the job.

When the supervisor found out about Raymond's age, he went to the personnel department and told them a person who can raise a bird dog that good needs a job at R.J. Reynolds Tobacco Company. The age limit was quietly waved and Raymond got the job.

The Young family still loves to tell the tale of Raymond's bird dog getting him his job at Reynolds.

In the early 1960's Raymond switched his preference of hunting from bird hunting to fox hunting. Fox hunting had become a big time sport in the southeast during this era. Dozens of farmers around the Kernersville-Colfax-Oak Ridge community, including his brother-in-law, Pete Flynt had dog lots full of fox hounds behind their houses.

Raymond carefully selected the best blood lines and raised his own pack of dogs from pups to go hunting with. He traveled all over the country hunting his hounds and his dogs were some of the best there were.

In 1964 Raymond's dog, Haw River Joe, won the U.S. Open Field Trials in Mississippi.

Two years later another one of his dogs, Haw River Rufus won the National Futurity Field Trials, which were sponsored by the national fox hunting magazine, "The Chase".

Raymond continued hunting for the next few years, but in 1966 his prized hound, Haw River Joe was stolen. The entire fox hunting community helped Raymond search for the great hound, but sadly he was never found.

Although Raymond continued to have good hunting dogs he never had another one like Haw River Joe.

In 1980 at age 62 Raymond retired from Reynolds. After retiring, Raymond and Ruby bought a cabin on the North Carolina Coast. Raymond enjoyed going to his cabin to fish, hunt, and visit friends. Raymond even helped to start a nearby hunting club and enjoyed hunting down there for several years.

Ruby also enjoyed the cabin and spending Raymond's retirement years back home in Oak Ridge. She spent her time growing flowers and cooking some of her famous home cooked meals for her now married children when they and the grandchildren came home to visit.

Sadly Ruby passed away on May 1, 1989. She was buried next door to her house at the Union Grove Baptist Church Cemetery. Raymond would never remarry.

Afterward, Raymond continued to enjoy time at his cabin on the North Carolina Coast and visiting family and friends around his home in Oak Ridge.

Raymond really enjoyed spending time with one of his friends, Jack Blaylock. Raymond and Jack had been best friends since their baseball playing days back in the late 1930's. While Raymond was a pitcher for the semi-pro team Jack was the catcher. Jack went on to be a successful player and coach at Kernersville High School. Jack remembers spending time with Raymond over the years cooking chicken stews, planting gardens together, going to auctions and visiting with friends and neighbors.

Raymond was known in the community for his frequent visits. He may not stay long but he always brought a smile and a basket of fresh vegetables from his garden to share.

Raymond passed away one month before his 93rd birthday on May 12, 2010. He was buried next to his wife, Ruby on the hill above their house at Union Grove Baptist Church.

Raymond and his siblings taken in the early 1920's in front of one of the Young family's tobacco fields. Raymond is on the left with Annie, Hubeart, and his younger sister Hazel standing in the front.

Ruby standing in front of her parent's house on Hwy 68 in Oak Ridge in the early 1930's

This picture was taken of Raymond and Ruby Young soon after they were married in the late 1930's in front of his parent's house on Pepper Road in Oak Ridge, NC.

This family portrait from the mid 1950's was taken in front of Grandpa and Grandma Young's house standing in Pepper Road. On the Back row from left to right are Raymond, Ruby, Ken, and Gary. On the front row are Ronnie and Linda.

Raymond in the mid 1960's with his fox hound, Haw River Joe. He was the United States Chamapion Fox Hound when he won the US Open in 1964.

Ruby making buttermilk biscuits and Raymond frying cornbread on the stove in their kitchen in February 1988.

Raymond and two of his best friends, Charlie McGee (left) and Jack Blaylock (right), telling stories at Raymond's 91st Birthday party in 2008.

Raymond celebrating his 88th Birthday in 2005 with his family. Back row from left to right is Kenny Crews, Ken & Betty Young, and Sue & Ronnie Young. Front row from left to right are Linda Crews, Raymond Young, and Gary Young.

Kenneth Ray Young

On November 15, 1938 Ruby and Raymond Young had their first child, Kenneth Ray Young. He would be called "Ken" by the family. Raymond was recently hired with Mock Judson Hosiery Mill in Greensboro, North Carolina and a couple of months after Ken's birth they were able to declare their independence and rent their own home. Ken's first memories were of Raymond and Ruby living across the road from Elias and Alma Young when they lived at the Case Place on Highway 68 just north of Oak Ridge, North Carolina.

When Ken was six he started first grade at Oak Ridge Elementary School and would go there his first four years. That same year Raymond and Ruby bought their first home at 5412 Union Grove Church Road in Oak Ridge. This would always be home for Ken. Soon after moving to their new home Ken made friends with a baby crow he found in their back yard. Ken loved playing with his new pet, but Ruby also enjoyed sewing in the back yard. The little crow had a habit of stealing her thread and flying away with it. Ken recalls, "Mama said the crow had to go, but she ended up letting me keep him". This would be the first of many pets in Ken's life. He has loved animals his entire life.

When Ken started the fifth grade he transferred to Kernersville School and would continue there for grades 5 – 12. By the time Ken was 12 Raymond started assigning him more responsibilities. At the time, Raymond was employed at Southern Silk Mill in Kernersville, NC and was also raising 3 ½ acres of tobacco at the same time. Half an acre was at their farm on Union Grove Church Road and three acres were at Grandpa Young's at the Lowery Place on Pepper Road.

During the summer months while Raymond was at work he put Ken in charge of Gary and Ronnie working the tobacco fields while he was not there. The three boys spent a lot of time working in those tobacco fields with Grandpa Young during this time. Raymond gave Ken 25 cents a week for his efforts. A lot of times Ken would go to the store and buy himself a Pepsi and a big honey bun.

When Ken turned 15 he started getting some odd jobs around the community to earn a little extra money. After saving for several months he was able to buy an old Model "A" Ford. Ken loved that old car. He only had one problem. He couldn't afford to buy gas for it. When Ken was 17 he got his first job in downtown Kernersville at Musten & Crutchfield Grocery Store. His first weeks pay was $11.00. Ken was so proud he grabbed a shopping cart and went all around the store buying groceries. He went home that day with $10.50 worth of groceries and gave them to his family.

It was also about this time that Ken met Betty McBride. She was three years younger than Ken and was in his brother, Gary's, grade at school. Ken and Betty started dating and would continue for the rest of his time in high school. In June of 1957 Ken graduated from Kernersville High School and he continued dating Betty after he graduated.

On February 6, 1958 Ken and Betty drove to Chesterfield, South Carolina with a couple of friends and got married. Betty still had two years of high school left.

In November of 1958 Ken was drafted by the U.S. Army. While Ken was away Betty lived with Ruby and Raymond and the other children. At first Ken was stationed in Fort Jackson, South Carolina and then it was on to Fort Seal, Oklahoma. Afterward he was stationed at Fort Bragg, North Carolina and would spend the rest of his time there.

Ken was in the Eleventh Air Assault and learned how to repel out of helicopters. He acquired the rank of E4 before his two years of service were up.

After Ken got out of the Army he and Betty found a place of their own. It was an apartment above a store in downtown Kernersville near the Justice Theater. They paid $35.00 a month for rent.

After the couple got settled in to their new home Ken went back to school at Guilford Technical Community College in Greensboro, NC on the G.I. Bill. Ken's course of study was Machine Shop Practices.

A few months later Ken got an opportunity to go to work at Duke Power Company. Ken gave up his machine shop schooling and gladly took the job. He would work there for the next 10 years. During his career with Duke Power Ken worked on a line truck and as a meter tech.

In 1981 Ken made a major career decision to leave Duke Power and go into business for himself. He and a partner opened a bakery in Burlington, North Carolina called Paul's Pastries.

Betty and her mother also helped at the bakery. Their hopes were so high, but the business did not make enough money and it was closed a year later.

Afterward Ken and Betty moved back to Kernersville and bought a house on Main Street. Although the bakery was not a success Betty and Ken learned a lot about the proper way to run a business from the experience.

Betty wanted her and Ken to take that knowledge and start a new business running a florist out of their home. Ken's father, Raymond liked the idea and gave Betty $100 to buy supplies to start the business. It started in the front room of their house, but business was so good it began to take over other rooms of the house. Before long they ran out of room in the house and decided to build a brand new building behind their house solely for the floral business. After the new building was completed Ken and Betty sold their house and had it moved to another location giving their floral business a large parking lot out front. It was a proud day for both Ken and Betty when they opened the doors to the new building for Young's Florist.

After selling their house Ken and Betty moved to a home they had bought on Warren Road in Kernersville. They both enjoyed living back in the woods along a winding stream. It was here that they relaxed after a long day at the florist.

After opening the new building Betty hired more help to make the flower arrangements. While some customers came to the shop to purchase their flowers, Ken found he had a full time job delivering the rest of the flowers. Ken and Betty had found the right combination and the business grew and grew.

While Ken made deliveries around the Kernersville area he was also a volunteer fireman for the local Piney Grove Fire Department. He had started volunteering with the fire department in the 1970's. If a call came in he would here it on his CB radio and would head right to the scene of the fire or emergency.

On the morning of December 15, 1986 Ken was out making a delivery when he saw smoke and flames coming from a house. He quickly called the Kernersville Fire Department and then made his way through the front door of the house. The smoke was thick but he crawled on the floor until he found a young boy running around. He grabbed his legs and pulled him out of the house. That is when he found out there was another boy inside the house. He went back in as flames were pouring out of the windows and found him asleep on the sofa. He woke the boy up and brought him out of the house as the fire department was arriving. Although Ken didn't consider himself a hero the town of Kernersville did and made January 21st Kenneth R. Young day in his honor.

Over the years Ken would go on many calls. One day Ken got a call that an elderly woman at a local nursing home was missing. They searched and searched but she could not be found. Finally they gathered several people from the surrounding neighborhood and they searched late into the night before finally finding her. After the rescue, Ken gave this particular call a lot of thought. How many young people and elderly people could be saved if these volunteers had better methods of tracking lost people down?

Then, Ken had a great idea. If they had a dog with a great sense of smell they could track the person down using the scent of a piece of that person's clothing. Ken and fellow members of the Piney Grove Fire Department, Bo Hopkins, James Johnson, and Danny Westmorland did a search and found a bloodhound that was just perfect for the job. His name was Joe.

After getting Joe, Ken formed the Forsyth County Search and Rescue Team. The unit was strictly voluntary and was joined by several interested friends who wanted to help as lost person emergencies arose in the community. Ken would serve as Captain of the team. Years later this team would change its name to Triad Bloodhounds. Ken continued his duties as Captain and was later made Major of the team.

Ken spent long hours training Joe to track and find the lost victims. Ken gives much of the credit of his knowledge of dogs to his father, Raymond who was so good at training bird dogs and fox hounds while Ken was a young man in the 1960's.

As time went by, Ken would raise and train many dogs for himself and others on the team. His dogs often traveled in the van with Ken on floral deliveries and everywhere else he went. If it was a hot summer evening and Ken and Betty went out to eat after a hard days work, you would see the van running in the parking lot with the air conditioner on just for their pets to keep cool.

Over the years Ken got thousands of calls and logged many more hours training and working with his dogs. The stories are too numerous to tell of the recues the team made.

And you can bet if a late night call came in, Betty would be right by Ken's side as he went on the calls. Over the years, Ken and Triad Bloodhounds have trained several other bloodhounds for the search and rescue team and have traveled all over the southeast searching for lost and missing people. Ken and his fellow members have always volunteered their time and have never charged anyone for their service. While members have come and gone over the years Ken and Danny Westmoreland are still with the team. Ken has now retired from going on calls with the bloodhounds, however he is still a vital part of the team.

While Bloodhounds are a special part of Ken's life he has always loved all types of animals. From the baby crow he had as a child to his bloodhounds to a skunk and everything in between. When you pull into Ken's driveway you never know what type of animal will greet you at your car.

In 2011 a sad day came for Ken and his family. The love of his life, Betty passed away after a short illness on March 3, 2011. For 50 years they had spent almost every moment of their lives together.

Ken continues to work with Triad Bloodhounds and he still owns Young's Florist, but has retired and leaves the day to day operation to his niece, Tina Compton.

Ruby with Gary and Ken(Ken is standing on the right) in their family's Model A Ford. Raymond would later recall how hard it was for the entire family to fit in the small front seat of the Ford, but at the time they didn't have a choice.

Ken & Betty in 1959 after they were married. Ken was in the US Army at the time and had thumbed his way home from Fort Bragg, NC to Oak Ridge to visit his family and new wife.

Ken with his dog, Bear, in 1998 working with the Triad Bloodhound Team.

Ken & Betty Celebrating their 50th Wedding Anniversary with their friends and family in February 2008.

Gary Wayne Young

On April 12, 1942 Ruby and Raymond Young had their second child, Gary Wayne Young. When Gary was born Raymond and Ruby lived on Bunch Road in Oak Ridge, North Carolina. When Gary turned three they bought a farm and home at 5412 Union Grove Road and he would spend the rest of his childhood growing up there.

Gary remembers growing up there so well. "It was just a small house; 2 bedrooms, living room, kitchen, front and back porch, attic and a basement. I had to sleep with my brother, Ken. What an experience that was. After Ken got married and moved out I finally got some sleep!"

By the time Gary was nine he was helping Ken cut firewood for the house. At the time they needed wood for both Ruby's wood cook stove and the wood heating stove to heat their home.

They would choose a tree in the woods behind their house and using a crosscut saw, Ken and Gary would saw the tree down. They would continue using the crosscut saw and later an ax to cut and chop the wood to the size needed. Gary remembers on cold winter days the house was cold, however if you were near the wood heater it was toasty warm.

Gary remembers he loved the outdoors when he was young. If he and Ken were not working in the farm fields or doing chores they were playing baseball together or riding their bikes. "We rode bicycles a lot. It must have been a 100,000 miles."

One of Gary's chores was to get the mail every day. The mail box wasn't in front of the house at the time. Gary would walk the quarter mile to the end of the road where the mail box was on Highway 150 to get the mail.

Gary smiles when he thinks back. "We never got an allowance for doing our choirs. I had never even heard of an allowance. You just pitched in and helped." He does remember his dad giving him a nickel or a dime now and then.

Gary grew up right on the Guilford-Forsyth County line on their farm and at the time could go to either Oak Ridge or Kernersville School.

Gary started out at Oak Ridge Elementary School in grades one and two and then switched to Kernersville School through the seventh grade. He then went back to the eighth grade at Oak Ridge School.

He would spend his high school years at Kernersville Senior High School, graduating in 1961.

Gary has fond memories of his grandparents, Grandpa and Grandma Young. They were both a big influence on Gary.

He remembers Grandpa Young having more patience than anyone he knew. "He had to have a bunch to put up with me, Ken and our cousin, MK Moore."

Gary remembers spending a lot of nights at Grandpa and Grandma Young's house when he was growing up. Grandpa Young was a quiet man, he never said much. He would just give you one of those looks and you knew what he meant. Grandma Young was very special. She loved all of her grandchildren and had a way to make each one feel special.

Gary recalls working in the fields with Grandpa Young and several of his cousins. They would work in the tobacco fields all morning and around noon they would ask Grandpa what they were going to do after dinner?

Grandpa would say with a grin, "I think we will help Gus this afternoon."

They never knew who Gus was, but they sure liked him. What it really meant was they would go fishing at Blaylock Pond that afternoon.

Gary did not know his grandparents on Ruby's side of the family nearly as well as he knew the Youngs. Ruby's mother, Nancy Sizemore had passed away in 1931 before Gary was born and Gary only remembers his Grandpa Thomas Sizemore when he very young. Grandpa Sizemore lived in a house in Oak Ridge that sat behind where Oak Ridge Methodist Church is today.

After graduating from high school in 1961, Gary worked during the summer with his father and Grandpa Young raising their crops of tobacco.

In October of 1961 Gary applied for a job at R.J. Reynolds Tobacco Company in Winston-Salem, North Carolina and was immediately hired. He started the new position as a carpenter. Gary liked the job and would work there until June of 1962.

Then he decided to join the U.S. Navy. In late June of 1962 he signed up and was sent to boot camp in Illinois. After boot camp he was stationed in Jacksonville, Florida for eight months.

In October of 1964 he was sent to Iceland for 13 months. Finally, in November of 1965 Gary was able to come back home and spend about a month with his family back in Oak Ridge, NC.

Then, Gary was given orders to report to the USS Saratoga Navel Aircraft Carrier. Gary would spend the rest of his time in the Navy on the Saratoga.

Finally Gary was sent to Philadelphia, Pennsylvania. There he was discharged from the Navy after four years of service in August of 1966 as an E3 Airman.

Gary remained in Philadelphia for about two weeks after being discharged and visited with an old Navy buddy he had served with in Iceland a couple of years back.

It was during this time Gary was introduced to his buddy's sister-in-law, Joy Dixon. Gary really liked Joy and the two promised to keep in touch after Gary went home. Then Gary moved back to his home town in Oak Ridge, North Carolina.

Gary and Joy kept in touch by telephone and mail over the next few months and later that year Gary moved back to Pennsylvania. On January 18, 1967 Gary and Joy were married.

The couple decided to make their home in Philadelphia.
After getting married Gary found a job in Philadelphia driving heavy construction equipment. He would spend the next seven years driving pans, bulldozers and backhoes building everything from ponds to college dormitories.

Joy and Gary had their first child, Holly on December 20, 1967. Gary remembers her as being a tom boy all through her childhood.
In 1974 Gary went to work with the Amtrak Railroad System in Philadelphia. He was hired as a welder and his job was building and repairing railroad bridges and other repairs.

On May 12, 1975 Gary and Joy had their second child, Trevis. Trevis was a typical boy, always getting into things.

In 1983 Gary and Joy decided to go their separate ways. Gary would continue living in Pennsylvania working for Amtrak until 1987. Then Gary moved back to Oak Ridge, North Carolina.

Upon his return, Gary went to work with North American Van Lines driving one of their moving trucks. He worked with them until 1989.

From 1989 to 1991 Gary worked at Trailmobile in Kernersville, NC making trailer repairs and then for Thomas Freight from 1991 to 1994 driving one of their tractor-trailer rigs.

In 1994 Gary went to work with Loflin Concrete based in Kernersville, NC. For the first year Gary drove a cement truck and afterward began driving a dump trailer. Gary would work for 10 years with Loflin Concrete before retiring.

Over the years Gary tried to model his life after some of the most important people in his family. He was always close to his mother, Ruby and admired her for all the love she had showed him. He also tried to pattern his life after one of the greatest men in his life, Grandpa Young.

Growing up one of his best friends was first cousin, MK Moore. They played, fought and got into trouble together all through their childhood. Even now when they get together they begin telling fond stories of each other.

A couple of years back Gary ran across an old girlfriend from high school, Peggy McCuston. Peggy had attended Stokesdale High School and Gary, Kernersville High School and the two dated for a while back then.

When Gary went into the Navy the two moved on with their lives. Then one day Gary read in the newspaper where her husband had passed away. It took Gary several months, but he finally got the courage to call her. As the two talked they realized they still had feelings for each other.

Today the two enjoy spending time together and Gary feels that Peggy is a very special part of his life.

Gary holding the two-man cross cut saw he used with his older brother Ken in their back yard. This picture was taken around 1950.

This late 1940's picture is of Gary Young on the right with his older brother Ken in the driveway of their house on Union Grove Church Road.

Hollye and Trevis fishing at their Grandparent's house in the late 1970's.

Gary with his two granddaughters, Delaney and Savana Wagner, on a trip to visit him in North Carolina.

Ronald Lee Young

On October 4, 1949 Ruby and Raymond Young had their third child, Ronald Lee Young. They would call him Ronnie. When Ronnie was born Raymond and Ruby lived at 5412 Union Grove Road in Oak Ridge, North Carolina and he would spend his entire childhood growing up there.

Ronnie remembers their house was quite small when he was a young child. There were only three rooms and an attic. When his younger sister, Linda came along sleeping arrangements had to be adjusted in the house. After that Ronnie slept in the bedroom with his mother, Ken, Gary and Linda. Raymond slept in the attic. Behind their house were two barns, a corn crib, dog lots, and a Johnny house. It was no ordinary Johnny house. The Young's had a two-seater.

When Ken and Gary were old enough to chop firewood Ronnie would help by doing his share. While his two brothers chopped away Ronnie would load his wagon, pull it to the house and load the fire boxes. Ronnie remembers those cold mornings when his father would throw a stick of wood on the hot coals in the wood stove. Before long it would heat the entire house.

Ronnie also remembers hand drawing water from the well on the back porch and using a metal dipper. The family would use this well until Ronnie turned 13. When they got running water.

As a child Ronnie was always outside playing. He had some blocks of wood that he would pretend were cars and trucks. He would drive those cars all over their dirt driveway behind the house.

One of his other pastimes was to stand in the gravel road in front of the house and using a tobacco stick to hit rocks down across the pasture. If he could hit one over the creek running through the pasture it was a home run!

Ronnie was the third child in the family and the youngest boy; however there were no advantages to being one of the youngest. Everyone had their own special jobs to do. His chores as a child were to gather eggs from the hen house, milk the cow and get in the firewood. As he got older he began working in the tobacco fields with his father, Grandpa Young, Ken, and Gary.

His mother was always sewing and mending clothes. She would make a lot of her own clothes and the children's clothing. She did all the cooking, but she taught him how to make beans and taters and his dad taught him how to make his own special recipe of fried cornbread. Ronnie still enjoys making Raymond's fried cornbread today.

When Ronnie or the other children were sick Dr. Walker would come from Kernersville out to their house. He did not send them a bill and there was not insurance to cover the cost of the visit back then. They would pay him with eggs, some of Raymond's cured pork meat from the smoke house, or some of Ruby's canned vegetables from the garden.

Growing up, Ken was 11 years older than Ronnie. While Raymond was working at the silk mill or in the tobacco fields Ken and his wife, Betty, would help out with Ronnie. They would take him to his little league baseball practices and to his games if Raymond and Ruby could not go. He would spend a lot of time with Ken and Betty over the years and would consider them his second mom and dad.

Ronnie did not get an allowance back then, but he would walk up the road to Paul Merritt's store in the evening where all the farmers from the community would gather. He remembers a local farmer named Clarence Beeson would be at the store and he would give him a nickel if he could climb to the top of the old metal pole that held the big Esso Gas sign.

It was hard to make it to the top, but when he could he would go home with a nickel in his pocket. And yes, that was big back then. Raymond did get the family a TV when Ronnie was young and at night they would watch it if they could find a station. The antenna had to be turned just right if they wanted to find one of the three stations they had.

Ronnie started first grade in 1955 at Kernersville Elementary School and then switched to Oak Ridge Elementary for grades 2 – 6. Ronnie really enjoyed his time at Oak Ridge School and would often draw a circle in the dirt behind the school and shoot marbles with his friends. Ronnie was a good shooter and was hard to beat.

When Ronnie was 13 his older brother, Gary had joined the Navy and was stationed in Jacksonville, Florida. Ronnie and Ruby took a bus down to Jacksonville and spent some time with Gary. This was the first time he had been away from home.

Ronnie went to Summerfield School through the eighth grade and then Northwest Guilford High School where he played in the band. He graduated from Northwest Guilford in 1967.

In the spring of 1968 Ronnie got a job at Pierce Funeral Home in Kernersville working with Jack Pierce and Paul Morris. Ronnie only worked there for a few months, but while he did he met Paul's daughter, Sue Morris. Ronnie and Sue started dating and would continue to do so for the next two years.

In September of 1968 Ronnie applied for and accepted a position with Sechrest Funeral Home in High Point, North Carolina. The company liked Ronnie and after working in High Point for a while he was promoted to manager of Sechrest's new funeral home inThomasville, North Carolina.

On August 1, 1970 Ronnie and Sue were married at Fellowship Baptist Church in Kernersville. They later spent their honeymoon in Myrtle Beach, South Carolina.

Upon their return the two moved to Horneytown, North Carolina and lived near Smith's Store on Highway 66. Sue would continue working at Sears Mail Order Center in Greensboro, NC until the couple started having children.

On January 6, 1972 Sue and Ronnie had their first child, Scott, and on November 2, 1975 they had their second child, Sherri. Five years later in 1980 Ronnie and Sue built a new home in Wallburg, NC and the couple still lives there today.

All of Raymond and Ruby's grandchildren were growing fast and had started to school. For the first time in years Ruby did not have any babies to help take care of. That changed in 1983 and on September 4, 1983 Sue and Ronnie had their third and final child, Allen. Ruby was so excited to have another little boy in the family. Just as she did with all of her grandchildren they spent hours in the floor with a coloring book together.

Ronnie enjoyed going to the coast fishing with his father and father-in-law, Paul Morris. Every Fall they would pack up Raymond's truck and drive to his cabin in Stella, NC. Ronnie remembers those nights all too well. By 8pm everyone was in bed and it was not easy to fall asleep with Raymond in one room and Paul in the other room snoring. Early the next morning everyone was wide awake to the sound of Raymond banging pots and pans in the kitchen as he cooked his country ham and eggs.

Ronnie would continue working at Sechrest Funeral Home as the manager for the next 32 years. Then in December of 2000 Ronnie accepted a position with J.C. Green and Sons Funeral Home in Thomasville, NC. He was appointed the position of manager at the Wallburg, NC loacation. In 2006 he became a partner in the company and is Vice President of both locations. He has dedicated his life to serving families for over 43 years.

Ronnie and Sue really enjoy life and today like traveling when they get the chance and spending time with their children and grandchildren.

Ronnie Young walking home from the pond after an afternoon of fishing in the early 1960's.

Ronnie and his father, Raymond sawing wood slabs on the back of a Ford Tractor in 1974.

Ronnie and Sue's Children and Grandchildren in 2011. On the back row are Stephanie and Allen Young. Middle row from left to right are Alicia Young, Alex Young, Sherri Byrd, and Scott Young. On the front row from left to right are Anna Young, and Tori and Linsey Byrd.

Ronnie and Sue Young with their dog Lacie in 2011.

Linda Gail Young

On September 2, 1951 Ruby and Raymond Young had their fourth and last child, Linda Gail Young. Just like Ronnie, Linda grew up on a small farm on Union Grove Church Road in Oak Ridge.

From an early age Linda has fond memories of Grandpa and Grandma Young. She remembers during the summer after school was out getting to go and spend a week at a time with them almost every year. Grandpa Young would cook breakfast every morning on an old wood burning cook stove.

She remembers Grandma Young would fill up two pans with warm water and she and Linda would sit in the doorway and soak their feet each night. Grandma Young said it would make them sleep better.

Linda was the baby in the family and the only girl. Although the boys worked hard on the farm she did not have many chores. She would help her mom with the housework and when she was little she would help to hand churn the butter. When she was older she would join the boys working in the tobacco fields.

One of Linda's fondest memories from childhood was going to the beach for a few days every summer with her brother, Ronnie, her mom and dad and Grandpa and Grandma Young.

In 1958 Linda's brother, Ken got married to his new bride, Betty and soon afterward was drafted by the U.S. Army. While away, Betty lived with Raymond and Ruby.

During this time Ruby, Betty and Linda would go to Greensboro on Saturday mornings to go shopping. Sometimes Linda's dad would give her $20 to go shopping with. This made Linda feel like she was rich.

"You could buy a lot for $20 back then." Linda recently recalled.

One Christmas in the early 1960's, Linda woke up and found a beautiful new doll under the Christmas tree. At the time Ken was working at Duke Power Company and used his money to buy the doll for Linda. He never told her it was from him.

While growing up, Linda went to Union Grove Baptist Church next door to her house with her mom. She always looked forward to Bible School every summer at the church. Children came from Kernersville and Oak Ridge to attend Bible School at Union Grove.

Linda went to Oak Ridge Elementary School for grades 1 – 7. She then went to the eighth grade at Summerfield School and graduated from Northwest Guilford High School.

Linda got her first job at P&N Dime Store in Kernersville in 1966. She worked every Saturday and made $7.00 per day.

While Linda was attending high school, she met a young man named Wayne Burchett and they started dating. They would continue dating all through high school.

Linda graduated from Northwest Guilford High School in 1969 and on October 10, 1969 she and Wayne were married at First Baptist Church in Summerfield, North Carolina. After they were married they moved into a mobile home in Summerfield for a few months. After that they moved to Pepper Road in Oak Ridge, NC and lived in the same big white house Grandma and Grandpa Young had lived in for about five months. The couple were then able to buy a home in Summerfield.

After Linda and Wayne were married Linda worked at Sears Mail Order House in Greensboro with her sister-in-law, Sue Young. A couple of years later Linda started working at Oak Ridge Methodist Church with their daycare center.

In 1971 Linda and Wayne had their first child, Wayne Burchett, Jr and In 1976 they had their second child, Tina Burchett.

In 1977 Linda started working with her brother, Ken and her sister-in-law, Betty at Young's Florist in Kernersville. She worked with the florist until 1986 when she started her own florist shop out of her house in Summerfield.

A few years later Linda and Wayne went their separate ways. In the spring of 1991 Linda started dating a man in the Kernersville area named Kenny Crews. Kenny owned Crews Wrecker Service and if you lived there and had car trouble you knew Kenny was the man to call.

On December 14, 1991 Linda and Kenny were married and have been happily married ever since.

Kenny and Linda started an auctioneering business called Crews Auction Company and held auctions throughout North Carolina.

In the early 2000's Linda and Kenny moved to a house next door to Kenny's mother's home on Main Street in Kernersville and they still live there today.

This early 1950's picture shows Ken with his younger siblings Ronnie (left) and Linda (right) in their back yard on Union Grove Church Road.

Christmas morning in the mid 1950's was an exciting time for the Young's. This year Linda'a brother Ronnie got a new bicycle, and Linda found a doll under the tree. Years later she found out her oldest brother Ken had bought the doll for her and put it under the Christmas Tree.

Tina and Wayne enjoyed spending time with their cousins at Raymond and Ruby's house during the summer. From left to right are Tina, Trevis, Ruby, Hollye, and Wayne.

Kenny and Linda Crews soon after they were married at a Young Family Reunion in the early 1990's.

Chapter Ten

The Hazel Young Moore Morris Family

On December 21, 1919 Elias and Alma's fourth child, Mary Hazel Young was born. She would be called Hazel by the family and would be another one of the beautiful Young sisters. Hazel spent the first three years of her childhood growing up on the McGee Farm, which was Alma's parent's farm just west of Walkertown, North Carolina. In 1922 Elias and Alma moved the family to the Wicker Farm. It was located in the Belews Creek Community near Goodwill Church east of Walkertown, North Carolina and down the road from Elias' father, Hester Young's farm.

In 1926 Hazel started first grade at Walnut Cove School and would spend the first through fourth grades there.

In 1930 when Hazel was 11 Elias and Alma moved their family to the Case Place farm on Hwy 68 in Oak Ridge, North Carolina. Hazel would continue her schooling through the eighth grade at Oak Ridge School.

Hazel remembered this time in her life well. There was little money during the depression. Fortunately Elias and Alma were farming nine acres of tobacco on the large 200 acre Case Place farm during this time and part of the deal was the Young family could live in the old Case homeplace. They could also grow all of their own food.

The family had a milk cow, chickens for eggs and meat, raised two hogs each year for meat and lard, and had two large gardens. Alma canned hundreds of quart jars of vegetables, fruits, jellies, and jams each year, and Elias was a great game hunter.

Most of Hazel's clothes during the 1930's were made on Alma's foot pedal powered Singer Sewing Machine. Alma often got the fabric for free from the fancy printed feed sacks their animal feed came in. Alma would often make matching dresses for the girls if she had enough fabric. One time she made two dresses that were alike for Hazel and Edna. The girls did not like the color and pattern that the dresses were made out of so they took them to a field one day behind the house, dug a hole and buried them. It worked out fine for a while, until Elias went out one morning to plow the field and plowed up the dresses.   The girls learned their lesson that day to be thankful for what they had.

Hazel enjoyed playing a game with her sisters they called Mother and Child. The older sisters would pretend to be the mother for their younger siblings. When they played, Edna would be the mother to Opal and Elsie always wanted Hazel to be her mother. They played this game often when they were children.

In 1937 Hazel met a young man from Stokesdale, North Carolina named Marvin Moore. The two started dating and soon fell in love.

Marvin's father was Herbert "Bud" Moore originally from Reidsville, NC and his mother was Alice Clark Moore originally from Winston-Salem, NC. Bud made his living working for the Railroad and running a saw mill, but had passed away at the young age of 53 in 1917. Marvin's mother now owned a tobacco farm in Stokesdale and Marvin helped her raise tobacco on the farm to make his living.

On April 9, 1938 Hazel and Marvin were married. Since it was during the depression and jobs were hard to come by the couple lived with Elias and Alma for the first two and a half years of their marriage.

Hazel and Marvin received a special Christmas present on December 25, 1938 when their first child Norma Jean Moore was born. Two and a half years later on April 15, 1941 the couple had their second and final child Marvin Kitchen Moore Jr. He would be called M.K. for short.

In 1943 Marvin got an offer to become the Chief of Police in Gibsonville, North Carolina. Marvin gladly took the job. The new position gave Hazel and Marvin the opportunity to move away from the

Case Place farm and have their own home in Gibsonville. It was a beautiful five room house.

In 1946 Marvin and Hazel decided they wanted to run a business of their own. They moved to Marvin's mother, Alice's, farm in Stokesdale, NC and rented a house on the farm. They built a new building on the farm and opened a country store. Hazel and Marvin worked together keeping the store open from early morning until late in the evening. The two would run their country store for the next seven years.

In 1953 Marvin and Hazel closed the store and moved to Greensboro, North Carolina and lived with Marvin's mother. Later in 1954 Hazel and Marvin decided to go their separate ways and Hazel, Norma, and M.K. moved back to Oak Ridge, NC to live with Elias and Alma in the big white house on the Lowery Farm.

Hazel and the children lived on the Lowery Farm until 1957 when Elias and Alma bought the little green house next door. The house was much smaller so Hazel decided to buy a mobile home and moved it beside the new house for her, Norma, and M.K. to live.

Hazel worked at Adams-Millis Hosiery Mill in Kernersville, NC during this time.

In 1958 Hazel met a man in the Oak Ridge community named Conrad Morris. He was a carpenter and was good at his trade. He lived down the road from Elias and Alma's house on Pepper Road. The two started dating and enjoyed spending time together.

On February 14, 1959 Hazel and Conrad were married. They moved Hazel's mobile home across the road to Conrad's farm and lived there.

About a year later Conrad's brother, who delivered the mail in Oak Ridge, became ill. His health situation kept him from doing his job. Hazel and Conrad started delivering the mail until he was healthy enough to get back to work. Their efforts saved his job.

In the mid-1960's Conrad and Hazel retired to a beautiful cabin on the North Carolina Coast in Stella, North Carolina. Their cabin was next door to her brother, Raymond's, cabin. They would call this home for the next several years until Conrad passed away on April 13, 1973.

After Conrad passed away Hazel moved back to Kernersville to be closer to her family.

A short time later, Hazel got a job at the Oak Ridge Military Academy in their cafeteria and became a favorite with the students. She made her famous angel biscuits every day for the students and they loved them. Hazel worked with the academy until she was 62 and then retired. Hazel enjoyed retirement and often traveled to the beach with family and friends.

Sadly Hazel passed away on July 2, 1990. She was a much loved member of the Young family.

This is a picture of top row, Marvin and Hazel Moore and bottom row Norma and M.K. Moore. This picture was taken in the mid-1940's in front of Grandpa and Grandma Young's house on Pepper Road.

This is a picture of Hazel and Conrad Morris shortly after they were married in 1959.

M.K. Moore when he was on the USS Tioga County LST – 1158 amphibious landing and supply ship when he was in the U.S. Navy in the mid-1960's. M.K. is a Vietnam Veteran.

This is a picture of from left, Raymond Goins, Edna Young Goins and Hazel Young Moore Morris. Edna is Hazel's younger sister. This picture is circa the middle 1960's.

This is a picture of Norma Jean Moore when she was 22 years old.

To the left is a picture of M.K. Moore fixing his famous Pinto Bean Recipe at a Young family get-together in 2010.

Norma Jean Moore

On December 25, 1938 Hazel and Marvin Moore had their first child, Norma Jean Moore. At the time Norma was born, Hazel and Marvin lived with Hazel's parents, Elias and Alma Young. Mothers did not go to the hospital for their children to be born at the time so Norma was born in the old home place on the Case Place farm in Oak Ridge, North Carolina.

Immediately afterward Hazel became very ill and had to go to the hospital where she almost died. One night while there, Hazel overheard a nurse say, "I wonder if Hazel will be with us in the morning?" Hazel thought the nurse meant she would be going home, not that she would not make it through the night. Fortunately Hazel did make it through the night and a few days later she was able to go home. It took Hazel several months to recover after returning home. While Hazel was recovering Grandma Young looked after Norma.

In 1940 Norma's father was hired as the Police Chief in Gibsonville, North Carolina and he was able to move his family there. This was a big change for him, Hazel, and Norma. Now they had running city water and indoor plumbing.

In 1941 Norma's brother, M.K. was born. Norma and M.K. would share a bedroom while living in Gibsonville.

Four years later in 1945 Norma started first grade in Gibsonville. The next year in 1946 Marvin and Hazel moved to Marvin's mother's farm in Stokesdale, North Carolina. Marvin and Hazel rented a house on the farm and built a new building on the farm to start a country store. The store was open from early morning until night time and was long hours for both Marvin and Hazel. Norma remembers being at the store waiting until closing time so she could go home and go to bed. She could hardly keep her eyes open on those long nights.

Norma started the second grade in Stokesdale and would continue going to school there through the eighth grade. One of the treats Norma remembers from this time was her parents giving her a nickel so she could buy ice cream in the afternoon at school.

In 1954 Marvin and Hazel moved to Greensboro, North Carolina and lived with Marvin's mother for a while. While there Norma went to the ninth grade at Greensboro Central Middle School. The school was only two blocks away and an easy walk for Norma. She was also able to eat lunch at home every day.

On many days after school Norma walked a few blocks up town with her friend, Carolyn, to Woolworth's Five and Dime Store and sat at the counter and ordered a Coke.

In 1955 Hazel and Marvin went their separate ways. Afterward, Hazel, Norma, and M.K. moved back to Oak Ridge, North Carolina to live with Elias and Alma on the Lowery Farm on Pepper Road.

After the move Norma went to Summerfield High School for the next three years and graduated in 1957.

After graduation Norma went to work for Sears Mail Order House in Greensboro. It was a good job for Norma and she prided herself on being on time every day. She was living with Elias and Alma at the time and one morning she walked out to the little car she was driving to find it had a flat tire. Norma had never changed a flat tire before and she and Grandma Young were the only ones at home that morning.

Grandma Young came out and looked at the situation and said, "I've never changed a tire before, but I've seen it done several times. Norma, I think we can do this".

With that Grandma Young started giving instructions and Norma went to work changing the tire. A few minutes later the spare tire was secured in place on the car. Norma was 15 minutes late for work that day, but she was there. That was a proud day for Norma and it also gave her a special respect for Grandma Young, who could just look at things and figure out how to do them.

After settling into her job at Sears, Norma moved to Greensboro and rented an apartment with a friend named Kathleen. Norma would live there for the next several years.

One day in May of 1966 Norma and her roommate went to the Boar and Castle Drive-in Restaurant in Greensboro for a sandwich. When they pulled up a car with two young men pulled in beside them and they started talking. It turned out that one of the guys had worked with Norma's Uncle, Clyde Young, at Lorillard Tobacco Company. Before leaving, the young man asked Norma for her telephone number.

The next day the young man, Paul Campbell, called Norma and asked her for a date. The two started dating and on December 17, 1966 Paul and Norma were married. The wedding ceremony was at Union Grove Baptist Church in Oak Ridge, NC.

After their honeymoon the couple returned to Greensboro where they rented an apartment on Castlewood Drive for about six months and then they bought a home on Amber lane in Greensboro in 1967.

While they lived in Greensboro, Paul worked for Dow Corning Corporation and Norma worked for Pilot Life Insurance Company.

On August 7, 1969 Norma and Paul had their first and only child, Douglas. After graduating from high school Doug continued his education at the University of North Carolina at Greensboro. He graduated from UNCG with a degree in History. Today he is one of Greensboro's finest working as a police officer in Greensboro, NC.

In 1976 Paul was transferred by Dow Corning to Midland, Michigan. While living in Midland, Norma decided to continue her education and get a college degree. She first attended Delta College and later Central Michigan University for the next several years to accomplish this. Norma and several other housewives from Midland carpooled the 35 miles to Mt. Pleasant, MI three days a week during this time. They scheduled their classes so they could get home before their children were out of school. Norma graduated on December 16, 1985.

In 1986 Dow Corning transferred Paul back to Greensboro, North Carolina. When they got back to Greensboro Norma applied for a job with Southern Guarantee Insurance and accepted a position as an administrative assistant to the vice-president and eight underwriters.

In 1994 Norma and Paul decided to go their separate ways. While going through their divorce, Norma's Aunt Edna generously invited Norma to live with her in Oak Ridge. Norma will always be grateful to Aunt Edna for permitting her to do this.

Norma worked with Southern Guarantee Insurance until she retired in December of 2005.

Since retiring Norma has bought a townhome in Greensboro and she enjoys living there. Some of her retirement activities include day trips, classes at the Shepherd's Center, Ahoy exercise classes and lunches with her son, Doug and other friends.

Here are pictures of Norma's two granddaughters. From left are Samantha and Adelaide (Chrystal).

This is a picture of Norma Moore Campbell and her son, Doug. Today Doug is a police officer with the Greensboro Police Department.

Marvin Kitchen Moore, Jr.

On April 15, 1941 Hazel and Marvin Moore had their second and last child, Marvin Kitchen Moore Jr. He would be called "M.K." by the family. At the time M.K. was born Marvin Sr. was working as the Police Chief in Gibsonville, North Carolina. M.K. and his family would live in Gibsonville the first five years of his life.

In 1946 Hazel and Marvin moved the family to Stokesdale, North Carolina to live on Marvin's mother's farm. Hazel and Marvin opened up their own country store while there and ran it for the next eight years. The house they rented from Marvin's mother did not have a well and while living there they had to carry their water from a neighbor's house that was about a hundred yards away.

In 1947 M.K. started first grade at Stokesdale School and would be there through the seventh grade.

In 1954 Marvin and Hazel moved the family to Greensboro, North Carolina and lived with Marvin's mother. A year later in 1955 Hazel and Marvin went their separate ways. M.K., Hazel, and Norma moved back to Oak Ridge, North Carolina to live with M.K.'s Grandpa and Grandma Young on the Lowery Farm on Pepper Road.

While living in Oak Ridge M.K. attended Oak Ridge School for the eighth grade.

M.K. spent a lot of time with Grandpa and Grandma Young. Grandma Young was a second mother to him. He always considered himself lucky to have two great mothers.

Grandma Young believed in keeping her yard clean. Every Saturday morning she and M.K. would go out in the front yard with their homemade brush brooms made from tree branches and sweep the yard. M.K. remembers Grandma putting on a record by the gospel quartet, The Chuck Wagon Gang, while they swept.

M.K. also spent a lot of time in the tobacco fields working with Grandpa Young. One day Grandpa told M.K. it was time for him to learn to plow the fields. Grandpa hooked up his old workhorse, Dan, to a cultivator and let M.K. plow the weeds between the rows of tobacco. M.K. struggled and struggled, but could not get the cultivator to plow in the right place. Grandpa showed him the proper way and before long M.K. was plowing like a pro.

M.K. always enjoyed spending time with Grandpa Young. They enjoyed working hard and relaxing at the local fishing hole. M.K. always thought of Grandpa Young as a father.

No matter what jobs Grandma and Grandpa Young had for M.K. on Saturday mornings, they took Saturday afternoons off. That is when they went to Oak Ridge to see Uncle Clyde Young play baseball.

M.K. attended Summerfield High School. After finishing school M.K. went to work at Adams-Millis Hosiery Mill in Kernersville, NC. He would work there for the next two years as a lot boy.

While at Adams-Millis M.K. noticed a beautiful young woman named Lucy Dollarhite who also worked there. He kept asking her for a date and finally, she said yes.

Later M.K. went to work for Harry Gardner Plumbing in Oak Ridge, NC as a plumber's helper. M.K.'s Uncle Hubert Young also worked there as a sheet metal fabricator. M.K. would spend the next year working here.

In the spring of 1962 M.K. and his cousin, Gary Young, decided to join the Navy together on the buddy system. By doing this they could stay together at least through basic training while in the Navy. They both went to sign up, but a problem with M.K.'s paper work caused him to go home and return a month later. Gary Young was taken immediately and their plans of going through basic training together were ruined.

Finally on July 29, 1962 M.K. joined the U.S. Navy. He was sent to Great Lakes Boot Camp where he spent 11 weeks doing basic training. Then he got to return home for two weeks before being assigned to a ship.

He was sent to California and assigned to the Naval Ship USS Tioga County LST-158. The ship was 384' long and its primary functions were to transport and land tanks, amphibious vehicles, combat vehicles, and other equipment onto a beach during an amphibious assault. M.K. was assigned to this ship just as the Vietnam War was beginning and within a few months he and his fellow crewmen were delivering tanks, combat vehicles, and supplies up the Saigon River and to the shore line in Vietnam. His job on the ship was to maintain and shoot a 3 inch 50 caliber twin mount gun. He was a Gunners Mate Third Class.

During this time M.K. kept in touch with the beautiful young woman, Lucy Dollarhite, he had met at Adams-Millis a few years back. M.K. knew this was the woman he wanted to marry and he thought she too, deep down inside, wanted to marry him. Finally in 1964 M.K. talked Lucy into marrying him and they were engaged.

In May of 1966 M.K.'s ship landed in California. He had just got back from a tour overseas and was given a 30 day leave. While home, Lucy and M.K. were married on May 28, 1966 in Mt. Airy, North Carolina in the living room of the preacher's house. M.K. had thoughts of making a career in the Navy and tried to convince Lucy to go back to California with him. Lucy liked North Carolina too much and told him she would rather stay here.

After their honeymoon M.K. went back to California by himself and 77 days later he was discharged from the Navy.

When M.K. got back home he and Lucy needed a place to live. As luck would have it, his Uncle Pete and Aunt Opal Flynt had just bought a small farm and needed to sell their home on Bost Street in Kernersville. M.K. and Pete struck a deal and the sale was made. M.K. and Lucy would live on Bost Street for the next 15 years.

M.K. also needed a job. At the time his Uncle Raymond Goins had recently gone to work for the City of High Point in nearby High Point, NC. Raymond drove heavy equipment there and was one of the best motor grader drivers around. Just as M.K. got back from the Navy Raymond got a promotion to Assistant Superintendent of the city's street department. Raymond needed to hire some new employees and asked M.K. to come to work for him. M.K. would work in High Point for the next two years driving heavy equipment.

On April 28, 1968 Lucy and M.K. had their one and only daughter, Robin. Needless to say M.K. and Lucy have been proud of Robin over the years. After high school she got a Bachelors Degree from Appalachian State University in Boone, North Carolina and in 2007 she got her Masters Degree at William and Mary University in Virginia. Today she teaches school in Williamsburg, Virginia.

Also in 1968 M.K. had the opportunity to go to work with Roadway Express in Kernersville, NC. While he liked working in High Point the pay and benefits were much better at Roadway. M.K. would work at Roadway for the next 30 years before retiring.

Over the years Lucy worked for Sears. She spent 27 years at their mail order house in Greensboro, NC and another seven years at their parts and service center in Greensboro.

In 1981 M.K. and Lucy bought a home on Piney Grove Road in Kernersville. The couple still lives there today.

Before they retired they were able to travel some with M.K.'s Uncle Clyde and Aunt Nora Young. After they retired they continued to travel with Clyde and Nora about once a year to places they thought they would never be able to visit. M.K. greatly appreciates being able to spend these amazing vacations with them.

Both Lucy and M.K. enjoy their retirement. M.K. has a wood working shop behind his house and enjoys working on special projects for the family. They both still enjoy traveling. They like going to the beach, Williamsburg, Virginia to visit their daughter, or visiting his old Navy buddies all across America.

Each fall when the Young family has another get-together at Clyde and Nora Young's house you will find M.K. outside cooking another cast iron pot of his famous pinto beans. If you have time sit down with M.K. You will have excellent food and hear some great Young family stories.

On May 28, 1966 M.K. and
Lucy Moore got married in
Mt. Airy, North Carolina.

This is a picture of
M.K. and Lucy Moore
today.

This is a picture of Robin Moore Jones' family. From left are her husband, Chris, Robin, her daughter, Kathryn and her son, Will.

Chapter Eleven

The Edna Young Goins Beeson Family

On March 14, 1922 Elias and Alma Young had their fifth child and third daughter, Edna Lucille Young. Elias and Alma had recently moved their family to the Wicker Farm before Edna was born. It was located in the Belews Creek Community near Goodwill Church east of Walkertown, North Carolina and right next to Elias' parents, Hester and Mary Young's farm.

In 1928 Edna started first grade at Walnut Cove School and would spend the first and second grades there.

In 1930 when Edna was 8, Elias and Alma moved their family to the Case Place Farm, which was located about two miles north of the community of Oak Ridge, North Carolina just off NC Highway 68.

Edna would continue her schooling at Oak Ridge Elementary School through the eighth grade.

Edna grew up during the Great Depression in the 1930's. Times were hard during this time and money was really hard to come by.

As her brother, Hubert Young would say of the decade, "You couldn't buy a job."

Edna did have one major thing going for her during this time. The strength and bond of a strong and loving family. Elias was a great provider. Although he did not own his own farm he did rent a large tobacco farm and he could grow all the garden, wheat, oats, and corn they needed. He had his own work horses, milk cows for milk, chickens for eggs and meat, and he also raised a couple of hogs every year for meat and lard.

Along with Alma's ability to look after the family's daily food supply they survived these hard times. During the summer Alma fed the family from the garden, their daily milk from their cows, eggs from their chickens, and any game Elias brought home from a hunting trip.

Alma was also a forward thinking woman and made sure she canned enough food to get the family of nine children through the winter months.

Everyone in the family pitched in during this era doing their fair share of the work. Although the family did not have much money they did always have plenty to eat and good warm house to live in.

Alma needed a lot of help from her daughters when it came to cooking for such a large family. One day she asked Edna and Hazel to go to the garden and pick her a large paper bag of salad greens so they could have them for supper.

When the two sisters got to the garden they began picking, but soon got tired of all the work needed to fill such a large bag. So they fluffed up the greens they had picked to make the bag look full and returned to the house.

When they gave the bag to Alma she immediately saw what they had done. Alma pushed the fluffy greens down and saw the bag was only about one quarter full. She gave the girls a good scolding and sent them back to the garden to finish the job.

Edna worked hard while growing up. Her father raised nine acres of tobacco every year and that took help from everyone in the family. Their house did not have electricity or running water so everyone had plenty of chores to keep the house running smoothly. The strong work ethic Elias and Alma taught Edna while she was growing up would be beneficial to her throughout her life.

After Edna finished the eighth grade at Oak Ridge School she decided she had enough school and did not go back the following year. For the next couple of years she helped the family around the farm.

In 1940 Edna got her first job at Adams-Millis Hosiery Mill in Kernersville, NC. Edna worked there with her sister-in-law, Annie Mae Rierson Young. Annie Mae had married Edna's brother, Hubert, 4 years earlier in 1936. The two rode to work together and also ate lunch together. At the time Edna's other brother, Raymond Young and his wife, Ruby lived in an upstairs apartment in a house on Salisbury Street in Kernersville. Every day at lunch Edna and Annie Mae would get in their car and drive to Raymond's house where Ruby would have lunch ready. The three would eat lunch together and then

Edna and Annie Mae would return to work. They saved a lot of money by eating at Ruby's house instead of the cafeteria at work.

In a recent interview Annie Mae recalled, "Ruby Young was a great cook. She would always have lunch cooked for us when we arrived and she would have a pie for desert."

Later in 1940 Edna met a young man named Raymond Goins. Raymond was about five years older than Edna and worked as a welder with a local construction company. Raymond almost immediately won Edna's heart. The two started dating and would continue to do so for the next several months.

He was a smart young man and had the ability to learn mechanical systems and equipment quickly. In addition to a car, Raymond also owned a motorcycle. Edna loved for him to come and pick her up on his motorcycle. She would hop on the back and the two would go riding all over the countryside.

On February 15, 1941 Edna and Raymond went to the Justice of the Peace on Bethel Church Road in Kernersville and were married. This was a very happy moment in Edna's life.

For the first few months of their marriage they lived on the Case Place Farm in Oak Ridge with Elias and Alma. They both kept their jobs and started saving their money.

Then on December 7, 1941 the Japanese bombed Pearl Harbor and everything changed. The next day the United States declared war on Germany and Japan and World War II began.

Raymond sat down and had a long discussion with Edna after this happened. He knew for America to fight such a large war on two fronts they would need a tremendous amount of equipment. Raymond was a welder by trade and wanted to apply his skills toward the war effort to help his country.

Raymond knew the country would need a lot of ships to transport troops and supplies once the war got into full swing. There was a huge shipyard less than a hundred miles away in Newport News, Virginia and Raymond wanted them to move there so he could help build ships for the U.S. Military.

The following weekend the two drove up to Newport News to visit the shipyards. Raymond talked to a company there and was immediately hired.

They began to look around to find an apartment to rent near his new place of employment. The problem was they could not find anything. Then Raymond noticed there were a lot of campers parked at a nearby location and stopped to see why.

Other people had also found it hard to find apartments to rent and had bought campers for a place to live instead.

Raymond and Edna looked at each other and shared a big grin and decided to do the same thing. They went to a nearby camper dealership and picked one out, bought it, hitched it to the back of their car and headed back to Oak Ridge.

They quit their jobs at Adams-Millis and the construction company. They filled their camper with their personal belongings and were back on their way to Newport News, Virginia.

While Raymond worked long hours building large cargo and troop transport ships Edna looked after the home front. If they wanted to come back home to Oak Ridge to visit Alma and Elias for a weekend, they simply hitched their camper onto the back of the car and they were on their way back home.

Edna and Raymond lived in Newport News for the rest of the war helping their country. They were both so proud of their efforts.

After the war Raymond and Edna moved back to Oak Ridge, NC. Upon their return Raymond went to work with Thompson-Author Paving and Construction Company in Greensboro, North Carolina. Raymond knew with all of the new houses being built after the war new roads and bridges would need to be built all over the state.

Raymond's career switched from being a welder to driving heavy construction equipment. One day he may have been hauling large tractor-trailer loads of dirt or gravel and a few days later he may have been driving a motor grader building a new road. Raymond could use practically any type of equipment they had.

In 1948 Edna and Raymond bought a small piece of land just down the road from where Elias and Alma lived on Pepper Road and built a new home. It was a beautiful four room cottage with a large two car garage built behind the house. The two were able to pay for the house with their savings.

A short while after building their new home Edna decided to go into business for herself. She purchased a knitting loom, had it installed in one of her bedrooms in their new home and began making socks. She was able to make several hundred pairs of socks every day and had a very good business. If the loom needed a repair, Raymond would take care of that for her after he got home from work. Edna would run this business for several years.

During the 1950's Edna and Raymond settled into living in Oak Ridge. They shared many of their favorite hobbies together.

On a Saturday night you may find them at Bowman-Gray Stadium in Winston-Salem, North Carolina watching a NASCAR race. Raymond liked the brashness of driver Curtis Turner who did not take anything from anyone on the track. Edna liked the driver brothers, Billy and Bobby Myers.

Raymond even talked of being a stockcar driver himself, but Edna would have none of that.

Raymond also enjoyed rabbit hunting. He had a big lot full of small beagles he had raised from pups and trained himself. Raymond really did not enjoy catching rabbits as much as he liked listening to the dogs barking during the chase. He did however eat what he caught.

The couple did not have any children, but they did enjoy being around young people. Both Edna and Raymond loved their nieces and nephews. They enjoyed them visiting and on many occasions they may spend the weekend with them. There was always something to do. Edna may cook a special recipe, they may go skiing in their ski boat up at Philpot Dam Lake, or they may go roller skating at the Roller Rink in High Point, NC. If you stayed at the Goins house a niece or nephew knew they were going to have fun.

Several of the nieces and nephews have special memories of Edna and Raymond. Phyllis Crutchfield remembers when she graduated from high school Edna bought her a leather bound white Bible with gold lettering on it. It's one of her special keepsakes from her childhood.

Lynn McCormick remembers them taking her to the High Point Roller Rink to learn to skate. Lynn would later teach her daughter to skate and later in life that daughter would compete nationally in roller skating.

M.K. Moore remembers Edna bought him his first Sunday go-to-meeting suit. Gracie Flynt proudly brags Aunt Edna was my official Godmother.

Moochie McCormick remembered Edna and Raymond had a beautiful tropical fish tank with dozens of colorful fish inside. He would enjoy watching it for hours.

Anytime a niece or nephew visited, Edna always gave them a sweet treat to take with them. Yes, Edna and Raymond were a special aunt and uncle.

In the late 1950's Edna gave up her sock making business in her home and went back to work at Adams-Millis in Kernersville. She would continue working there for the next four or five years.

In 1961 Roy and Helen Nelson and their son, Neal, who were nearby neighbors to Edna, went to Florida for a vacation. On the way Roy and Helen were sadly killed in a car crash.

Neal, who was in the back seat at the time, did survive; however he was badly injured. Because the tragedy was so sudden, Neal didn't have anyone to look after him except for nearby neighbors when he returned home. He would find a place to stay later, but for the short term Edna and other neighbors pitched in and began assisting in nursing him back to health. Neal still remembers how much help Edna and Raymond were to him and his sister during this time.

As Edna helped she began to think how important it was to know proper methods of looking after those who are sick or injured. Edna realized just how little she actually knew and then her thought process evolved into what if I made nursing my profession in years to come. Edna knew she would need more education, but how much and how could she do it? Edna discussed the idea with Raymond and got his full support. "Do whatever it takes." Raymond said.

When Edna researched the requirements she found first she would have to get the equivalent of a high school education. Edna had quit school back in 1936 in the eighth grade. This first step alone would take her over a year. Next to become a North Carolina Licensed Practical Nurse she would need to attend technical school for another full year. And it was not just the schooling. She would also need to pass the North Carolina State Board Nursing Exam. Edna was 39 years old at the time and never dreamed she would go back to school. Her entire thought process would have to change. All these years she had used her hands to make a living. Now she would have to use her mind to learn medical techniques, uses of prescription drugs, and so much more.

In 1962 Edna started back to school working toward getting her General Equivalency Diploma (GED). Since she had quit school in the eighth grade she would need to take a lot of courses. For over a year she took math, English, history, and many more classes that were required. It was tough but finally in 1964 Edna got her diploma.

In 1964 Edna entered school at Guilford Technical Community College in Greensboro, NC to get her Licensed Practical Nursing Degree. It was a long hard grind, but Edna was up to the task. She graduated in the summer of 1965. Immediately afterward Edna took the North Carolina State Nursing Board Exam and passed. Edna had set a major goal in her life and now she had accomplished it. It was a proud moment in her life.

Later that year Edna applied for and accepted a position in High Point, North Carolina with the Guilford County Health Department as a visiting nurse. Edna's responsibilities included visiting patients in their homes who were sick, disabled, or elderly. She took vital signs, gave medical advice, and helped maintain the well being of her patients. She kept well documented records of the patients to make certain they were taking their medicine properly and making improvements in their health. Edna visited several patients a day and most loved seeing her come. She had a way of establishing feelings of trust with her patients.

Also in 1965 Raymond switched jobs for the first time in several years. He too went to work in High Point for the City of High Point as a heavy equipment operator helping them maintain their streets, bridges and highways. Within a few months Raymond proved himself to be an expert at leading others and getting jobs done on time and was made Assistant Superintendent of the Street Department for the city.

With Edna and Raymond now both working in High Point, they decided it would be wise if they moved there. A few weeks later they sold their house on Pepper Road in Oak Ridge and moved to a beautiful brick home on Eastchester Drive in High Point. The two would live there for the next several years.

In 1978 Raymond came down with a terminal illness. Edna did what she could to comfort Raymond during this time, but there was nothing she could do to save him.

On November 3, 1979 Raymond passed away. The entire Young family would miss their favorite uncle and it would be a sad time for Edna as well. Raymond and Edna had done everything together for the last 38 years. It would be hard living without him.

The employees of the City of High Point would also miss Raymond, whom they had enjoyed working with for the past 13 years.

Edna continued living in High Point and working for Guilford County as a visiting nurse. Her work of assisting so many people in need helped her through this time. Another outlet was her involvement in her church.

Back in Oak Ridge an old friend of Raymond's over the years started thinking about how he would like to ask Edna out to dinner.

Clarence "Big" Beeson owned a tobacco farm about two miles from where Edna and Raymond had lived in Oak Ridge and had actually been close friends with Raymond. Both he and Raymond enjoyed getting together and taking their rabbit dogs hunting when they had free time.

Clarence's wife, Reba had passed away in 1977 and he knew what Edna was going through. Clarence wanted to ask so badly, but he also wanted to use proper etiquette. He did not want Edna to feel he was pushing her, however he did not want to wait too long either.

Edna was a beautiful woman and had the highest quality and standards as a person. He did not want to lose his opportunity to another gentleman.

Four months after Raymond's passing Clarence asked Edna on a date. Edna also did not want to use improper etiquette. She wanted to go, but would it be right? Edna took time to think about this and talked to Clarence as well. Clarence said he understood and he waited as long as he could but he could not stand to wait any longer.

Edna knew right away she had met the right person and their courtship began. The two were married in 1980. After they married, Clarence moved to High Point to be with Edna. Clarence had recently retired from farming and was working with a golf club managing their greens at the time.

The two lived in High Point for a while and then they decided to move back to Oak Ridge. As luck would have it a long time friend of Edna and Clarence, Charlie Tuttle had his beautiful brick home for sale in Oak Ridge. The house was right across the road from where Edna and Raymond had lived on Pepper Road. Edna would live there the rest of her life.

In 1984 Edna retired from her job of nursing in High Point. She had proudly worked for the Guilford County Health Department for 19 years.

The next few years would be very enjoyable for Edna and Clarence. With both retired they had plenty of time to visit family and take vacations and trips whenever they wanted. The couple was very happy together.

In 1991 Clarence found out he had an incurable disease. Edna did all she could to make Clarence comfortable the last months of his life. Edna felt so blessed to have had two wonderful husbands in her life. Clarence passed away on August 12, 1992.

Over the next several years Edna did her best to enjoy every day of her life. She became a strong member of Union Grove Baptist Church in Oak Ridge and attended church every Sunday.

She also sang with a gospel group at the church known as the Sugar Sticks. Her brother, Clyde Young and her sister Elsie Marshall were also members of the group.

Edna did volunteer work at Piedmont Triad International Airport assisting passengers with any needs they had at the airport. She also kept physically fit by joining the YMCA in Kernersville and she loved water aerobics.

Anytime Edna had a chance she loved to travel. She enjoyed going to the Virginia Mountains and while there she had to get four or five lottery tickets. She enjoyed going on group bus trips and once went on a cruise with her nieces JoAnne Crutchfield Sapp and Maggie Crutchfield Brenden Taylor.

Edna remained independent and looked after herself for almost all of her retirement years. She was a very strong and healthy woman.

In December of 2006 Edna moved to Kerner Ridge Assisted Living Home on Hopkins Road in Kernersville. She would spend the last few months of her life there.

Sadly Edna passed away on May 26, 2007. She was 85 years old.

Edna was one of the finest you would ever meet and she spread joy and happiness all her life.

This is a picture of Edna when she visited the house where she was born in 1922 on the Wicker Place east of Walkertown, North Carolina. This picture was probably taken in the 1950's.

Edna and Raymond Goins lived in Newport News, Virginia during the World War II era where Raymond was a welder building troop transport and cargo ships for the U.S. Military. This is a picture of them while they lived there around 1943.

This is a picture of Raymond and Edna Goins on a Sunday afternoon visit to Elias and Alma's house on Pepper Road in Oak Ridge, North Carolina. This picture is from the early

Here is a picture of Edna and Raymond Goins visiting Raymond Young and his family in Oak Ridge in the late 1950's.

In this picture Edna Goins is piloting their ski boat at Philpot Dam Lake. The two loved to take their nieces and nephews water skiing there. This picture is from the early 1960's.

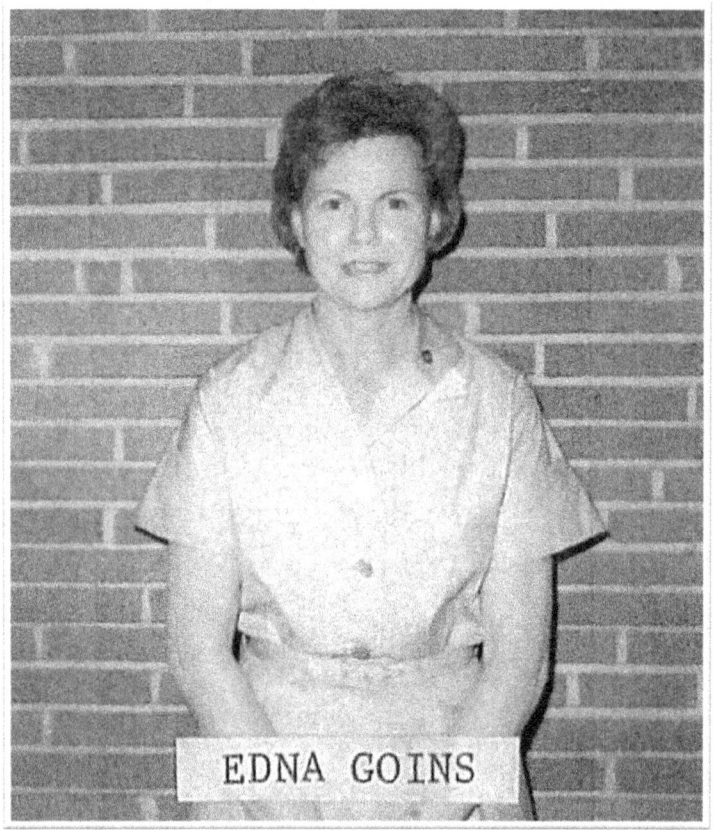

EDNA GOINS

Here is a picture of Edna Goins soon after she became a Licensed Practical Nurse for the Guilford County Health Department. This picture was taken in 1967.

This is a picture of Clarence and Edna Beeson a few months after they were married in 1980.

This is a picture of Clarence and Edna Beeson in the later years of their marriage. This picture was taken in 1990.

In this picture Edna Beeson is at a Young Reunion sharing fond memories of days gone by with her niece, JoAnne Crutchfield Sapp. This picture is from the late 1990's.

This is a picture of Edna Beeson with her sister, Elsie Marshall, when they sang with 'The Sugar Sticks' Gospel Group at Union Grove Baptist Church in Oak Ridge, North Carolina. This picture was taken in the early 2000's.

Chapter Twelve

The Opal Young Flynt Family

The date was February 16, 1925 and it was a happy day for Alma and Elias Young. On this day their sixth child and fourth daughter, Opal Alene Young was born. Opal was a cute little baby and over the years would become another one of those beautiful Young girls.

Opal spent the first five years of her childhood growing up on the Wicker Farm. The farm was right next to Elias' father, Hester Young's farm. Elias and Alma's main source of income while living there was raising tobacco.

In 1930 on Opal's fifth birthday Elias and Alma moved their family to The Case Farm in Oak Ridge, NC.

Opal still remembers the morning of the move like it was yesterday. The entire family was up at 5:00 A.M. After a hardy breakfast Elias, and Opal's brother Hubert, hitched up their two-horse wagon and began loading the family's bedroom and living room furniture. They had to hurry for they needed to make two trips that day to get everything moved.

While this was going on Alma and the rest of the five children packed their dishes and cookware and loaded them into the family's 1927 Model 'T' Ford. Opal still remembers her brother, Raymond at the front of the car using a hand crank to start it. His head bobbed up and down, up and down. Finally it gave a chug, chug, chug and they were off to the Case Farm.

Mr. and Mrs. Case were an older couple and needed someone to raise their nine acres of tobacco. The agreement they made with Elias and Alma was if they would raise the nine acres of tobacco and give them half of the profits they could live in a house, the old Case home place, on their 200 acre farm and could also raise gardens and animal feed to support their family and work animals.

The old homeplace house was over a hundred years old, yet was quite sturdy. It did not have electricity or indoor plumbing and their water was hand drawn from an outside well.

Since it was the depression era and jobs were so hard to come by this was a great deal for the Young family. In addition to growing the nine acres of tobacco each year, Elias grew two half-acre gardens, ten acres of corn, and five acres of wheat. He also had a milk cow and raised two hogs, which provided plenty of meat and lard for cooking.

Alma did her fair share canning hundreds of quart jars of vegetables and fruits to last them over the winter months.

A year after moving to the Case Farm Opal started first grade at nearby Oak Ridge School. She still remembers those days at the school and how class conscience some of the students were. Opal had a lunch pail that had only one handle. Some of the richer kids had lunch pails with two handles. Opal got penny pencils to go to school and some of the richer kids got two for a nickel pencils. Opal still laughs about how snobbish these kids were back then over those simple things.

Looking back now Opal realizes just how fortunate she was to have the loving family she had and the fact they lived on a huge farm and could grow anything they needed meant their family never saw a hungry day during the entire depression era.

Opal would spend all of her school years at Oak Ridge School.

On December 7, 1941 the Japanese attacked Pearl Harbor bringing the United States into World War II. Opal was 16 years old at the time. She saw several changes after that. For one, the depression ended and jobs started opening up for family and friends.

There was also the concern of who would be needed to go and fight for the military in Europe and the South Pacific. Opal did not know it at the time, but this would affect her directly three years later.

In 1942 Elias and Alma had an opportunity to buy a farm about five miles from where they lived on the other side of Oak Ridge. The farm was called the Lowery Place and was a beautiful 200 acre farm. Elias would pay for the farm by raising nine acres of tobacco each year on the farm. Mr. Lowery and Elias shook hands and the deal was done.

Opal will never forget how happy she was that their family was going to finally own the land and home where they lived. Opal remembers herself and her sister, Elsie running through the house singing, "We're going to own our own home, we're going to own our own home!!"

When a nephew to Mr. Lowery found out about the deal to sell the farm to Elias and learned they had only made a handshake to seal the deal, the nephew went to a lawyer to see if he could buy the farm out from under Elias. The lawyer told the nephew if he would put a deposit down on the farm he could buy the farm himself and Elias could do nothing about it. The nephew did just that and stole the farm from Elias.

Opal remembers how mad she was the day she heard the sad news.

"I went to the back screen door and tried to kick it off the hinges!!" Opal sighed.

Putting a deposit down on a purchase would be something Opal would never forget.

By 1943 Opal had started dating and on many occasions she and her sister, Elsie would go on double dates. On night two boys came by their house to take Opal and Elsie dancing. One boy was from Oak Ridge and the other boy, James "Pete" Flynt was from nearby Kernersville. Opal was supposed to date the boy from Oak Ridge and somehow on the way to their car Opal and Elsie switched dates.

Ironically this twist of fate was a life changing event for Opal. She and Pete started dating regular and soon fell in love.

Pete was 19 at the time and knew it was only a matter of time before he would be called by Uncle Sam to serve his country. For now he was still living at home in Kernersville helping his father farm tobacco.

One evening Pete came to see Opal and told her the bad news. I got a draft notice and I have to go into the Army next week. They knew this would be a rough time for both of them. With all the lives being lost in the horrendous battles in Europe there was even an unspoken concern he may not come back. But they never talked about that.

"Honey, I'll write you every day!" Pete promised.

"And I'll do the same!!" Opal replied.

Before they knew it Pete was taking nine weeks of basic training at Fort Bragg, North Carolina. Then after a short stay at a base in Maryland he was transferred to Fort McClellan Army Base in Anniston, Alabama.

Opal and Pete both knew this would be the last stop before Pete was shipped overseas, most likely to the front lines in Europe.

Pete did not want to wait until he got back from overseas to marry Opal and Opal did not want to wait either.

A formal proposal and a couple of passionate love letters later the final decision was made. Opal was going to Alabama to marry Pete.

Opal packed her suitcase and quickly made plans to go. Her first stop was to spend the night in Greensboro, NC with her sister, Annie and Annie's husband, Clifton Crutchfield.

After a good night sleep Clifton drove Opal to the train station where she bought her ticket to Anniston, Alabama. Opal still remembers the train traveling the back woods areas of South Carolina and Alabama and seeing how rundown the old depression era houses looked. It gave her a new appreciation for the quality of life her Mama and Papa had given her.

When Opal got to Anniston Pete was beaming from ear to ear. All of the plans had been made. Opal would spend the night at a nearby boarding house and the next day they would be married.

Everything worked as planned and Pete's Army buddies made sure the couple had some privacy the next couple of days at a nearby bungalow.

Sadly, it was short and sweet and then Opal was on her way back to North Carolina.

Pete got his orders a week later and was on his way to Europe via a Navy ship. When he got there he was immediately sent to Belgium. There the Allied forces were in a major battle with the German forces known as The Battle of the Bulge.

Pete, whose job was to carry a bazooka, recalled the fierce fighting on the battle fields during that time. He once had a large fir tree right beside him blown to tiny bits by an enemy mortar shell.

One night while attempting to get some sleep in a freshly dug fox hole, Pete's unit was overrun by the Germans. He and eight other members of his platoon were captured. During the confusion Pete raised his hands and a German soldier shot him in his left hand.

Pete and his fellow captures were taken to a nearby make shift basement prison where they waited to see if they would live or die.

Over the next few days Pete and his fellow captors noticed the German guards were taking one prisoner out of the basement every day and that prisoner did not return. They came to realize they were killing these prisoners because the basement was so crowded.

Pete and his buddies decided they had to make their escape now or they would soon all be dead. The next day when the guard came down to the basement to get another prisoner, one of Pete's buddies made a loud diversion. When the guard looked away Pete attacked the guard wrestled his gun away and shot him. It was a life or death situation. It was what he had to do.

Pete scrambled up the ladder from the basement shooting as he went with the other prisoners close behind. They all made it out of the makeshift prison and back to the allied lines.

Back home Opal received word from the Army Pete was missing in action, but that is all she knew. She did not even know if he was dead or alive.

It would be six weeks before she would hear anything from anyone about Pete's condition. Then one day she got a letter in the mail. It was from Pete!!

"Hi Honey, I'm in an allied hospital in France. I got captured by the Germans and I got shot in the hand. I'm OK and they say in a couple more weeks they're going to let me come home."

It was the spring of 1945. Opal was so glad to hear the news. Pete was coming home.

When Pete got home it was a very happy reunion for him and Opal. Pete had survived the Great War and now it was time for them to get on with their lives.

Pete had always been a farmer and it was what he wanted to do now. He and Opal rented a small farm in Sandy Ridge, North Carolina where he raised their tobacco allotment for a living.

Their first child, Shirley was born there and they were so proud to finally be starting a family.

Opal did not like it in Sandy Ridge. It just did not feel like home. She wished they could live a little closer to their families in Kernersville and Oak Ridge.

In February of 1948 Pete was offered a job in Kernersville, NC and this also pleased Opal very much.

Mr. Kenneth Greenfield owned a farm on the north side of Kernersville and also owned a farm and garden center in uptown Kernersville called Cash Feed Store.

Mr. Greenfield needed someone to tend his five acre tobacco allotment and in addition needed someone to deliver feed, seed, and fertilizer from his store to tobacco farmers and cattle growers around the area.

There was an additional perk that would come with the move. Mr. Greenfield was building a brand new rental home on his farm and that is where he wanted Pete and Opal to live.

It was the post World War II era and the U.S. Army was tearing down a military base they no longer needed in Greensboro, North Carolina.

The lumber was perfect for building the framework for new homes and Mr. Greenfield bought a large truckload to build his rental home.

While Pete and Opal were waiting on the new home to be completed, they had their second child, Jimmy.

Soon after Jimmy was born the new house was completed and Pete and Opal moved their family into the new home. The house was really nice. It had indoor plumbing, a new electric stove and a new refrigerator.

Pete and Opal settled in to their new home and were quite happy living there. They would live there for the next seven years.

In 1955 Opal had a pleasant surprise for Pete. She was expecting their third child who would be coming in May.

Although Pete enjoyed farming, renting a crop of tobacco instead of owning a farm simply could not support a family of five. Too much profit had to be shared with the owner. He had to find a job that would be stable and earn more money.

As luck would have it R.J. Reynolds Tobacco Company in Winston Salem, NC needed a carpenter and Pete applied for the job. He felt sure he would get the job, but he was turned down. The bullet wound from World War II to his hand kept Pete from being able to close his hand all the way and the person doing the hiring was afraid Pete would let a hammer slip out of his hand and injure someone. It was such a disappointment to Pete.

Pete had a neighbor and close friend, George Fontaine, who was a Forsyth County Deputy Sherriff and a respected man in the community. He had recommended Pete for the job and simply couldn't believe he was not hired. The following day he stopped by Reynolds and asked to talk with the personnel manager.

"Pete Flynt is one of the finest men I know. He's a World War II veteran and one of the hardest workers I know. There must be something you can do." George said.

The personnel manager replied, "Well, we do have an opening in plant security. If he'd like it we can hire him. It will be a lot of nighttime work."

When Pete returned to Reynolds the next day he was hired on the spot.

In May Pete and Opal's third child, Gracie was born. Opal and Pete were very proud of her.

They were also proud of the fact that with the new job Pete was able to buy a three bedroom home on the south side of Kernersville on

Bost Street. It was the first home Opal had ever owned in her life and it was a proud day when they moved in.

Pete liked his job at the largest manufacturer in Forsyth County. Opal stayed quite busy as well raising 3 children and managing the household.

Opal and Pete lived at this residence for 10 years, and then another opportunity came their way. It was a 20 acre farm about half way between Kernersville and Walkertown. It was being sold by a family whose mother had recently passed away.

Pete made an offer and the person handling the deal said lets just shake hands and we will do the paper work later.

Opal remembered what had happened to her father when he only shook hands. He lost the opportunity to buy a farm.

"Pete", Opal said, "Put $500.00 down on this place. If you don't the same thing that happened to Papa could happen to us!"

So they did.

As luck would have it one of the children in the family did not want to sell the farm and did everything he could to stop it. Opal's wisdom protected their offer and they got the farm.

Pete and Opal were so proud to own their own farm. It had an old farmhouse, a barn, and several acres of pasture. Pete even bought a horse for Gracie to ride while they lived there.

Seven years later in 1972, two doctors approached Pete and Opal about buying the farm and they offered good money for the place.

While Opal and Pete did not want to give up the land, the money they were offering could allow them to build a brand new brick home that would last them the rest of their lives.

The deal was too good to pass up and the farm was sold.

Shortly afterward Opal and Pete built their dream home on Vance Road east of Kernersville. The home had three bedrooms, two bathrooms, a full basement and a carport.

Pete also bought an additional five acres of land to go with the house. The land had a three acre pasture with a small stream and an old tobacco barn at the top of the hill.

A short while after moving in Pete built a fishing pond inside the pasture. The family enjoyed catching bass and brim there for years.

Pete and Opal enjoyed their new home over the years. It was almost perfect for their needs.

Pete continued working at R. J. Reynolds until 1988 when he retired with 33 years of service.

After retiring Pete had one more special thing he wanted to do for Opal. She had always dreamed of owning a cabin in the mountains. Pete wanted to do her one better and build her a cabin in the woods behind their house. This way she could walk to it any time she wanted.

Pete looked over the old tobacco barn that came with the five acres of land he and Opal had purchased and found it was still a very strong structure.

Pete hired a contractor and worked with him every day until it was just what Opal wanted. They built a new second floor so Opal could have a bedroom upstairs. The downstairs had an old wood cook stove Just like Opal's Mother, Alma used to own, a kitchen sink, a kitchen table and a new bathroom just outside the kitchen.

Opal loved it and spent thousands of hours there over the years.

In 1996 Opal lost Pete due to a sudden heart attack. It was a sad time for the entire family. The first Christmas without him the family was lost at the family Christmas Eve get-together. Who was going to fix Pete's famous turkey dressing?

Over time Opal and her children moved on and learned to enjoy life again as time went by. They knew that is what Pete would want them to do.

Over the past several years Opal's favorite hobbies have been going to the mountains, shopping, going to yard sales, or a trip to Goodwill to find another special item for herself or one of her family members.

Life has been good to Opal over these many years and she feels truly blessed to have the life she has had.

This is a picture of Opal and Pete Flynt in 1944 right before they were married.

Pete Flynt when he served in the U.S. Army during World War II. He saw action in Europe in 1944 and 1945 and was involved in The Battle of the Bulge.

Opal and Pete Flynt with their three children. On the front row are Jimmy, left and Shirley, right. Pete is holding Gracie. This picture was taken in 1956 on a Sunday afternoon visit to Grandma and Grandpa Young's.

Opal and Pete Flynt's oldest daughter, Shirley. This picture was taken in the early 1990's.

After Pete retired from R.J. Reynolds Tobacco Company in 1988 he converted an old tobacco barn behind their house into Opal's own personal "Cabin in the Woods". Above is a picture of Opal standing in front of her cabin. This picture was taken in the early 1990's.

Some of Opal's favorite pastimes over the years have been shopping for bargains at yard sales, Goodwill and other outlet shops. Here is a picture of Opal at a Goodwill Store in Mt. Airy, North Carolina while she was on a trip to the Virginia Mountains looking for some more special bargains. This picture was taken in 2009 when she was 84 years old.

Shirley Ann Flynt

On September 3, 1945 Opal and Pete Flynt had their first child, Shirley Ann Flynt. She was a happy baby and made Opal so proud, now that she was starting her own family. Shirley spent the first three years of her childhood living in Sandy Ridge, North Carolina.

Then in 1948 Pete and Opal moved to the Kenneth Greenfield Farm in Kernersville, North Carolina. Shirley really liked it there. Mr. Greenfield had just built a new house for them and it had several new modern conveniences.

The house was four rooms with coal burning stoves in the kitchen and living room. There was an open porch in front and an enclosed porch out back. There was also a pantry off the back porch. Shirley still remembers the 100 pound bag of pintos stored there that Pete bought each year after selling his crop of tobacco.

There was a new electric stove and refrigerator in the kitchen and a new wringer washing machine on the enclosed back porch. The house had indoor plumbing and a tub in the bathroom.

Shirley's father made his living raising five acres of tobacco for Mr. Greenfield and also worked at Mr. Greenfield's Cash Feed Store in downtown Kernersville.

In 1951 Shirley started the first grade at Kernersville Elementary School and went there for the next nine years. The school bus always stopped right in front of her house and Shirley was glad about that.

As Shirley got a little older she helped out in many ways on the farm. She helped her daddy with the tobacco crop as needed and she helped her mother with keeping the house clean and by washing the dishes and hanging clothes on the clothes line.

Shirley and her family went to Kernersville Moravian Church. It was an easy walk from their house. Palm Sundays were really special back then. Shirley would always get a pretty new dress to wear that day.

On many Saturdays she would walk with her younger brother, Jimmy in tow to the Justice Theatre to watch a movie. She would get a quarter from Opal to pay admission. That would buy two nine cent tickets with enough left over to purchase a large bar of candy.

Shirley remembers family was very important back then. On Sundays Pete and Opal would load up their 1950 Ford after church and go to Grandma and Grandpa Young's. There were always plenty of cousins to play with when they got there.

Pete had several brothers and sisters who enjoyed visiting each other back then, too. On many occasions they would have a great game of Rook or they may cook out on a charcoal grill having hotdogs and hamburgers and some great Musten's chili.

In 1955 Shirley's sister, Gracie was born and the Greenfield house became too small for a family of five.

Soon after, Pete got a job at R.J. Reynolds Tobacco Company in plant security. The new job, which paid more money allowed Pete and Opal to buy their own home on Bost Street on the other side of Kernersville.

Shirley really liked it there. There were many girls her age in the new neighborhood and she made several of them her friends.

She also liked it because after living there for a while Shirley got her own bed. She was sleeping with Gracie, but Shirley kicked in her sleep and that made Gracie afraid. Opal decided to get them two beds.

By the time Shirley was 14 she was babysitting to earn some extra money for herself.

At age 15 she got her first job at Moody's Restaurant in Kernersville. She enjoyed being around all the people there.

Shirley spent her sophomore and junior years of high school at Kernersville High School. Then she went to East Forsyth High School her senior year. She was part of East Forsyth's first graduating class in 1963.

After graduating, Shirley got her first full time job at Jefferson Life Insurance Company in Greensboro, North Carolina. She worked in the accounting department on claims and policy renewals.

Soon after starting to work Shirley bought her first car. It was a 1965 Ford Mustang.

Later in 1965 she got a job at R.J. Reynolds Tobacco Company in accounting. She would continue working there for more than 25 years.

In 1968 Shirley met a young man named Ronnie Crim Prater, who also was employed at Reynolds. Ronnie worked in the air conditioning department as a technician. Soon after, they started dating and on December 20, 1968 they were married. Ronnie and Shirley lived in the Belews Creek community in the old Crim home place for a while and afterward bought a mobile home.

On January 6, 1974 Shirley and Ronnie had their first and only child, Duane Kelly Prater. Duane loved life from the start and was always into something. Shirley had told Pete and Opal she wanted to have five children of her own. After Duane she decided one was enough. Pete laughingly referred to Duane as 5-in-1 after that.

In 1976 Ronnie and Shirley bought some land and built a new home. It was brick with three bedrooms, a full basement and a two-car garage. Shirley and Ronnie were so proud of this purchase.

In 1984 Shirley and Ronnie decided to go their separate ways. Shirley purchased her own home soon afterward on Lake Drive in Kernersville. She still lives there today.

In 1985 R.J. Reynolds Tobacco Company merged with Nabisco to become RJR- Nabisco. The infamous Ross Johnson of Nabisco headed up the merger and soon afterward became Chairman and CEO of the new firm.

Over the next decade many changes were made at the new RJR-Nabisco. Most of the changes helped management and hurt the older RJR workers.

In 1995 after several changes, Shirley ended up with the Planters-Lifesavers group in their accounting department.

In a surprise move the entire Planters-Lifesavers department was dissolved. Shirley was given no options and lost her long term career at Reynolds.

Undeterred, Shirley took several courses at Forsyth Tech to improve her skills and in 1996 went to work at Machine and Welding in Winston-Salem, North Carolina in their accounting department.

A year later she applied for employment at Pepsi Bottling Group, in Winston-Salem and got the job in their accounting customer service group. Shirley continued working there until she retired in 2006.

Shirley loves being retired. She said one of the best things about it is you do not have to report to anybody. Over the last several years Shirley has enjoyed shopping, yard sales, traveling and going to the North Carolina and Virginia mountains.

One thing has always stuck in Shirley's mind her daddy, Pete told her over the years, "Look after Mother."

Opal is 87 now and needs assistance in her day to day life. Shirley is right there by her side helping her as she needs it.

If Pete were here today he would be so proud of Shirley and what she is doing.

Opal and her daughter Shirley in late 1945.

Shirley and her brother Jimmy standing in Pepper Road in front of Grandpa and Grandma Young's house. in the early 1950's.

Shirley and Jimmy Flynt in 1954
posing for a family portrait.

This is a picture of
Shirley Flynt Prater and
her son, Duane Prater.

James M. Flynt, Jr.

On February 16, 1948 Opal and Pete Flynt had their second child, James M. Flynt, Jr. Pete and Opal were so proud to have a son. He would be called "Jimmy" by the family.

Jimmy was born right at the time Pete and Opal moved to the Kenneth Greenfield Farm in Kernersville, North Carolina.

Some of Jimmy's fondest memories during his early childhood were of growing up on that farm. By the time Jimmy was old enough to walk he was following his daddy everywhere he went.

When Jimmy was three, Pete got a brand new Ford Tractor with all the plowing implements to tend the farm. Jimmy had a special place to ride on that Ford Tractor, sitting against the right finder with two hands clutching tight to the edge of the finder.

Jimmy rode everywhere Pete went. There was lot happening on the farm back then. Pete was raising five acres of tobacco and also had a big garden beside the house. He also raised about five acres of corn and three acres of wheat.

The farm had several extra buildings behind the house and each had a special use. There was a big red feed barn where Pete kept his milk cow. It had to be milked twice a day. He also raised a few head of cattle and they stayed in the barn at night. There was a large hayloft for storing hay for the animals and a feed storage area for storing the animals oats and store bought feed. There was also a black cat that lived in the barn to keep the mice away.

Right behind the house was a chicken coop to house the laying hens that gave the family an endless supply of fresh eggs. Back in the woods there were two wood fired tobacco barns that were used each fall to cure Pete's tobacco crop. Jimmy loved curing time because he got to stay with his daddy at night while he was curing the tobacco. That was a time for wild tales and good father and son talks.

Every once in a while Jimmy and Pete would ride up to Harvey Bodenheimer's store and get some link hotdogs for their evening meal. Jimmy liked going with Pete to the woods and cutting two forked branches from an old hickory tree to be used to roast the hot dogs over the tobacco barn fires. There was also a apple orchard on the farm. Every fall Pete hitched his tractor to a large trailer with wooden side boards and pulled it from tree to tree under the apple tree limbs. He then shook the limbs and gathered several bushels of apples from the orchard.

Mr. Greenfield had his own cider mill and he and Pete would spend an afternoon grinding the apples, collecting the juice and then making several gallons of apple cider.

In 1954 Jimmy started the first grade at Kernersville School and spent grades 1 – 9 there. The bus came right by his house all nine years.

In 1955 Pete went to work at R.J. Reynolds Tobacco Company allowing him and Opal to buy their first home on Bost Street on the other side of Kernersville.

Jimmy really liked the move. There were a bunch of boys his age in the new neighborhood and he made friends with several of them.

This was the era of collecting baseball cards and all the boys in the neighborhood did so. Jimmy had quite a collection. His favorite cards were the 1958 Topps All-Star Baseball Cards. These cards had stars all over them and the top players of the time included Mickey Mantle, Hank Aaron, and Ted Williams.

Jimmy remembers carrying 15 to 20 of these cards in his front pocket all summer long that year. He ended up wearing the faces off the cards from all the wear of them rubbing together in his pocket, but that was OK. All that summer they made him feel like the King of baseball card collecting.

When Jimmy was 10 he got a new Western Flyer bicycle for Christmas. Pete and Opal purchased it from the Western Auto Store in downtown Kernersville. It was a pretty bike and Jimmy would ride it everywhere he went until he was 16.

When Jimmy was 12 he got a job at the Justice Theatre in Kernersville. It was his first job. His Western Flyer bicycle was his sole transportation to work the three years he worked there.

He started out selling Cokes and then progressed to the candy counter. Later he got to operate the popcorn machine at the entrance to the theatre.

During this era Pete raised about three acres of tobacco every summer in addition to working at Reynolds. Jimmy had plenty to do back then helping his daddy with the tobacco crop and working at the theatre.

In the fall of 1963 Jimmy started going to the new East Forsyth High School. He was a sophomore and would go there for the next three years. During that time Jimmy made both the football and wrestling teams and lettered in both sports.

When Jimmy turned 16 he got his drivers license and Pete bought a silver-gray 1952 Plymouth for him to drive. Jimmy loved the freedom of having his own car. He could drive to school, stay for football or wrestling practice and not have to depend on anyone to take him somewhere or pick him up.

Jimmy earned his spending and gas money during this time by working at Greenfield Farm and Garden Store in Kernersville. The same Mr. Kenneth Greenfield that Opal and Pete had rented the farm from when Jimmy was little also owned this store. Jimmy would work part time there all through high school.

Jimmy graduated from East Forsyth in 1966. It was a proud moment in his life.

After graduating Jimmy went to the beach with some close friends and the guys had some wild parties. One morning while there, Jimmy woke up and found someone had poured peroxide all over his hair during the night. The end result was a carrot orange head of long hair.

When he got home he had to face his father. When Pete saw his carrot top son he was not happy with his son. Jimmy was supposed to go for a job interview at R.J. Reynolds in three days and there was no way Pete was going to let him go there looking like that. The following morning Jimmy was escorted to the barber shop by Pete, where he got a G.I. haircut. Jimmy was a little embarrassed by the short hair and wore a hat for a month afterwards. A couple of days later Jimmy went for the interview at R.J. Reynolds. The interviewer must have liked such a clean cut guy, because he got the job.

It was also about this time Jimmy's childhood friend, Gary "Ralph" Watson was dating one of Jimmy's friends from childhood, Donna Southern. Donna was a senior at East Forsyth High School and had a pretty friend, who was also a senior there. Her name was Becky Petticord.

Ralph and Donna invited Jimmy and Becky to an East Forsyth football game to get to know each other. The two liked each other from the start and started dating.

Back at Reynolds Jimmy's new job was working second shift inspecting cigarettes. When a cigarette machine made cigarettes they came down a conveyor and he had to pick out the bad ones and put the good ones in an aluminum tray. It was a boring job, but it paid well.

A couple of months later a man with a handful of papers came by Jimmy's machine and said, "Your test scores show you have a high aptitude in mechanics. We want to put you on Reynolds' mechanics special training program on first shift."

It was also during this time Jimmy got his 1-A draft notice from Uncle Sam. The Vietnam war was in full swing by then and Jimmy knew it was only a matter of time before he would be called.

One day while on break at the Reynolds machine shop an older machinist struck up a conversation with Jimmy. "You know you're getting ready to be drafted. Do you want to go into the Army with no skills or do you want to go across town to Forsyth Tech and study for a year to become a machinist. You can get a deferment while you go to school."

This got Jimmy to thinking. He discussed his options with his soon to be bride, Becky and decided he would be much better off with a technical skill. He went to Forsyth Tech and applied for the one year machinist program. Sadly it was full for the next year, however they did have a new program titled Manufacturing Engineering Technology. It expanded on the machinist program and studied things like electronics, hydraulics, and drafting design. It was a two year course and he could get an Associates of Applied Science Degree in it.

Jimmy thought long and hard and decided to go with the new program. He thought he could continue working at Reynolds during the two years, but he knew it would be hard.

On May 5, 1968 Jimmy and Becky were married. The marriage was at Pisgah United Methodist Church in Kernersville and was a beautiful wedding. They were both very happy together.

Becky was recently hired in data processing at McLean Trucking Company in Winston-Salem and she planned on working there while Jimmy went to school.

Three months later Jimmy started school and found out right away he could not work at Reynolds and go to school at the same time. Without studying at least four hours per night he would flunk out the first quarter. Becky was very understanding during this time and paid most of the bills while Jimmy went to school. Jimmy graduated in 1969.

After graduating Jimmy went to work at Kester Machinery Company in Winston-Salem, North Carolina. They were an industrial mill supply company. It was while working at Kester in May of 1970 Jimmy and Becky's first and only child, Andy was born. Andy was their pride and joy.

In the fall of 1970 Jimmy accepted an offer to go to work as a draftsman at Burlington Industries Research Center in Greensboro, North Carolina. This turned out to be a big opportunity for Jimmy. He got to work directly with engineers drawing plans for parts of large machinery. Jimmy liked his job and hoped he could make his career there. Then one day in 1972 management called a meeting of all the Research Center employees and informed them they had sold the building to another firm and would no longer be in business in a few months.

Jimmy had to scramble or he would be jobless very soon. As luck would have it some lab technicians from the Research Center went across town to Lorillard Tobacco Company and applied for a lab technician job there. They were turned down but said they heard there was a job opening for a mechanical designer. Jimmy went and applied and got the job. Lorillard is where they make Newport, Kent and Old Gold cigarettes.

For the next nine years he did mechanical drawings for Lorillard's senior staff engineers.

In 1980 Jimmy was able to advance to Lorillard's new Planning Department. Jimmy really liked this job. It was thrilling to see some lines on a drawing turn into a new production line of modernized equipment.

In 1985 Jimmy was promoted to Maintenance and Construction Supervisor. In this job Jimmy supervised Lorillard's mechanics, machinists, welders, carpenters, electricians, painters, pipe fitters and sheet metal men that kept the plant running. He would do this for the rest of his career at Lorillard.

In 1988 Andy graduated from East Forsyth High School. The following fall he started college at High Point University majoring in English. He graduated with honors in 1992. A few years later Andy continued his education at The University of North Carolina Greensboro and graduated with a masters degree in Library Science.

In 1994 Jimmy and Becky decided to go their separate ways.

A few months later during the Christmas season Jimmy went to Hanes Mall in Winston-Salem. While paying for his purchase he noticed how cute the woman cashier was.

Jimmy just blurted right out, "Are you married?" The woman said no and Jimmy asked her for a date.

The woman's name was Carolyn Wallen and she, like Jimmy, was a graduate from East Forsyth High School. Carolyn at the time was going through a divorce herself.

In 1995 Jimmy and Carolyn were married. Carolyn was a fun loving person who really enjoyed life. One of her favorite things to do was make Jimmy laugh.

In 2001 Jimmy and Carolyn started thinking about early retirement. Jimmy would have 30 years at Lorillard in 2002 and could retire. Their dream was to retire to Corpus Christi, Texas. Carolyn had lived there before and found life to be so much fun on the Gulf shoreline. They went down to look at homes and found a beautiful one and put down a deposit. The deposit was contingent on selling their home in Winston-Salem.

When they went back home and put their house up for sale, to their surprise it sold in less than a week. Jimmy still had a year to work at Lorillard, so Carolyn moved down ahead of him.

Two weeks after moving Jimmy tried to call Carolyn and could not get an answer on the phone. Finally, he called the police and asked them to go over to the house to see what was wrong. When they got there the doors were locked and they called Jimmy to see if they could break a lock. Jimmy told them yes and waited on the phone to see what was wrong. About 20 minutes later they came back on the phone with the sad news. Carolyn had unexpectedly passed away during the night. The news was heartbreaking for Jimmy. It was a sad time.

A few months later Jimmy sold the house in Texas and moved his belongings back to North Carolina. For a while Jimmy lived with his mother, Opal. Opal enjoyed Jimmy living there and also liked for Jimmy to take her shopping.

One Saturday they stopped by a country store that sold vegetables and fruits. Jimmy noticed a pretty woman about his age working there. Opal bought several items and Jimmy needed assistance getting all the stuff to the car. When the woman finished helping Jimmy load the car he asked, "Do you and your husband own this place?" "That's not my husband!", the woman responded. "I'm not married." That was the answer Jimmy wanted to hear. Her name was Judy Freeman Gash, originally from Lumberton, North Carolina and her husband had passed away a few years earlier.

Jimmy started dating Judy and about six months later in April of 2002 they were married. Jimmy today says proudly that Judy is the love of his life.

In 2005 after 33 years of employment Jimmy retired from Lorillard. He has enjoyed retirement ever since.

Today Jimmy and Judy love going to yard sales, going out to eat or going for a country drive. Quite simply they love being together.

East Forsyth linemen (left to right), guard James Flynt, guard Roger Pinnix and center David Swaim get ready for the final game.

Jimmy Flynt on the left playing football at East Forsyth High.

Jimmy's son Andy with his grandfather Pete Flynt when he graduated from East Forsyth High in 1988.

Jimmy and Judy Flynt.
This picture was taken
at the 2002 Young
Christmas Party.

This is a picture of Andy
Flynt with his wife, Amy
and their sons, Caleb, left
and Keelen, right. This
picture was taken in 2010.

Grace Elizabeth Flynt

On May 2, 1955 Opal and Pete Flynt had their third and last child, Grace Elizabeth Flynt. She would always be known as her Daddy's girl. She would be called "Gracie" by the family.

Gracie was born on the Kenneth Greenfield Farm in Kernersville, North Carolina. However they soon moved to a new house Pete and Opal had bought. Gracie really liked where they lived. She and her sister, Shirley shared a bedroom and each had their own bed.

In 1961 Gracie started first grade at Kernersville Elementary School. She would continue going there through the ninth grade.

Gracie was a pretty little girl in her grammar school days and she was tough, too. Kernersville Elementary School's third grade bully once bragged, "I can beat up anybody in the third grade except Gracie Flynt!"

In 1964 Pete and Opal bought a 20 acre farm on Old Valley School Road. It was part of the Old Swaim Farm. This place was a real treat to Gracie. It had an old white farmhouse with lots of room, a large red barn and plenty of pasture land. A short while after the move Pete surprised Gracie with her own horse.

Gracie would saddle up and ride all over the community. She even rode to downtown Kernersville a few times. Gracie loved all types of animals and living on the farm allowed her to have several pets.

In 1972 Opal and Pete sold the farm and built a new brick home on Vance Road in Kernersville.

There was also another perk from selling the farm. Pete bought Opal a new 1973 Chevrolet Camaro in the fall of 1972. It had a big V-8, was silver gray and had a black vinyl top. Of course Gracie got to drive the new Camaro her senior year of high school.

In June of 1973 Gracie graduated from East Forsyth High School. It was one of her proudest accomplishments.

Soon after graduating Gracie met a young man named Mack Little. They had several things in common. For one Mack had just become employed at R.J. Reynolds Tobacco Company where her daddy worked. Another interest they each enjoyed was local Saturday night stock car racing.

Mack was a very smart young man, particularly in the area of auto mechanics. Mack's daddy, Roy Mack Little, Sr. was the chief mechanic at McLean Trucking in Winston-Salem, North Carolina at that time and taught Mack quite a bit about making auto repairs and how to fine tune a car engine. Mack would later take that knowledge to the race track where he could make any car he worked on a winner.

A few months later Gracie and Mack were married. They purchased a new mobile home and an acre of land and lived in Winston-Salem near where Mack's parents lived for several years. A few years later they built a new brick home right down the street and still live there today.

About a year after their Marriage Gracie and Mack had their first and only child, Roy Mack Little, III. He looked just like his father and later the two would be known as daddy, "Big Mack" and son, "Little Mack". The names have stuck over the years.

Gracie's own interest in mechanics later earned her a job at Doug Jones Enterprises in Walkertown, North Carolina where she was hired to sell John Deere riding lawn mowers.

Customers loved to come in and talk to Gracie. With her down home style they may talk about racing, horses, or farming for a while, and then they would talk about lawn mowers.

Gracie could explain the mowers in detail from headlight to trailer hitch and many times the costumer walked out with a new lawn mower.

Both Big Mack and Gracie loved racing and most Saturday nights during the 1970's and '80's you would find them at a local short track somewhere across the region. They could be at Bowman Gray Stadium in Winston-Salem, Caraway Speedway on the other side of High Point, NC or even at Martinsville Speedway in Martinsville, Virginia.

While Gracie's husband, Big Mack was helping local greats like Gerald Compton and Jay Hedgecock make their mark in the local modified division, Gracie choose to follow her family kin, first cousin, Phillip Smith and his modified racing career. Phillip was one of the best. He won races all over the southeastern United States. Gracie was his score keeper at almost every race. She got to sit in a special room next to the press box to officially count his laps and she carried her own pit crew radio to keep up with all the action.

Gracie also enjoyed Winston Cup Racing during this era. Her favorite drivers in that division were Buddy Baker and Harry Gant.

In 1995 after Little Mack graduated from high school, he too got the bug to go racing. But for Little Mack the want was different. He did not want to sit in the stands and watch or keep score or even be a race car mechanic. He wanted to drive the race cars!

This would be a life changing event for both Gracie and Big Mack. No longer would Gracie be keeping score for her cousin, Phillip Smith and no longer would Big Mack be a mechanic for local modified drivers. Instead they would be forming their own race team.

And Little Mack would have to make some major commitments himself. He would need to spend dozens of hours every week committed to helping his father make his race car the best on the track.

After some hard soul searching Little Mack, Big Mack and Gracie made the commitment to give it their best shot and formed the family race team, Mack Little Racing.

Together they cleaned out the one-car garage at their home on Reidsville Road and turned it into a race shop.

With some help from friends and family they built Little Mack his first race car and he began his racing career at Bowman Gray Stadium in Winston Salem North Carolina.

Little Mack took some bumps, however he quickly learned his skills as a driver well. Before long he was winning races and quickly became a crowd favorite.

Over the years Little Mack has won dozens of races and division championships at Bowman Gray Stadium, Hickory Motor Speedway and Caraway Speedway.

During the past few years Gracie has dealt with some health issues which have prevented her from going to the race track and see her son race. It was just too hard for her to make the long walks from the parking lots to the stands.

A couple of months ago Big Mack and Little Mack had a surprise for Gracie. It was a RV with all the comforts of home. Now Gracie can go see Little Mack race any time she wants.

Gracie and Jimmy Flynt with their dog in the late 1950's

Gracie Flynt in her 3rd grade school picture.

Gracie Flynt's High
School Picture

This is a great picture
of Big Mack, Little
Mack and Gracie
Little. This picture is
from the late 1970's.

Chapter Thirteen

The Elsie Young Marshall Family

On April 13, 1927 Elias and Alma's seventh child and fifth daughter, Elsie Young was born. Over the years Elsie would grow to be a beautiful young woman.

Elsie spent the first two years of her childhood growing up on the Wicker Farm, located in the Belews Creek Community near Goodwill Church east of Walkertown, North Carolina. The farm was a couple of miles from Elias' father, Hester Young's farm. Elias and Alma's main source of income while living there was raising tobacco.

In 1930 Elias and Alma moved the family to The Case Farm about two miles north of Oak Ridge, North Carolina just off NC Highway 68. Elsie was only two years old at the time. On that cold February morning she was held by her mother in the front seat of their Model "T" Ford as they moved to the new farm.

The Case Place was a large 200 acre farm and Elias and Alma had moved there to grow nine acres of tobacco for Mr. and Mrs. Case. In return the Young family could live there rent free and could grow all the food they needed for their family and farm animals if they gave half the profits each year from the tobacco crop as rent.

The Great Depression had just started and the times were hard, but the Youngs were a proud family and made the best of this bad situation. Elsie would spend the next 12 years of her childhood growing up on The Case Farm.

In 1935 Elsie started first grade at Oak Ridge Elementary School. She did not have to wait out in the cold for her bus ride to school back then. That is because her brother, Raymond, drove the school bus. He kept the school bus parked in their front yard and each morning the Young children were the first ones on the bus. Elsie attended Oak Ridge Elementary School through the seventh grade.

During the later 1930's one by one Elsie's older brothers and sisters started getting married. Hubert, Annie, Raymond, Hazel, and Edna were all married by 1940 and all had moved out on their own.

That left Opal, Elsie, Clyde, and Wonnie still living at home when World War II started in December of 1941. Elsie would be closest to her sister, Wonnie, over the coming years.

In 1942 Elias and Alma moved their family to the Lowery Farm and the Big White House on Pepper Road in Oak Ridge, which was only about five miles away from the Case Farm. Elsie would spend her teenage years and young adult years growing up there.

Also in 1942 Elsie changed schools and attended Summerfield school for the eighth grade.

In 1943 Elsie changed schools again and went to Colfax High School until she graduated.

While at Colfax High School Elsie met an athletic young man named Reavis Marshall. They were in the same grade and at the time Reavis was more interested in playing baseball than he was in girls, but Elsie knew she liked Reavis from the first time she saw him.

Reavis was raised on a tobacco farm a few miles up the road from Colfax School. His parents were Glen and Mary Marshall.

Elsie tried her best to get Reavis to ask her out on a date, but it never happened. The two would remain close friends all during high school.

In June of 1947 Elsie graduated from Colfax High School. This was a monumental event in the Young family for it was the first time one of Elias and Alma's children had graduated and had a high school diploma.

Elsie would set a new standard for the next generation of Youngs. All of the Young grandchildren in the future would be expected to get their high school diplomas.

Soon after graduating high school Elsie got a job at Sears Mail Order in Greensboro, NC. Elsie did not have a car and rode to work with a friend.

Elsie's sister, Wonnie, who was still in high school at that time remembers Elsie buying the Young family their first refrigerator while working at Sears. Before that the family had an ice box.

About a year later Elsie's friend got a new job and Elsie had to quit working at Sears because she did no have a way to get to work. Elsie's brother, Raymond, found out about the situation and got Elsie a job where he worked at Southern Silk Mill in Kernersville, NC. Now she was able to ride to work with Raymond.

While Elsie was pursuing her career, Reavis Marshall was doing his best to fulfill his dreams of becoming a Major League baseball player. In 1948 he played Class 'D' baseball with the Mt. Airy Graniteers of the Blue Ridge League in Mt. Airy, North Carolina. His team had a tremendous season that year winning the league pennant and then going on to win the playoffs from a team in Galax, Virginia.

The Boston Braves minor league system really liked Reavis' potential and in 1949 advanced him to their Sumter, South Carolina Class 'B' baseball team in the Tri-State League.

By the spring of 1950 Reavis had become a solid .300 hitter and was a key player on the team. He had visions of some day playing in the Major Leagues with other up and coming players in the Braves organization like Hank Aaron, Eddie Mathews, and Warren Spahn.

Then later in 1950 the United States went to war with North Korea and young men all over the country Reavis' age were drafted into military service.

Reavis thought long and hard about his options and thought he would much rather be on a U.S. Navy ship than being in a foxhole facing the enemy in a cold country like Korea. A couple of weeks later he joined the Navy.

Reavis first went through basic training and then on to several training classes. While Reavis was in the Navy, he and Elsie sent letters back and forth to each other continuously. They had come to realize they were truly in love and wanted to be married. The only thing preventing this was Reavis' time remaining in service. Neither could wait for him to get out.

In 1952 he was assigned to the Navy ship USS LSMR 527 and went overseas to the coast of North Korea. He would be in the Korean War conflict for the next several months.

In 1953 an admiral at the Coronado Navy Base in San Diego, California found out baseball star Reavis Marshall was on one of his ships stationed off the coast of Korea. His Navy Baseball Team was in bad need of an outfielder and he asked if Reavis could be sent immediately to his base in San Diego. Reavis was given a letter from the admiral by the commanding officer on his ship and was sent on his way to find the quickest route back to California.

Reavis went to a nearby Navy base and was granted a flight to the next island across the pacific. At that base another naval passenger was bumped and Reavis flew to Hawaii. The next day Reavis got a flight to San Diego and was playing for the Navy Baseball Team the following day.

He was able to take the trip in three days that would have taken at least two to three weeks by normal channels Reavis was able to complete in three days. It was amazing for Reavis to see what a person can do when they have the right connections from higher ups.

In July of 1954 Reavis was discharged from the Navy and he returned home to Colfax, North Carolina. When he got home he could hardly wait to see his love, Elsie. The two were glad to be together again and soon after getting home Reavis proposed marriage. Elsie of course said yes.

On January 15, 1955 Elsie and Reavis were married. The wedding was at Elsie's sister, Edna Young Goins', home and the entire families from both Elsie and Reavis' sides were there. It was a wonderful day.

After they were married Reavis and Elsie moved to a house on Marshall Smith Road in Colfax, NC previously owned by Reavis' Uncle Ed Marshall.

In February of 1955 the Milwaukee Braves Baseball Farm System wanted to sign Reavis to a new contract to play with the South Atlantic league in Jacksonville, Florida. This would be an advancement to Class 'A' baseball and would put Reavis much closer to being able to play in the Major Leagues.

Reavis thought about how this may be his pathway of reaching his dreams of being a Major League star. Then he thought of being away from Elsie again. He had to make a choice. This time the decision was easy for Reavis, he chose Elsie.

At the time of their marriage Elsie was working at Adams-Millis Hosiery Mill in Kernersville and Reavis was recently hired with Southern Silk Mill in Kernersville.

There was only one problem. They each worked a different shift. After all those years of being apart while Reavis was in the Navy, here they were only seeing each other for a few minutes a day. Reavis would have none of this. He loved Elsie too much to be away from her all the time again. Soon afterward Elsie quit her job at Adams-Millis and came home so she and Reavis could start raising a family.

On October 8, 1957 Elsie and Reavis had their first child, Lisa Gaye Marshall. The two were so proud of their daughter.

It was also around this time Reavis got a job with Atlantic Oil Company at the gasoline tank terminal located across from the Piedmont International Airport in Greensboro, N.C. To keep the job Reavis had to have a telephone so he could be called in to work when needed in cases of special shipments or emergencies.

At the time Southern Bell did not have a telephone line down Marshall Smith Road and Reavis did not have a phone. He ended up renting a house at the end of the road on Highway 421 that had a telephone.

When Reavis went to Southern Bell to see how he could get a line ran down their road the company told him if 10 people on his road would buy a $100 worth of Southern Bell stock they would run the line.

Within a week Reavis got enough neighbors to buy the stock. While they were running the line Reavis inquired with AT&T about getting a telephone for their house. As luck would have it telephones were in short supply and were on backorder. They told Reavis there was a building being built and was almost completed in Greensboro and if he would go and reserve their phone he could get it after the building was completed. That is the hoops Reavis had to jump through to finally get his family a phone so he could move back home.

Reavis worked with Atlantic Oil Company for approximately two years and the company went out of business. The experience with Atlantic was helpful. After their company closed Reavis was hired by Shell Oil Company located in the same tank terminal across from the Greensboro Airport.

Reavis started out in Shell's warehouse ordering and selling supplies such as tires, oil, and other items to service stations in the Piedmont Triad area.

About a year later he received a promotion with Shell to the position of terminal receiver. At this time Shell, Exxon and other oil companies received all of their gasoline from their refineries in Louisiana through the Plantation Pipe Line. This line was a large underground pipe from their refineries in Louisiana directly to the tank terminal in Greensboro. Any gasoline put in this line took seven days to make the 1000 mile journey.

It was Reavis' job to know exactly when Shell's gasoline was going to be received and to open the proper valves to fill the proper tanks in Greensboro. Reavis would work with Shell for over 30 years doing this job.

On April 25, 1960 Elsie and Reavis had their second and final child, Reavis Devon Marshall, Jr. He would be called R.D. by his family and he was so much like his father.

After settling into his job at Shell Reavis and Elsie had several activities they enjoyed as a family over the years. Reavis loved having a big garden every year. He would plant at least a half acre and in it he had Tomatoes, corn, okra, onions, potatoes, green beans, water melons, cantaloupe, and much more.

Behind the garden he had a grape arbor, black berry bushes, fig bushes, apple trees, and other fruit trees.

He and other gentlemen on Marshall Smith Road enjoyed having a friendly competition of who had the best looking garden. There was always plenty to eat for the summer and Elsie would can dozens of quart jars of vegetables and fruits for the winter just like her mother, Alma, had done many years earlier.

Any extras were given to friends and family or to fellow church members at Colfax Baptist Church.

Another activity they enjoyed was going to the Marshall family cabin in Swansboro, North Carolina. Reavis remembers well when he was a young teenager helping his father, two uncles, and two other friends of the family buy land and build a cabin on the Carolina coast. It was a beautiful setting. You could see the lights of the city of Swansboro across the bay at night. It was a relaxing place to be.

The Marshall family hung on to this cabin over the years and used it regularly. Every spring and fall Reavis, Elsie, Lisa, and R.D. would pack up and be off to Swansboro. There were so many fun things to do there. They could go fishing, flounder gigging, or simply enjoy a few days in the sun.

In the early 1990's Reavis retired from Shell Oil Company. This gave Elsie and Reavis more time to do the things they wanted to do. They enjoyed traveling and spent a lot of time in the mountains or on the coast at their cabin in Swansboro.

They continued their church activities, and Elsie and Reavis sang in the Colfax Baptist Church choir.

They also enjoyed visiting family and going to the Young get-togethers. Whether it was a Young Christmas Party, a family reunion, or a chicken stew at Clyde and Nora's house, you could count on Elsie and Reavis being there.

In the early 2000's the couple joined the singing group, 'The Sugar Sticks'. Also in the group were Elsie's brother, Clyde, her sister Edna and friend of the family, Roger Howerton. The group sang all over the Piedmont at church events.

On August 18, 2008 Reavis passed away after a long illness. Elise felt so blessed to have had such a wonderful husband over the years.

Today Elsie does her best to enjoy life every day. She enjoys spending time with her children, Lisa and R.D. One of her favorite pastimes is going with Lisa to local thrift stores and finding another clothing bargain or something special for her home.

Here is a great collage of Elise Young Marshall's pictures through the years.

Here is a picture of Reavis Marshall in his baseball uniform when he played for the U.S. Navy at Coronado Navy Base in San Diego, California in 1953 and 1954.

This is a picture of from left Reavis and Elsie Marshall and their nephews, Gary Young and M.K. Moore. This picture is from the mid-1950's.

This is a picture of Elsie with her daughter, Lisa. This picture was taken in 1958.

Here is a picture of Elsie and Reavis Marshall with their children Lisa and R.D. This picture was taken in the mid-1960's.

This is a picture of Reavis and Elsie Marshall freezing strawberries for winter. This picture was   probably taken around the year 2000.

To the left is a picture of Reavis Marshall preparing a big iron pot of his famous chicken stew recipe at a Young get-together at Clyde and Nora Young's house. This picture was taken around 2003.

This is a picture of the Reavis and Elsie Marshall Family taken in 2006. From bottom left are Lisa, Reavis and Elsie. From top left are Doug, Jason Marshall, Jordan Marshall, Kempy Marshall and R.D.

Lisa Gaye Marshall

On October 8, 1957 Elsie and Reavis Marshall had their first child, Lisa Gaye Marshall. When Lisa was born Reavis and Elsie had recently purchased their home on Marshall Smith Road in Colfax, North Carolina from Reavis' Uncle Ed Marshall. Lisa would spend her entire childhood here.

Lisa felt blessed to have two wonderful sets of grandparents when she was growing up. Maw Maw and Paw Paw Marshall lived just down the road from her house and Lisa enjoyed riding her bike over there to spend time with them. She remembers Paw Paw Marshall enjoyed rabbit hunting. He kept a big lot of beagles behind his house. Lisa can still see him in a field near their home sitting under a shade tree and taking a break with his dogs after they had just finished chasing another rabbit.

Lisa also enjoyed visiting Maw Maw Marshall. Especially on those days when she had just baked a pound cake and had it sitting in her window to cool. She recalls the aroma was heavenly.

Another fond memory Lisa had of her grandparents was helping them put in a barn of tobacco. Her job was to hand the green tobacco leaves to the person who was stringing them onto the sticks.

It was also a treat to visit Grandma and Grandpa Young. They had both recently retired and lived in the little green house on Pepper Road in Oak Ridge, North Carolina.

Lisa, her brother, R.D. and her parents would always visit on Sunday afternoons after church. There were always family members there and plenty of cousins for her and R.D. to play with. Lisa was especially close to her Uncle Clyde Young's children, Rhonda and Clyde Jr. Lisa's Aunt Wonnie McCormick also had a son, Moochie who was Lisa's age and another daughter, Lynn, who was a little older.

They had a lot of fun talking, playing games, roaming the woods, and just having fun.

When Lisa was six years old she started the first grade at nearby Colfax Elementary School. She would attend Colfax through the sixth grade. She enjoyed getting ice cream in the afternoons at Colfax Elementary. Fudgecicles were seven cents and ice cream sandwiches were a dime.

While Lisa was growing up she enjoyed having a close and loving family. They attended Colfax Baptist Church almost every Sunday. Her father was a Sunday school teacher and both Reavis and Elsie sang in the church choir.

On weekends and during vacation time they enjoyed traveling. They may go to the North Carolina Mountains to visit the Cherokee Indian Reservation or one of the amusement parks along the way. At other times they may visit the Marshall Family Cabin on the North Carolina Coast in Swansboro, North Carolina. No matter where they traveled the Marshall family always had fun.

Lisa later attended Northwest Guilford Junior High School in the ninth grade and Northwest Guilford Senior High School through the twelfth grade.

On the weekends when Lisa was a teenager she enjoyed going to Greensboro and visiting her cousins, Clyde Jr. and Rhonda Young. On Saturdays they enjoyed getting ice cream from the neighborhood ice cream truck and on Sundays Lisa would go with the Young;s to Florida Street Baptist Church in Greensboro.

In 1975 Lisa graduated from Northwest Guilford High School. She later attended Jefferson College in Greensboro, NC and graduated with an Accounting Degree.

Lisa was hired at Jefferson Pilot Insurance Company where she worked in their department for Group Insurance Rates and Underwriting.

In the 1980's Lisa met a man named Doug McLaughlin in the singles class at Florida Street Baptist Church. It wasn't long before they began dating. One day at Carolina Coffee Shop in Greensboro Doug asked Lisa to marry him. She gladly said yes and on September

27, 1985 they were married at the same place they met, Florida Street Baptist Church in Greensboro.

Doug was working as an engineer with Gilbarco in Greensboro, North Carolina when he and Lisa were married and he still works there today. The company builds gasoline pumps for service stations and Doug's responsibility is writing software for those gasoline pumping systems.

On February 28, 1989 Lisa and Doug had their first and only child, Melanie. Lisa and Doug have been proud of Melanie over the years. She is a recent graduate of the School of Communications Arts in Raleigh, North Carolina and today is employed in web and graphic design. Melanie has recently decided to advance her education and is now attending Wake Technical Community College in her spare time. She currently lives in Wake Forest just north of Raleigh.

Lisa worked with Jefferson Pilot Insurance Company for 20 years and then moved on to become an employee at the University of North Carolina in Greensboro. Today she is an Administrative Assistant at UNCG's Bryan School of Business and Economics.

Lisa and Doug have enjoyed traveling over the years. Doug and Lisa are also avid photographers. Doug purchased one of the first digital cameras made many years ago and has taken thousands of pictures ever since. While they like still and scenic photography, the Youngs and Marshalls also appreciate all the pictures they take at family get-togethers over the years.

Whether at a reunion, a Christmas party, a chicken stew or just when the families are eating out together to share old memories you can find Doug and Lisa there with their cameras. The photographs they have of the Young's and Marshall's over the years are true treasures.

Today, Lisa enjoys spending time with her mother, Elsie. One of their favorite pastimes is going to local thrift stores and shopping.

This is a series of pictures of Lisa Marshall McLaughlin from the time she started first grade at Colfax Elementary School until she graduated from Northwest Guilford Senior High School in 1975.

Above is a picture of Lisa, Melanie, and Doug McLaughlin today.

Reavis Devon Marshall, Jr.

On April 25, 1960 Elsie and Reavis Marshall had their second and last child, Reavis Devon Marshall Jr. He would be called "R.D." by the family. When R.D. was born Reavis and Elsie lived on Marshall Smith Road in Colfax, North Carolina. R.D. would spend his entire childhood living there.

From his early childhood R.D. has some fond memories of going to visit Grandma and Grandpa Young. His grandparents lived in the little green house on Pepper Road in Oak Ridge, NC when R.D. was born.

He remembers going there on Sunday afternoons after church and having several cousins his age with whom to play.
R.D. and cousins, Clyde Young, Jr. and 'Moochie' McCormick really enjoyed those afternoons they used to spend together.

There was a big shed behind Grandma and Grandpa Young's house they enjoyed climbing on top of. When they got to the top on a clear day they could see all the way to Hanging Rock. On one side of the tin roof they could climb over and pick cherries from a big black heart cherry tree in the summertime. On the other side the tin roof was much steeper and the boys enjoyed using it as a sliding board.

They also liked to walk down a dirt road behind their Grandpa and Grandma Young's house that led to the woods and a large creek. On several occasions they dammed up the creek and played in the cold water.

R.D.'s Uncle Raymond and Aunt Edna Goins lived down the road from Grandma and Grandpa Young's and Reavis and Elsie would visit them on Sundays as well. Raymond had a big dog lot of beagles in his back yard and often on Sunday afternoons he and several family members would go hunting. It would not be unusual to see twenty or more of the family men watching Raymond's dogs chasing rabbits.

Edna and Raymond enjoyed water skiing and kept a

camper and a ski boa at Philpot Dam Lake. One Sunday afternoon when R.D. and his family were visiting the lake Raymond asked young R.D. if he wanted to learn to ski.

Raymond spent a lot of time explaining to him the techniques of getting up on the skis as the boat was taking off. Then Raymond put the skis on R.D., handed him the ski rope, and started the boat. R.D. was up on the first try and continued to ski for four or five miles. R.D. was so proud of himself that day.

When R.D. was six years old he started first grade at Colfax Elementary School. He would go there through the sixth grade and Northwest Guilford Middle School through the ninth grade.

R.D. was proud of the half acre garden his daddy grew each year while he was growing up. There was plenty of food for their family during the summer and Elsie canned dozens of quart jars of vegetables to last them over the winter months.

R.D also remembers his parents loved taking time out of their day to day routines to travel. Sometimes they would go to the mountains in western North Carolina. Reavis always wanted to get an early morning start when they did and around breakfast time he would stop and pull their grill out of the trunk of the car. He would then set up and fix bacon, eggs, and all the trimmings for their breakfast.

R.D. attended Northwest Guilford Senior High School and proudly graduated in 1978.

After graduating R.D. went to work at Custom Industries, a machine shop in Greensboro, NC and worked there for two years.

Later he was hired by Gilbarco in Greensboro. Gilbarco made gasoline pumps for service stations and convenience stores all across the nation. While R.D. worked there he was a digital tester. His job was to make sure the digital meters in the pumps worked properly after they were manufactured and before they went out to the customers. R.D. worked for Gilbarco for six years.

In the early 1980's one of R.D.'s favorite pastimes was playing church league softball at the Colfax School baseball field. In 1984 while R.D. was playing a softball game one night, he noticed a beautiful young woman in the stands. She was so pretty he just had to talk to her.

Her name was Kempy Holmes. As it turned out she was the younger sister of a girl R.D. had graduated from high school with in 1978.

The two liked each other from the start and began dating. On April 13, 1985 Kempy and R.D. were married before many of their family and friends at Shady Grove Wesleyan Church in Colfax.

After they were married the couple moved to Kernersville. While living there Kempy, who had recently graduated from Guilford Technical Community College with a diploma in dental assisting, went to work with a local dentist as a dental assistant.

R.D. continued working with Gilbarco for the next year and in 1987 got a job with Duke Power Company in Greensboro. R.D. knew this was where he wanted to spend his career and has been there ever since. R.D.'s areas of expertise at Duke are repairing and replacing transformers, substations and power surge reclosers.

A short time after starting to work at Duke Power, R.D. and Kempy moved back to Marshall Smith Road in Colfax and built a home where they live today.

On November 30, 1990 Kempy and R.D. had their first son, Jordan. Then on December 14, 1992 the couple had their second and final son, Jason. R.D. and Kempy have been very proud of their sons over the years.

Jordon, since finishing high school, has continued his education at Guilford Technical Community College in the study of electrical engineering. Jordon is also very proud of the fact he was recently hired at Duke Power as a lineman. He hopes when he completes his courses at GTCC he can advance his career at Duke Power into Electronics Engineering.

Kempy and R.D. are also very proud of their other son, Jason. Jason was very adventuresome as a teenager and one of his favorite hobbies was riding bulls.

Jason also went to Guilford Tech after finishing high school and graduated with a diploma in Heavy Equipment Operations. Today he works for Five Points Motor Company as a diesel mechanic..

R.D. and Kempy have been involved in their church over the years. Their main area of interest has been helping youth groups and other organizations.

This is a picture of from left, Reavis, Lisa, and R.D. Marshall when they were on a trip to the North Carolina Mountains in 1968. Reavis is cooking breakfast for the family.

Here is a picture of from left, Kempy, Jordan, Jason and R.D. Marshall when Jason graduated from high school in 2011.

Chapter Fourteen

The Clyde Hanes Young Family

The date was March 15, 1931 and it was a proud day for Alma and Elias Young. On this day their eighth child, Clyde Hanes Young was born. At the time Clyde was born Elias and Alma lived on The Case Place Farm, which was located about two miles north of Oak Ridge, North Carolina just off of NC Highway 68.

The Case Place brings back many fond memories to Clyde. Although the Great Depression brought hard times, Clyde had a wonderful family surrounding him when he was growing up. First there was his father, Elias. Elias was a great farmer and made sure his family was well provided for. He made his living growing nine acres of tobacco and he also grew plenty of food for his family.

In Clyde's eyes there was not a sweeter or harder working woman than his mother. Alma made sure the family had great meals every day. She was up every morning at 5:00 A.M., along with Elias, cooking breakfast and then on to doing anything it took to provide for her family. Alma sewed all the family's clothes on an old foot pump sewing machine and while she was not cooking or sewing she was canning food for the family to make sure they had plenty to eat over the winter months.

Clyde also had seven older brothers and sisters. Each were hard working and pitched in to help out around the farm anywhere they were needed. Clyde's younger sister, Wonnie, would come two years later.

Times were hard and there were very few jobs available. Clyde still remembers how proud the family was in 1934 when his older brother, Raymond, got a job driving a bus for the Oak Ridge School system. Raymond drove two routes every morning and afternoon delivering children to and from school.

In 1937 Clyde started first grade at Oak Ridge Elementary School and would continue going there through the seventh grade. It was also during this time that many of Clyde's older brothers and sisters started getting married. By 1941 five of his older siblings would be married and had moved away from home.

Then on December 7, 1941 the Japanese bombed Pearl Harbor and the United States of America went to war. Clyde, who was 10 years old at the time, still remembers all the changes back then.

For one, jobs opened up everywhere. The U.S. troops needed lots of clothing and other cloth materials so Clyde's mother, Alma and several sisters and sister-in-laws got jobs at local hosiery mills.

Not every male was needed in the military during this time. They were needed in other critical jobs as well. Although Clyde was only a young teen at the time he carried an adult share of the load helping his father raise tobacco. His brother, Raymond, worked at a local rayon mill where they made parachutes for the war effort. Clyde's brother-in-law, Raymond Goins, went to Newport News, Virginia and built troop transport ships and cargo ships for the military. Clyde's soon to be brother-in-law, Pete Flynt, went into the Army and served in Europe. Everyone pitched in during World War II and winning the war was a sense of pride for every member of the Young family.

In the fall of 1945 Clyde changed schools and started the eighth grade at Colfax Jr. High School. He would go there for two years through the ninth grade.

During his time at Colfax, Clyde developed an interest in playing baseball. He acquired a first baseman's mitt and started playing first base for the Colfax School team. Clyde was a strong young man, who was quick with his hands and feet, and could hit the ball a country mile.

In the fall of 1947 Clyde switched schools again, this time going to Summerfield High School. The Summerfield Baseball Team welcomed Clyde to their team.

During his playing time there Clyde became the best first baseman in the school conference and made the "All Guilford County Baseball Team". Considering that included all the boys from the big cities of Greensboro and High Point, that was quite a feat. Although Clyde would never brag about his accomplishment, it was one of his proudest moments. Clyde proudly graduated from Summerfield High School in June of 1950.

In the summer of 1950 Clyde continued his post high school education at Oak Ridge Military Academy. Although Clyde loved farming, he knew the importance of furthering his education in the post war job market. The academy also wanted Clyde for their baseball team.

Clyde continued to help his father on the farm during this time and he also continued living at home. Oak Ridge Military Academy was only a few miles down the road from where they lived.

Late in the fall of 1950 a friend of the Young family, Corey Lowery, was in the hospital and unable to tend his farm. With winter coming and no wood in their wood shed to heat their home, the men of the Oak Ridge community decided to take a Saturday and cut wood for the Lowery family. They figured a long days work could supply them with enough firewood for the winter.

Elias asked Clyde if he wanted to stay home and tend the farm or help with the wood cutting. Clyde wanted to help his neighbor in need and went with his father. In a recent interview at his home, Clyde looked up on his living room wall and said, "That crosscut saw hanging on the wall there is the one I carried that day." Clyde's job that day was to help Elias with the crosscut saw to cut the tree trunks into lengths just the right size to fit into the Lowery's fireplace. Others would then split the lengths into firewood.

A little later in the morning someone took Clyde's place on the crosscut saw and Clyde began using an ax to clear the trees of branches so the tree trunks would be easier to cut.

Clyde was in mid swing at another branch when suddenly the tree started to roll. The sudden shifting caused Clyde's ax to miss the branch and its sharp edge landed across the top of his foot and almost cut it off.

One of the neighbors helping that day was Pink Dwiggins. He quickly took charge of the situation. Pink saw how badly Clyde's foot was cut and also saw how much he was bleeding. Pink put one hand on the back of Clyde's ankle and the other at the bottom of Clyde's foot and held his foot tightly together. This helped to reduce the bleeding.

The rest of the men carried Clyde to a nearby car and then on to the doctor. All the while Pink Dwiggins held Clyde's foot tightly together. Clyde would later say, "Pink probably saved my life that day."

The injury took several months to heal, but fortunately for Clyde he made a full recovery. Clyde did not return to Oak Ridge Military Academy after that. He decided instead to help his father full time farming his nine acres of tobacco. Elias could use the help since almost all of his children were married and moved on.

Clyde continued playing baseball with the Oak Ridge Bulls, a local Oak Ridge semipro team, and the family loved watching him play. No matter what farm work needed to be done, on Saturday afternoon Elias stopped everything and all the extended family went to the Oak Ridge School baseball field to watch Clyde play.

On February 7, 1954 Clyde was drafted into the U.S. Army. Although he didn't really want to go, Clyde knew it was his patriotic duty and he proudly served his country for the next two years.

He first went to Fort Jackson, South Carolina for his basic training and then it was on to Fort Benning, Georgia for infantry school. Next Clyde spent six months at Fort Bragg, North Carolina.

From Fort Bragg he was sent to Germany and would spend his final year of service there. Clyde enjoyed his time in Germany and got to see things he had never seen before.

Finally, in the spring of 1956 Clyde was discharged from the Army and returned home to Oak Ridge. Clyde was excited to be back home with his family and friends.

Soon after returning home, Clyde met a beautiful young woman named Shirley Smith. The two began dating and a few months later were married. After they were married Clyde and Shirley moved to a house on Highway 68 on the other side of Oak Ridge.

Clyde went to work at Lorillard Tobacco Company in Greensboro, NC in 1956. Clyde was hired as a researcher in Lorillard's Research and Product Development Department.

This was a great opportunity for Clyde. Lorillard had just finished building a large new cigarette manufacturing facility in Greensboro and the factory was one of the most modern tobacco plants in the country.

The company even advertised their research efforts on national television. Who did they get to be in their advertisement? It was none other than Clyde Young. Some of the older Youngs still remember Clyde's Lorillard advertisement airing on the famous TV game show of the late 1950's, "The 64,000 Dollar Question".

Lorillard developed two new brands from their research. The first was Kent Filter Cigarettes. This brand would be a major seller for the company during the 1960's – 1980's. The second cigarette they developed was Newport Menthol Filter Cigarettes. This brand sold well from the start and in the early 1990's became the nation's No. 1 best selling menthol brand. Newport still holds that No. 1 sales ranking today. Clyde was proud to be a member of this research team and would work for Lorillard for the next several years.

On July 25, 1957 Clyde and Shirley had their first child, Clyde Young Jr. The couple was still living in the house on Highway 68 when Clyde Jr. was born.

In 1959 Clyde moved his family to an apartment above a store in Oak Ridge. The store was located across the road from Oak Ridge School. There were two apartments above the store and a long time friend of Clyde's, Roger Howerton and his family, lived in the other apartment.

On August 18, 1959 Shirley and Clyde had their second child and first daughter, Rhonda. Rhonda and the rest of the family would spend the next three and a half years living in the apartment in Oak Ridge.

In 1963 Clyde was hired by the U.S. Postal Service to be a mail carrier in the Guilford College – Quaker Village area of Greensboro, North Carolina.

Soon after landing the job, Clyde moved his family to Greensboro to be closer to his work. Clyde enjoyed his new job and the people on his route liked Clyde, too. Clyde knew he had found where he wanted to be for the rest of his career. Clyde would work with the postal system for the next 28 years until he retired.

On May 21, 1969 Clyde and Shirley had their third and last child, Gina.

Later in 1971 Clyde and Shirley went their separate ways.

Clyde and Clyde Jr. moved back to Oak Ridge and lived in the little green house on Pepper Road where Clyde's parents, Elias and Alma, had lived until they passed away. A short time after moving Clyde purchased the house and he and Clyde Jr. lived there for the next three years.

In 1974 Clyde added a new stop on his postal route. Gate City Savings and Loan had just completed a new branch office building in the Guilford College area and Clyde was assigned the duties of delivering their mail. The first thing Clyde noticed when he began the mail deliveries was their beautiful new branch manager, Nora Ballew. She literally took Clyde's breath away.

When Clyde found out she was not married he asked her out on a date. For the two it was love at first site and they knew they were meant for each other.

On March 27, 1975 Clyde and Nora were married and Nora moved with Clyde on Pepper Road. A few months later Clyde sold the little white house to a neighbor. Clyde kept the land the house sat on and the neighbor moved the house across the road and still lives in it today.

Later in 1975 Clyde and Nora built a beautiful new brick home where the old house had stood.

In 1976 Nora had an opportunity to go to work with Emory Wilson in Greensboro. They needed a controller to look after their finances. The firm sold Gorman-Rump water pumps to municipalities all over North Carolina, South Carolina, and Virginia. The pumps were used to supply water to communities, businesses, and homes.

Over time the owner realized Nora was not only good with financial numbers, but understood the sizing and inner workings of the water pumps as well. He then moved her into sales and had her travel across three states to make sales. Nora would continue working with Emery Wilson until she retired.

Clyde and Nora had many interests other than their working careers over the years.

One of Clyde's main goals was to keep the Young Family together. He was responsible for the Young Reunions. Every year the family would get together at Country Park in Greensboro or Kernersville Lake Park in Kernersville, NC. Clyde was responsible for the reunions for over twenty years. Although the family no longer has reunions they still get together at least five or six times a year for chicken stews, pinto bean suppers, eating out at local restaurants or the Young Family Christmas get-together. Clyde and Nora still have a major hand in these activities.

Clyde and Nora loved to square dance over the years and were members of the dance team, *"The Star 8's"*. They were active members for 10 years.

The two also enjoyed traveling. They went to Florida almost every year. Other trips included going to San Francisco, the Grand Canyon, West Virginia and to Montana.

After retiring Clyde enjoyed gospel singing and was a member of *The Oak Ridge Old Time Gospel Quartet*. Clyde was the group's tenor. The other three members of the group were friends, Roger Howerton, Leonard Stafford and Gary Blackburn. Gary's wife Myra played piano for the group and also sang. They sang for churches all over the central North Carolina.

Clyde was also a member of the gospel singing group, The Sugar Sticks. Other members of the group included Clyde's sisters, Edna and Elsie, his brother-in-law Reavis Marshall and old time friend, Roger Howerton.

To this day Clyde and Nora still make sure the Young Family gets together often. This fall he invited the entire family to his house and his nephew M.K. Moore brought out the cast iron pot and cooked pinto beans for the family. It brought a smile to Clyde's face to see the Young's gathering in his back yard, the same back yard where his mother and father hosted family events years earlier.

Above is a picture of Clyde Young in front. In the rear are his brothers from left, Hubert and Raymond. This picture was taken in 1939 or 1940 At the Case Place Farm in Oak Ridge, N.C where Clyde was born.

To the left is a picture of from left, Elias Young and his sons, Hubert, Clyde and Raymond. This picture was taken on Mother's Day in 1944 or 1945 at the Lowery Farm on Pepper Road in Oak Ridge, N.C.

To the left is a picture of Clyde Young when he was in high school. This picture was taken in 1949 or 1950. Clyde is standing in front of the Big White House on Pepper Road in Oak Ridge, N.C.

Above is a picture of Clyde Young, far left, in the dugout with several teammates when he played for the Oak Ridge Bulls in the early 1950's. If you look closely in the upper left hand corner you will see Clyde's father, Elias Young, in the stands.

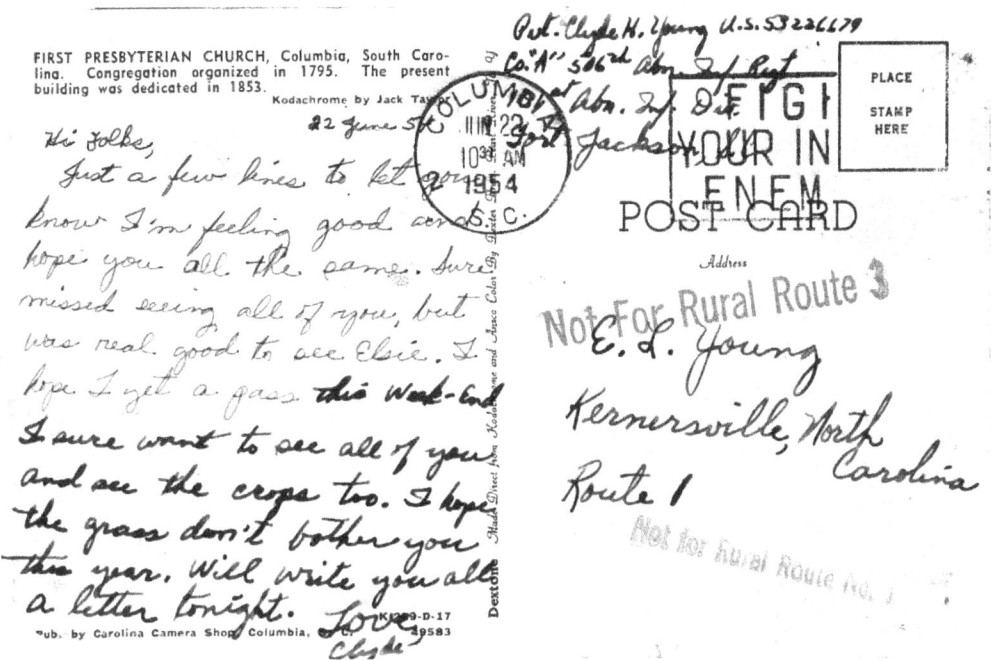

FIRST PRESBYTERIAN CHURCH, Columbia, South Carolina. Congregation organized in 1795. The present building was dedicated in 1853.
Kodachrome by Jack Ta...

Pvt. Clyde H. Young U.S. 53226679
Co. "A" 506th ...
...Jacks...

POST CARD

PLACE STAMP HERE

Hi Folks,
Just a few lines to let you know I'm feeling good and hope you all the same. Sure missed seeing all of you, but was real good to see Elsie. I hope I get a pass this Week-End. I sure want to see all of you and see the crops too. I hope the grass don't bother you this year. Will write you all a letter tonight.
Love Clyde

Address

E. L. Young
Kernersville, North Carolina
Route 1

Pub. by Carolina Camera Shop, Columbia, S. C.

Above is a letter home from Clyde Young to his father, Elias Young, while Clyde was in the U.S. Army in 1954.

Here is a picture of from left top row, Clyde Sr. and Shirley and bottom from left, Clyde Jr. and Rhonda. This picture was taken in 1961 or 1962 at the little white house in Oak Ridge, N.C.

This is the house Clyde, Shirley, Clyde Jr., Rhonda and Gina lived in when they lived in Greensboro during the 1960's and early 1970's at 2323 Kersey Street.

To your left is a picture of Clyde Jr. and Rhonda Young taken in the late 1960's.

Above is a picture of from left, Nora Young and Clyde Young and friend of the family, Jack Blaylock. This picture was taken at a Raymond Young's 80th Birthday Party in the 1997.

Clyde and Nora Young looked after the Young Reunions for over 20+ years making certain the family stayed close over the years. Clyde is seated in the center of the front row in this 2004 picture.

Clyde Hanes Young Jr.

On July 25, 1957 Clyde Sr. and Shirley Young had their first child, Clyde Hanes Young, Jr. He would be called Clyde Jr. by the family.

When Clyde Jr. was born Clyde Sr. and Shirley lived on Highway 68 in Oak Ridge, North Carolina.

When Clyde Jr. was two years old his family moved to an apartment above a store in Oak Ridge. The store was located across the road from Oak Ridge School. The family would live there for the next three years.

In 1963 Clyde Sr. was hired by the U.S. Postal service to be a mail carrier in the Guilford College – Quaker Village area of Greensboro, North Carolina and he moved his family to Greensboro to be closer to his work.

Clyde Jr. had just turned six at this time and soon afterward started first grade at Foust Elementary School in Greensboro. He continued going to school there through the sixth grade.

Some of Clyde Jr.'s fondest memories of his younger years were of his family's visits to Elias and Alma Young's house in Oak Ridge on Sunday afternoons after church. That was when Grandpa and Grandma Young lived in the little green house.

Clyde Jr. had several cousins his age that also visited at this time and they all played together the entire afternoon. He and first cousins Lisa Marshall, R.D. Marshall, and Moochie McCormick became very close friends over the years. They would climb onto the tin roof of the shed behind the house and eat cherries off the cherry tree. If they were feeling brave they would slide down the roof and jump off the end.

In 1971 Clyde Jr.'s parents decided to go their separate ways. Since Grandpa Young had passed away in 1970, his house in Oak Ridge was available and Clyde Sr. purchased the home and he and Clyde Jr. moved there.

Clyde Jr. spent the rest of his teenage years growing up in Oak Ridge. In seventh grade he started school at Northwest Junior and later attended Northwest Senior High School where he Graduated in 1975. While in the 11th and 12th grades at Northwest Guilford, Clyde Jr., drove the school bus for the Guilford County School System. He remembers well parking the school bus in the yard at the little white house.

Clyde Jr. has fond memories of growing up in Oak Ridge. One of his favorite pastimes was he and his father going rabbit hunting with Uncle Raymond Young and Uncle Raymond Goins and cousins, Ronnie Young and M.K. Moore.

Clyde Jr. looked up to his older cousin, Ronnie Young, and really enjoyed spending time with him while he was growing up in Oak Ridge. The Young family has so many cases of older family members mentoring younger family members over the years.

Ronnie would pick up Clyde Jr. and they would spend the day together. He also enjoyed spending the night or sometimes entire weekends at Ronnie's parents, Uncle Raymond and Aunt Ruby Young's house. Often time he helped them with their tobacco crop while staying there.

After graduating from high school Clyde Jr. went to work at Varco-Pruden, a manufacturer of steel buildings. He started with the company as a machine operator and soon advanced to part of their management team. Clyde Jr. worked with Varco-Pruden for 31 years until the plant closed.

Clyde Jr. was married to Donna Wear in 1981 and on October 20, 1986 they had their first child, Zach. Zach graduated from Embry-Riddle Aeronautical University in 2009 and got his private pilots license. Zach enjoys flying multiple engine aircraft and some day hopes to be an airline pilot. Currently he is employed with Federal Express in Greensboro.

On March 8, 1990 Clyde Jr. and his first wife had their second and last child, Chelsea. After graduating from high school she began studying to become a Registered Nurse at the University of North Carolina at Greensboro and plans to graduate in 2013.

Clyde Jr. and his first wife would later go their separate ways.

In 2006 Clyde Jr. met a woman named Melanie Jean Curry. The two started dating and on September 29, 2006 they were married and enjoy living in Oak Ridge together. Melanie is employed as a Nurse at North Carolina Baptist Hospital in Winston-Salem, N.C.

Today some of Clyde Jr.'s favorite hobbies are playing golf, working in his yard, and he also enjoys painting as a hobby in his free time.

To the left is a picture of Clyde Young Jr. taken in 1961 when he was 4 years old.

Clyde Jr. with his dad at his Uncle Raymond Young's house in July 1965.

This is a picture of Clyde Jr's children Zach and Chelsea Young.

Above is a great picture of Clyde, Jr. and hias wife, Melanie.

Rhonda Sue Young

On August 18, 1959, Clyde Sr. and Shirley Young had their second child, Rhonda Sue Young. She would be called Rhonda by the family.

When Rhonda was born Clyde Sr. and Shirley had recently moved to an apartment above a store in Oak Ridge, North Carolina. The store was located across the road from Oak Ridge School. The family would live there for a little over three years.

In 1963 the family moved to Greensboro when Clyde Sr. was hired by the U.S. Postal Service.

In 1965 when Rhonda was six years old she started first grade at Foust Elementary School in Greensboro and would go there through the fifth grade.

One of her closest friends during this time was first cousin, Lisa Marshall. Lisa would on many occasions come and spend the weekend with Rhonda in Greensboro.

In 1971 Rhonda's parents decided to go their separate ways and Clyde Sr. and Rhonda's brother, Clyde Jr. moved back to Oak Ridge, NC. Rhonda and her sister Gina continued living with their mother in Greensboro.

Rhonda continued her schooling in Greensboro, going to Joyner Elementary School in the sixth grade and then Mendenhall School through the ninth grade.

Rhonda then went to Page High School for her sophomore year. The following year Rhonda and Shirley moved to Durham, North Carolina and Rhonda spent her junior and senior years at North Durham High School. She proudly graduated from North Durham High in 1977.

After graduating from high school, Rhonda went to ECPI University in Greensboro, NC and graduated with a degree in Computer Technology.

In the mid1980's, Rhonda met a man named Dave Irwin. The two dated for the next couple of years and were married in 1989. The couple settled in Greensboro and would live there for the next several years.

Later in 1989 Rhonda and Dave had their first child Brian David Irwin. After Brian finished high school, he continued his education at Appalachian State University graduating with a Master's Degree in Business Administration.

Dave and Rhonda had their second and final child, Mackenzie Nichole Irwin in April of 1994. Nichole recently finished high school and is currently attending college at the University of North Carolina – Wilmington in Wilmington, NC.

In 2009 Rhonda and Dave decided to go their separate ways.

Today Rhonda works for Vita Nonwovens in High Point, North Carolina. She is a Network Administrator with the company.

Rhonda continues to live in Greensboro today and enjoys cross-stitching and cooking.

Rhonda Young with her younger sister, Gina. This picture was taken in the late 1970's.

This is a picture of Rhonda Young Irwin today with her Yorkie named Axil Rose.

Gina Carol Young

On May 21, 1969 Clyde Sr. and Shirley Young had their third and final child, Gina Carol Young. She would be called Gina by the family. When Gina was born Clyde Sr. and Shirley had lived in Greensboro, North Carolina for several years where Clyde Sr. worked as U.S. Postal System mail carrier.

In 1971, when Gina was two years old Clyde Sr. and Shirley went their separate ways. Gina would live with her mother after that as a child and attended school in Greensboro. She is a proud graduate of Western Guilford high School. In school Gina became interested in math and did well in her math classes. After graduating from high school she attended the University of North Carolina at Greensboro and graduated with a Bachelors Degree in Mathematics.

After graduating from UNCG Gina applied for and received a position as a math teacher at Western Guilford High School in Greensboro and she would teach there for several years.

In the 1990's she met a young man named Matt Ambrosino and the two started dating. A few months later Gina and Matt were married at First Baptist Church on West Friendly Avenue in Greensboro, NC. After their marriage Matt and Gina made their home in Greensboro.

Gina had three children. Her first daughter, Colby, was born on February 5, 2001 and her second daughter, Sophia, was born on January 16, 2003. Her first and only son, Matthew, was born on December 28, 2004. During her free time Gina enjoys going to her children's sporting events. Colby plays volleyball at school, Mathew plays on the soccer team, and Sophia is a cheerleader at her school.

Today Gina works as a math teacher at Greensboro Middle College and continues to live in Greensboro.

To the left is a picture of Gina Young taken in the late 1970's.

This is a picture of Gina Young Ambrosino with her children from left Colby, Matthew, and Sophia.

Chapter Fifteen

The Juanita Young McCormick Family

The date was April 11, 1933 and Elias and Alma were welcoming their ninth and final child, Hattie Juanita Young into the world. She would be called "Wonnie" by the family. At the time Wonnie was born Elias and Alma lived on the Case Place, located about two miles north of Oak Ridge, North Carolina just off NC Highway 68.

The Case Place was a 200 acre farm. Elias and Alma rented the ld Case homeplace from Mr. and Mrs. Case. The family raised nine acres of tobacco and gave half the profit they earned from the crop for rent during this time. In addition the family could raise all the garden they needed and several acres of corn and hay to feed their work horses and farm animals. Elias had two work horses at the time, a milk cow, and he raised a couple of hogs every year.

The old homeplace was the old Case family home, which was built in the late 1850's. The house did not have electricity or indoor plumbing and their water came hand drawn from a well behind the house.

Elias was a great farmer and could grow almost anything. His gardens provided more than enough food for the family during the summer and Alma always canned hundreds of quart jars of vegetables, fruits, jellies and jams each summer to last over the winter months. There was also a large chicken coop behind the house, which provided plenty of eggs and fried chicken for Sunday dinners.

Elias and Wonnie's brothers, Hubert and Raymond cut a lot of wood during this time. They needed it to fire Alma's wood cook stove and to heat the house during the winter. One of Wonnie's chores during this time was to keep the wood boxes filled inside the house.

So many things were hard to come by during this time. There was not any extra money for the family to spend on things that were not a necessity. Wonnie still remembers Alma saving the feed sacks from chicken feed purchased from the local grist mill and using them to make dresses for herself and her daughters.

Since Wonnie was the youngest child she saw several of her brothers and sisters get married before she started to school. Between

1935 and 1939 Wonnie saw Hubert, Annie, Raymond, Hazel and Edna all get married and move away.

In the fall of 1939 Wonnie started first grade at Oak Ridge Elementary School and would continue going there through the eighth grade.

Two years later on December 7, 1941 Wonnie still remembers hearing the news on the family battery powered radio that the Japanese had attacked Pearl Harbor in Hawaii. The following day she heard the famous speech by Franklin D. Roosevelt asking congress to declare war on Japan and Germany.

In 1942 Elias and Alma moved the family to the Lowery Place over on what is now Pepper Road in Oak Ridge, NC. Wonnie would spend the rest of her childhood at this house.

In 1944 Wonnie's sister Opal got married. That left Elsie, Clyde and Wonnie still at home. Elsie and Wonnie became very close sisters during this time and would remain close over the years.

During World War II many jobs opened up for women all across America. With so many men at war they were needed to fill the work force. Alma got her first public job with Adams-Millis, and would work there for the next decade.

Wonnie smiles when she thinks back to that time.

"I had to learn to cook, then," Wonnie said. "We all had to do more at home when Mama went to work at Adams-Millis."

Wonnie did not get an allowance during her teen years. Sometimes she would did get a quarter to go to the movies on Saturday night at the Justice Theatre in Kernersville. These were great times in Wonnie's life. On many occasions she would go with her cousins Jo Anne Crutchfield, Norma Jean Moore, and Ila Mae Hester.

Wonnie also loved to go to her brother Clyde's baseball games. Clyde was a great first baseman and a powerful hitter. After high school he went on to play semipro baseball in Oak Ridge.

In 1948 Wonnie met a man named Rufus McCormick. Rufus and Wonnie loved each other from the start and knew they wanted to spend the rest of their lives together when they got old enough to get married. For now they would have to wait for a while.

Then in 1950 they drove to Chesterfield, South Carolina and got married. They stayed an extra week in South Carolina for their honeymoon. Wonnie was still in high school at the time and after getting married decided to drop out of school. Years later she would go back and finish high school to get her diploma.

Rufus at the time of their marriage worked at J.P. Stevens in Greensboro, North Carolina. The firm was one of the largest textile manufacturers in the southeast. Rufus' job at the plant was to repair and maintain the machines.

In 1951 Wonnie got her first job at the Blue Bell Factory in Greensboro, North Carolina where they made Wrangler Jeans. Wonnie's job was putting the bluing on the cloth for making their famous jeans.

It was also in 1951 that Rufus and Wonnie built a new home on Church Street in Greensboro, NC. This would be their home for many years.

In 1952 Wonnie and Rufus had their first child, Lynn. And in 1956 the couple had their second child, Gordon. When Wonnie and Rufus got home from the hospital their daughter, Lynn did not like the name, Gordon. She decided her brother should have the name of the popular Mickey Mouse Club Mouseketeer, Moochie. Although Wonnie said he could not be called that, the name stuck and he was called that his entire life.

Wonnie, Rufus, Lynn and Moochie were a happy family as the children grew up. They attended church regularly and Wonnie enjoyed being a member of the Methodist Womens group.

One of the family's favorite pastimes was going camping at White Lake, North Carolina.

Rufus and Wonnie would continue working in textiles for several years. Then Rufus decided to change careers and go to work for Moses Cone Hospital in Greensboro, NC. Rufus worked out of their maintenance shop making repairs to the hospital facilities.

Wonnie also decided to change her career from textiles to the medical profession. She would have to go back to school and get her high school education.

In 1986 she attended a Guilford Technical Community College satellite site near her home and got her high school diploma. That was a proud day for Wonnie.

It was not long before Wonnie began a new career also at Moses Cone Hospital in Greensboro in the Radiation Oncology Department. Radiation Oncologists are health care professionals who treat cancers and tumors through radiation therapy. Rufus and Wonnie both worked at Moses Cone Hospital until they retired.

Sadly Wonnie and Rufus lost their son, Gordon "Moochie" McCormick on January 1, 2007 after a short illness. Moochie is Elias and Alma's first and only grandchild, at the time this book was written, that has passed away.

Wonnie and Rufus enjoy spending time with their four grandchildren, Mohogany, Mariah, Morgan and Mason Headen.

Wonnie and Rufus are mainstays of keeping the Young family together as an extended family. Any time there is a Young Reunion, a Young Christmas party or a Young birthday celebration you will see Rufus and Wonnie there. It is always great to see them and if you sit and talk with them for a while they will share great memories with you.

Wonnie and Rufus recently celebrated their 62nd year of marriage together and expect many more to come.

To the left is a picture of Lynn and Moochie McCormick when they were young children. This picture was taken in 1959 or 1960.

On the right is a picture of Lynn and Moochie McCormick on a visit to Grandma and Grandpa Young's in 1959 when their Grandparents lived on Pepper Road in Oak Ridge, North Carolina. On the front row is Gracie Flynt. On the second row from left are Gordon "Moochie" McCormick and Lynn McCormick. On the back row from left are Linda Young, Cindy Sapp and Diane Bolin.

Here is a picture of Lynn when she attended Summerfield Elementary School in Summerfield, North Carolina in the early 1960's.

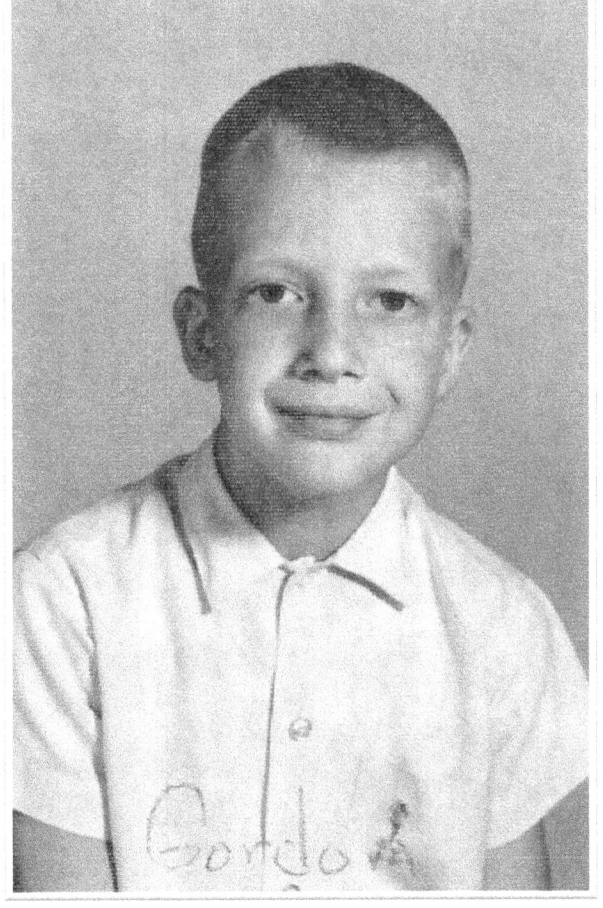

This is a picture of Gordon "Moochie" McCormick when he atteanded Summerfield Elementary School in Summerfield, North Carolina in the mid-1960's.

This is a great picture of Juanita Young McCormick taken in the 1980's.

Wonnie poses for this picture with her three living sisters in 2000. From left to right are Elsie, Opal, Edna, and Wonnie.

Above is a picture of Wonnie, far right, taken with her family in 1944 when Wonnie was 11 years old. From left to right on the bottom row are Elias and Alma. From left top row are her siblings Clyde, Hazel, Raymond, Edna, Opal, Hubert, Elsie and Wonnie. The little boy in the window of the car is M.K. Moore and the little boy on the fender is Gary Young.

Above is a picture of Rufus and Wonnie McCormick today.

Lynn McCormick

On November 9, 1952 Wonnie and Rufus McCormick had their first child, Lynn McCormick. Lynn felt like she grew up in the best of two worlds. Her parents had built a new home in 1951 on Church Street in Greensboro, North Carolina, which was located right beside her grandpa, Simon Peter McCormick's farm.

Grandpa McCormick had recently retired from the railroad and now raised chickens and sold butter and eggs to make his living. He also raised several acres of tobacco. Lynn enjoyed her visits next door getting to help out and play with his many animals.

Lynn also enjoyed visiting her other grandparents, Grandpa and Grandma Young. Lynn's fondest memories are from when Elias and Alma lived in the little green house on Pepper Road in Oak Ridge, North Carolina.

Most of their visits would be on Sunday afternoon after church. Wonnie would tell Lynn and Moochie on the way not to eat anything because there would be so many aunts, uncles, and cousins there. Alma and Elias could not afford to feed them all.

When they arrived and everyone had exchanged their pleasantries Grandma Young would secretly motion for Lynn to come and sit behind the kitchen door. Then with a big grin she would bring Lynn one of her delicious homemade cookies to eat.

Lynn also enjoyed spending the night at Grandma and Grandpa Young's. She would get to sleep with Grandma when she did. Grandma would always put some Watkins Ointment under her nose before going to bed. The ointment had eucalyptus oil in it and really had a strong smell.

When Lynn asked why she used it, Grandma Young would reply, "Because it makes you breathe good."

Another reason Lynn enjoyed visiting was because Grandma and Grandpa Young had a big black cherry tree in their back yard. In the summer you could climb up on a shed behind their house and eat your fill.

Lynn started first grade at Summerfield Elementary School in 1958 and would go there through the ninth grade.

During her early teen years Lynn enjoyed visiting her aunt and uncle, Edna and Raymond Goins. Edna was Wonnie's sister and they lived right down Pepper Road from Grandma and Grandpa Young's house. Edna and Raymond did not have children and enjoyed their nieces and nephews spending time with them.

Edna and Raymond were very active and enjoyed several hobbies. They had a beautiful dark wood panel ski boat and took Lynn skiing at Philpot Lake several times. They also enjoyed roller skating and took Lynn to the High Point Roller Rink where Lynn learned to skate.

In later years Lynn would teach her daughter, Hillary, to roller skate as well. Hillary would go on to compete in national competitions.

In Lynn's later teen years she attended Northwest Guilford High School. When Lynn turned 16 she got her drivers license. She then applied for a job to drive a school bus for the Guilford County School System. Lynn got the job and was assigned two routes to drive each day. As it would turn out they were the longest two routes in Guilford County. Lynn handled the task with skill and efficiency. She would drive both her junior and senior years of high school.

She also worked while in high school during the summer months at City Motors, an AMC car dealership, in Greensboro as their receptionist.

Lynn graduated from Northwest Guilford High School in 1970 and went to work at City Motors full time and would work there for about three years.

Lynn was married the summer after graduating from high school. During the marriage she had two children, Eddie Howie McLaurin and Hillary Leigh McLaurin.

Lynn liked her job at City Motors, however she hoped for a better career opportunity in the future. She knew to advance she would have to get more education. In 1971 Lynn went back to school at night at

Rockingham Community College in Wentworth, North Carolina. She graduated with an Associates of Applied Science Degree in Business Administration two years later.

Now Lynn was able to seek a better career. She applied for and was offered a position as a systems analyst at Cone Hospital in Greensboro, North Carolina. Lynn liked the new position and has worked there ever since.

Lynn's first marriage lasted for fifteen years and in 1985 the couple went their separate ways.

In 1988 Lynn met a man named Barry Thomas Bates. They started dating and would continue dating for the next several years. Then in 2000 the two were married.

Lynn's favorite hobby is working with leaded stained glass. A few years back Lynn went to an auction and purchased two beautiful stained glass panels. She liked them so well she wanted to start making her own.

She went to downtown Greensboro where the components were sold and asked if she could take classes but unfortunately they did not offer classes. Later she found a person in her community that had become a great artisan in the trade and asked if he would teach her the techniques. He said yes and she began classes.

Over time Lynn became very talented in the craft and now makes large colorful panels of her own.

A couple of years back Lynn wanted to buy pottery from a local craftsman. To Lynn's surprise the pottery maker didn't want to be paid money for his pottery. He wanted to barter with Lynn to make him a stained glass window.

Lynn knew she had become a craftsman in her own right when this happened.

Over the years Lynn has felt blessed that she has had a great job and a good quality of life. She is still employed with Cone Hospital, now 39 years and counting.

She and her husband, Barry built a new home recently and plans to one day retire and enjoy life.

This is a picture of Lynn and her Husband Barry.

On the right is a picture of Lynn's children, Eddie Howie McLaurin and Hillary Leigh McLaurin Headen.

Lynn's three Granddaughters from left Morgan, Mo, and Mariah.

This is Lynn's Grandson, Mason, when he was two years old.

Gordon "Moochie" McCormick

On February 9, 1956 Wonnie and Rufus McCormick had their second and final child, Gordon McCormick. He would grow to be a warm and caring person and would be called "Moochie" by the family. From an early age Moochie enjoyed going to Elias and Alma Young's. That is when they lived in the little green house on Pepper Road in Oak Ridge, North Carolina. There were always plenty of cousins there for him to play with.

One Sunday while on a visit to his grandparents, Wonnie and Rufus looked around and did not see Moochie. Where could he be? As it turned out he had walked down to his Aunt Edna and Uncle Raymond Goins' house for a visit. Their home was only a couple of hundred yards below Grandma and Grandpa Young's. When they found Moochie he was watching Edna's new tropical fish tank. He found all those colorful fish fascinating.

When Moochie was six he started to Summerfield Elementary School and would go there through the ninth grade.

Moochie then continued his high school education at Northwest Guilford High School, graduating in 1974. After graduating, Moochie started to work at a local machine shop thinking he may want a career there. A short time later Moochie met a pretty young woman named Gretchen Phillips and after dating for a few months the couple was married. They had two children, Ashley Ann McCormick and Zack Taylor McCormick.

Moochie later had an opportunity to go to work with the City of Greensboro with their water treatment division. He would spend his career working at the Mitchell Pumping Station which is located on Battleground Avenue in Greensboro.

Moochie's cousin and close friend, Kelly Young also worked with the City of Greensboro Water Division. On those special occasions when Mitchell Pumping Station needed a repair Moochie would make certain Kelly was called to do it. He knew Kelly would do it right.

Kelly was known for his neatly trimmed beard, but one day he decided to shave his head and trim his beard to almost nothing. When he arrived for a repair at the Mitchell Pumping Station he got out of his truck and quickly ran into the building to make the repairs. Moochie was really disappointed and said to a co-worker, "They didn't send Kelly". The co-worker knew ahead of time it was Kelly and took Moochie inside to meet the new repairman. "Moochie, I want you to meet your cousin, Kelly".

Moochie had several hobbies over the years including playing the banjo and the guitar. He worked hard at his job and always kept a smile on his face. If a co-worker was having a down day Moochie would find a way to cheer them up. He was simply a fun person to be around and to work with.

In 2006 Moochie started having headaches and knew something was wrong. He went to the doctor and after several tests they found he had an inoperable disease.

Sadly Gordon "Moochie" McCormick passed away on January 1, 2007. He was 50 years old. His funeral was attended by hundreds of family, friends and co-workers and he is missed by everyone that knew him.

Above is a picture of Gordon "Moochie" McCormick taken in 2006.

Chapter Sixteen

The Mary McGee Hester Walker Family

Mary Elizabeth McGee was born on June 17, 1905 to Robert Lee McGee and his wife, Lillian. To the Young family over the years she would be affectionately called "Lizzy". Lizzy's father, Robert, was Alma Young's brother. They were both born in Walkertown, NC.

In 1908 when Lizzy was three years old her mother, Lillian unexpectedly passed away. At the time Robert and Lillian had two children, Lizzy and Claudia. Robert was unprepared to raise two young daughters on his own so he asked his parents, John and Mary McGee to raise Lizzy and Claudia for him. John and Mary agreed and raised their grandchildren until John passed away in 1914. After that the two sisters lived with a McGee uncle for three more years.

In 1917 when Lizzy was 12, Alma went to visit the uncle and his family and found the living condition for Lizzy and Claudia were not up to the standards she thought they should be. While the uncle's family endured the two girls there was no real love for them and they had to work long hard hours in the fields every day to earn their keep.

When Alma returned home she talked to Elias and told him they needed to find a way to help Lizzy and Claudia so they could have a better quality of life.

On the next visit Alma took the two girls home with her. Alma had made arrangements for Claudia to live with her sister, Nann, and Lizzy would live with her and Elias. Lizzy lived with them for the rest of her childhood.

Years later Lizzy would say, "Aunt Alma Young was like my mother. She was the only Mother I ever knew."

And when it came to Alma's children Lizzy would always be considered a sister to each of them.

In the summer of 1923 when Lizzy was 18 she met a young man named Edgar Jones Hester. Lizzy liked Ed from the start. He had a good job with the county working on road construction jobs. The county was expanding their road systems to help commerce for the local businesses.

On November 25, 1923 Lizzy and Ed were married. They lived in the Goodwill Community East of Walkertown, North Carolina. It was a great time in Lizzy's life.

Lizzy and Ed had six children between 1924 and 1940. They were Grace, Ed, Ila Mae, Billy, Shelby and Faye.

During the 1920's and 1930's Lizzy and Ed developed a close bond with Alma and Elias. Ed and Elias enjoyed hunting rabbits together and Lizzy and Alma loved sitting and catching up on the latest gossip.

When Lizzy's children were old enough to spend the night, Alma and Elias would let them stay and treat them like their grandchildren.

Lizzy's daughter, Grace, has told many times of spending time during the summer with Elias and Alma. "Me and my sisters would come and stay for weeks during the summer. We helped Elias when he needed to put in a barn of tobacco and we helped Alma in the garden picking vegetables and later canning those vegetables for winter. The main thing was we lived in the city and sometimes food was not as plentiful as it should be. When we stayed with Elias and Alma you always got plenty to eat."

All went well for Lizzy and Ed during most of the 1930's. Although the Great Depression was hard on most people, Ed was working for the county and earned enough to support his family during these difficult years.

In the spring of 1939, Ed was driving a piece of construction equipment grading the dirt surface for a new road. Suddenly the equipment caught on fire. Ed was trapped inside and was severely burned. A few days after the incident he came down with pneumonia and on July 29, 1939 Ed Hester passed away. It was a very sad time for Lizzy.

The loss of Ed put Lizzy in a dire situation. At the time it was the hardest part of the depression. Lizzy was only 34 years old, had five children and was expecting her sixth child in March. How was she supposed to raise six children and earn enough money to feed them all?

Lizzy did everything she could to make ends meet. She took in laundry from neighbors and did their ironing as well. As each of her children grew older they started part time jobs and brought the money home for the family. With hard work and many prayers they were able to get by.

In March of 1948, Lizzy had another tragedy in her life. Her daughter, Shelby, who was nine years old at the time, was putting a stick of wood in the family fireplace. She was wearing a long nightgown and suddenly a sleeve caught on fire. Shelby got scared and started running as hard as she could. The running fanned the flames and caught the entire gown on fire. The burns were so severe she passed away a short time later.

Lizzy and her children continued helping each other during these years. Slowly one by one each child became adults and got married. In 1956 when Lizzy was 51 she met a man named Pink Walker. Pink was a painter by trade and the two were made for each other. They were married later that year.

Lizzy and Alma remained very close over the years. They were not only mother and daughter, they were the closest of friends and would remain that way the rest of their lives.

In 1965 when Alma passed away it was a hard time for Lizzy and the Young Family. Ironically, two weeks later Lizzy would pass away as well. She was 60 years old.

Although Lizzy was not born into the Young family she was a big part of Elias and Alma's family. This book would not be complete without sharing the story of her life.

This is a picture of Lizzy Hester holding Clyde Young in 1931.

In the picture is Lizzy with her two daughters, Faye, left and Shelby, right. This picture was taken in the early 1940's.

Here is a picture of Lizzy with Alma and all of her daughters. From left are Alma, Annie Mae; (Hubert Young's wife), Hazel, Wonnie, Annie, Lizzy, Opal, Elsie and Edna. This picture was taken in the early 1950's. The little boy sticking his head out is MK Moore.

This is a picture of all of Lizzy and Ed Hester's grandchildren.

Grace Hester

On December 14, 1924 Lizzy and Ed Hester had their first child, Grace Hester. In her early childhood Grace lived in the Goodwill community about five miles east of Walkerton, North Carolina. The family would later move to Winston-Salem, North Carolina and Grace spent her childhood there.

Grace grew up during the Great Depression. Only the strength and bond of a loving and caring family pulled them through it.

After Grace became a teenager she remembers spending many of her summer weeks at Alma and Elias Young's farm when they lived at the Case Place in Oak Ridge, North Carolina. She loved going there. There was a lot of farm work to do, but everyone pitched in and made the work seem more like fun.

Alma's daughter, Opal, was Grace's age and they were very close friends during this time. They still tell tales of running and playing in the woods after the chores were done for the day.

In 1941 Grace met a young man named Ed Everhart. She knew there was something special about him. They would date through the summer and fall and on December 20, 1941 they were married.

After they were married Grace went to work with Western Electric in Winston-Salem, North Carolina manufacturing telephone components for the Bell System.

Ed acquired a job working with R.J. Reynolds Tobacco Company also in Winston-Salem.

A couple of years after they were married they had their one and only child, Linda.

Grace and Ed loved their jobs, but had a dream of one day owning their own business. They kept noticing at their jobs how many supplies were needed for plant maintenance, particularly for janitorial services.

A short time later they started their own chemical business. They sold a wide range of supplies. Their lines included industrial cleaners, paper towels, toilet tissues, soaps, and other specialty items. Over time the business became a success for Grace and Ed.

While Ed passed away in 2009, Grace is still living today and at 88 is doing very well.

This picture of Grace and Ed Everhart was taken in 2002 when they attended the Young Family Christmas Party.

Ed Hester, Jr.

On May 9, 1927 Lizzy and Ed Hester had their second child and first son, Ed Hester Jr. In his early childhood Ed lived in the Goodwill community about five miles east of Walkerton, North Carolina. The family would later move to Winston-Salem, North Carolina.

Ed also grew up during the depression years and remembers the hardships of that era. Ed remembered a turn for the worse when his father passed away in 1939. After that Ed became the father figure in the Hester family. In the early 1940's Ed went to work as soon as he could and brought all of his money home to his mother, Lizzy.

Ed's younger siblings respected him and listened to what he said. His hard work and caring ways went a long way toward pulling the Hester family through this time.

In 1950 Ed met a beautiful young woman named Doris Tuttle. Ed Knew Doris was going to be the love of his life and they were married on December 22, 1950.

Ed and Doris decided to make their home with Lizzy so they could continue to help out the Hester family.

A couple of years later Ed and Doris decided it was time to move out on their own.

Soon afterward, they had their first daughter Joy, followed by their second daughter, Jill.

Ed worked in the construction business. He worked for Piedmont Construction Company in Winston-Salem and later worked for Santee Cooper in South Carolina as a business manager in their cement division.

Ed enjoyed his time at Santee Cooper and stayed with the company until he retired.

Sadly Ed passed away on August 28, 1992 shortly after he retired. He was 65 years old.

Above is a great picture of Ed Hester with his family. To the far left is his wife, Doris. In the middle are their two daughters, Joy and Jill.

Ila Mae Hester

On February 1, 1933 Lizzy and Ed Hester had their third child, Ila Mae Hester. She was only six years old when her father, Ed passed away. She learned early in life if you wanted to be successful you would need to work hard and have a strong business sense.

In 1949 she met a young man named Lacy G. Mabe. They started dating and were later married on January 28, 1950. Lacy and Ila Mae had two children, Karen and Lacy Jr. Soon after getting married Ila Mae was hired by Western Electric in Winston-Salem, North Carolina and worked there for several years.

Years later Ila Mae and Lacy decided they wanted to go into business for themselves. They moved to Emerald Isle, North Carolina and for a while ran a beach campground.

Next they ran a hardware store and then started their own pizza shop. The building where they ran the pizza shop is now Jordan's House of Seafood at Emerald Isle.

In 1981 they decided to move to Florida where Ila Mae worked in banking for the next 15 years before retiring. In 2000 Ila Mae and Lacy moved back to Winston-Salem to be closer to their family.

In the above picture on the left is Ila Mae Hester Mabe. This picture was taken when she attended Opal Young Flynt's birthday party on February 16, 2005. To the right is Ila Mae's sister, Grace Everhart

Billy Hester

On October 8, 1935 Lizzy and Ed Hester had their fourth child, Billy Hester. Billy was born in Winston-Salem, North Carolina and would spend his entire childhood living there.

Billy was only four years old when his daddy passed away from a construction accident in 1939.

Without a father, Billy grew up in a family that all had to pull together to make ends meet. Billy had a strong mother and she made sure her children had the necessities of life, but there were not a lot of extras.

By the time Billy was a young adult he truly understood the value of hard work and education.

By age 16 he was working at Farmers Dairy in Winston-Salem. They were one of the major milk producers in the area.

While he worked there Billy continued his education and graduated from high school in 1953.

A year later Billy decided he wanted to serve his country and volunteered for military service in the U.S. Air Force. Billy thought he would be in the Air Force for four years and would be out, however it did not work out that way. After completing his first four years he liked it so well he stayed in for another four years.

It was during this second four year term Billy met a beautiful young woman named Barbara Meadith. Billy knew this was the woman he wanted to spend the rest of his life with and they were married on August 16, 1958.

Billy and Barbara had two children, Belinda and Billy, Jr.

Billy continued as a member of the Air Force and retired after 20 years of service.

After retiring Billy and Barbara moved to Missouri. Billy started a new career in Missouri working in the state's lead mines as a mechanic. He would continue working there until he retired.

Billy and Barbara still live in Missouri today.

Above is a picture Billy Hester, far right. Also in the picture are his sisters, from left, Ila Mae, Faye and Grace. This picture was probably taken in the 1990's.

Shelby Hester

On January 7, 1939 Lizzy and Ed Hester had their fifth child, Shelby Hester. Shelby was born in Winston-Salem, North Carolina.

Sadly, Shelby would spend only nine years on this earth. On March 28, 1948 Shelby was putting a log in the family fireplace when her long night gown caught on fire. Shelby got scared and took off running as fast as she could. The wind blowing by her as she ran caused the entire night gown to become engulfed in flames. The burns were so severe Shelby died from the accident.

Shelby's sister, Faye was only eight years old when this happened. The two were so close and played together all the time.

When Faye was interviewed recently and asked about Shelby, she replied, "Shelby was full of fun and could climb anything. She would climb a street sign to the top and sit up there and just laugh."

This is a picture of Shelby Hester, left and her sister, Faye,a right. This picture was taken in 1943.

Faye Hester

On March 4, 1940 Lizzy and Ed Hester had their sixth and final child, Faye Hester. Faye was born in Winston-Salem, North Carolina and would spend his entire childhood living there.

Faye never got to see her father. Ed was in a construction accident and passed away five months before Faye was born. Fortunately she had a strong family that worked hard to help each other during her childhood.

In 1955 Faye met James Fincher. She knew right away he was the man she wanted to spend her life with. About a year later they were married.

Over the years they had four children; Jamie, Jimmy, Angie and Kathy.

James began a career with Bonson Company in Winston-Salem, NC. They were manufacturers of air conditioning systems for commercial buildings and manufacturing facilities. Later in life he was employed by Salem Carriers, a trucking firm in Winston-Salem, NC.

Faye worked at R.J. Reynolds Tobacco Company in Winston-Salem, North Carolina. Faye has the distinction of being the first woman sheet metal craftsperson at Reynolds. Later in her career she worked in Reynolds' tobacco research center.

Faye and James continue to enjoy their retirement together.

Above is a picture of Faye when she was 15 years old.

Chapter Seventeen

Tobacco Farming

"The Way It Used To Be"

For Generations the Young family has relied on their tobacco crop to pay the bills and help their family to survive. Raising tobacco is a process that starts early in the year and does not end until the fall when the tobacco is sold at auction. Although there were many advances in manufacturing and technology in the early 1900's tobacco farming remained much the same as it was many years earlier. It was not until the 1960's that modern equipment was beginning to be used. From the mid 1800's to the 1950's farmers used hand labor and mules to raise tobacco.

Carl Young is the oldest son of Hubert and Annie Mae Young and the oldest grandson of Elias and Alma Young. Carl grew up during a time when tobacco was the most important crop on your farm. They grew wheat and corn for animal feed, and a vegetable garden for the family, but without tobacco they could not pay their rent or other bills. It was essential for the family to grow a quality crop of tobacco to ensure it would bring top dollar at the tobacco warehouse auction.

Carl's father, Hubert, made his living as a farmer and Carl helped him every day doing his fair share of the work. Even during the school year Carl remembers grabbing a biscuit after school for a quick snack and going to help his father until sundown. Carl has provided us with a complete years worth of work as a tobacco farmer in the 1950's. It was never an easy job but like Carl, each member of the family growing up during these times pitched in and helped their family in the fields. The following is a description of a typical year on a tobacco farm.

Carl's farming history lesson starts in January and goes through December and would be repeated each year. Starting in January and February Carl remembers all the wood they had to cut. First there was firewood to heat the home. They did not have a chainsaw back then. All the wood was cut with a crosscut saw and an ax. The crosscut saw was a two-man job with Hubert on one side and Carl on the other. The ax was used for limbing the trees and later for splitting the wood. Usually they preferred to use good hardwoods like oak and maple for heating the home.

Then there was wood cut for the kitchen wood cook stove. They used the same tools here. The wood for the cook stove was cut much smaller than regular home heating firewood. Usually in one inch to two inch pieces. Dry pine and poplar were preferred. They burned much quicker and gave a hotter fire for the cook stove.

Finally they had to cut wood for curing the tobacco in their wood fired tobacco barns. Hubert could count on 10 to 12 barns of tobacco from his tobacco crop each year. Each barn required two wood furnaces being fired for six to seven days, 24 hours a day to completely cure the barn of tobacco.

This wood was cut different from the rest. Usually it came from good strait small trees with trunks three inches to five inches in diameter. The trunks were cut six feet to eight feet long and stacked vertically near the tobacco barns.

All the while they were cutting wood Hubert was looking for a suitable place to plant their tobacco plant bed in the spring. He preferred it on the south side of a hill if possible. This would allow more sun to hit the bed each day.

The area had to be clear new ground each year and needed approximately 400 square yards of area to plant enough tobacco plants for their 6 – 8 acre crop. The plot had to be grubbed and cleared of all weeds.

In mid-February Hubert purchased a few precious ounces of tobacco seed to plant their plant bed. The seeds were so small you could barely see them. They were like fine ground flakes of black pepper. Hubert would mix them with sand to make them easier to spread over the large plant bed area. The seeds were planted in the last two weeks of February.

Once planting was complete, Hubert and Carl covered the entire bed with a light mesh cheese cloth and then secured the cloth to the ground around the entire perimeter. The cheese cloth protected the sprouting plants from wind and rain and also filtered harsh sun rays from the sprouting plants.

Hubert kept a close eye as the plants began to grow. If weeds started crowding out the tobacco plants he and Carl would have to remove the cloth cover and hand pull out all the weeds. They would then recover the bed with the cheesecloth and secure it all the way around.

It generally took until the first week of May for the tobacco plants to get big enough for transplanting.

In March Hubert and Carl continued cutting firewood and hauling it to the house and the tobacco barns.

March was also the time they started preparing the land for their tobacco, corn, and garden crops. All of the plowing and tilling implements were pulled by horses and mules. They still did not have a tractor.

In mid-March they started planting the garden. Cabbage and onions were planted first. As the weather warmed and after the frosts ended, they planted the rest of the garden.

In April they started planting corn. Hubert's family needed a lot of corn. In addition to the corn used for cornmeal by the family it was also needed to feed the horses, mules, cows, hogs, and chickens.

Hubert and Elias liked to plant their tobacco crop between the 10th and the 25th of May. Each of their families had between six and eight acres of tobacco and they helped each other during this time planting the crops.

First the tobacco plants had to be pulled from the tobacco plant beds. This task had to be done carefully. Each plant was pulled out of the ground by tugging on the stem and making sure while pulling, the roots were left unharmed.

As the tobacco plants were pulled they were stored in wooden bushel baskets or crates. The plants had to be kept straight, making it easier for the person dropping the plants into the tobacco hand setter for planting.

Planting also required several 55 gallon metal drums of water at the field. They were hauled by wagon from a nearby creek.

At the time a hand tobacco setter was used to plant each seedling individually. The tobacco setter had two openings at the top. The larger opening was a reservoir, which was filled with water. The smaller opening was where the person assisting the hand tobacco setter operator would drop the tobacco plants in one at a time. At the bottom of the setter was a pointed round shoot, which could easily be plunged four to five inches deep into the freshly plowed soil. The round shoot remained closed until the operator pulled a lever. When the lever was pulled the round chute at the bottom opened dropping out the tobacco plant with the roots of the tobacco plant deep in the ground. The water reservoir also opened at the same time, giving the roots about half a cup of fresh water to help the plant get started growing. Once the setter was lifted up the operator used his toes to push soil around the roots of the newly planted tobacco plant. A skilled tobacco hand setter operator could plant at almost walking speed.

The plants in the plant bed did not all mature at the same time. Over a two week period Hubert, Carl, and Elias would get three pullings of plants, which were enough to plant their tobacco crops.

About three weeks after planting, the plowing and hoeing of the tobacco crop began. Over the next several weeks Hubert and Carl plowed the tobacco five or six times. The reason for plowing some old farmers of the time would say was to bring the moisture up out of the ground. If weeds got between the plants where the plow could not reach Carl and Hubert had to use a hoe to get those out.

The final plowing of the tobacco crop was termed, "Laying it by". That is when they used a plow known as a sweep which kept the weeds from growing between the rows of tobacco for quite a while.

During this time they kept the garden plowed and hoed as well. As the vegetables matured they were harvested for the kitchen table and any excesses were canned for the upcoming winter.

These flowers were broken off the top of each plant by hand to encourage the leaves to grow

By the first week of July the tobacco crop had almost reached maturity and each tobacco plant had a large pink flowering bloom in the top. These flowers had to be removed by a procedure known as topping. The tops were hand broken out of the top of the plant making certain to leave about 18 tobacco leaves on each stalk to continue growing.

After topping, the plant continued to grow and suckers began forming between the tobacco stalk and the stems of the leaves. These had to be pulled out by hand three or four times over the next month.

It was also during this time the family started harvesting or as it was commonly called, priming the tobacco crop.

Priming tobacco in the late 1950's from left, Ken Young, Hubert Young, M.K. Moore, Gary Young, Clyde Young, and Carl Young

Hubert and Carl knew the tobacco was ready to be harvested when the leaves started turning from green to yellow at the bottom of the stalk. They would usually pull three to four leaves from the bottom of the stalk up during each priming.

The entire immediate family along with extended family, and neighbors helped when it came time to put in a barn of tobacco. Hubert, Carl, and several older men primed the tobacco from the stalks in the fields, while the women and younger children strung the tobacco onto tobacco sticks at the tobacco barn. The tobacco primers used a horse or mule in the field to pull a tobacco sled alongside the primers to make it easy to lay the tobacco into the sled. They made sure to keep the tobacco straight as they laid their armloads of tobacco in the sled. This made it easier for the workers at the tobacco barn to string the tobacco.

Young family members working together to pull tobacco at a field in the late 1950's. The horse is pulling a sled full of tobacco that will be going to the barn to be strung onto sticks

When a sled was filled to the top a second horse or mule pulled the full sled to the barn.

When the sled arrived at the barn the tobacco was removed and laid on a large table made of wood planks and sawbucks. Three people worked together to string the tobacco onto sticks. There were two people handing leaves and one person using a stringing buck to string the leaves onto a tobacco stick. The handers handed three to four leaves at a time to the stringer who put 26 to 28 hands of tobacco on each stick. There were usually two teams of handers and stringers working at the barn.

The stringers had to string the tobacco tight onto the stick so leaves would not fall out while they were curing. Falling leaves could catch the barn on fire and potentially burn it down.

During a day's harvest the two stringers usually strung about 450 sticks of tobacco. Once the stringing was complete all the sticks had to be hung inside the barn. These were wood fired tobacco barns. Once the fires were lit they had to be maintained 24 hours a day during the entire curing process and that process took six to seven days.

Brenda Young on the right stringing tobacco onto sticks as Grandma Young (left) and Grandma Rierson prepares the tobacco in 1958.

Hubert and Carl had to spend every night at the barn keeping the fires stoked, and during the day they still had to do their regular farm work. Sometimes they would be suckering the tobacco crop, and other times they may be putting in another barn of tobacco. Every two to three hours one of them would have to stop, go to the tobacco barn where they were curing, and check the temperature and add wood to the fires.

After the sixth or seventh day of curing when the tobacco had turned into golden yellow leaves the fires were put out and the doors were opened on the barn. The tobacco leaves were really dry after curing, and handling them now would crumble the leaves into flakes and dust.

To prevent this Hubert and Carl's next task was to bring the tobacco into order. This process took about two days. Bringing tobacco into order meant letting the morning cool damp air add moisture to the leaves. By the second morning the added moisture made the tobacco leaves soft and pliable and the sticks of tobacco could then be moved out of the barn without being damaged.

When the sticks of tobacco were removed from the barn they were taken and stored in Hubert's pack house. The pack house was a big building large enough to store the entire cured tobacco crop for that season.

The above process was repeated 10 to 12 times until the entire crop of tobacco had been primed and cured.

The tobacco stored in the pack house had to be periodically restacked. If they did not mold could set in ruining the tobacco. This was done a couple of times during the remainder of the harvest season.

Fall of the year was harvest time for the feed crops as well and also took a lot of work. That was Hubert's favorite time of year. It was cooler then and those hot days of summer were all gone.

In all Hubert planted between 25 to 30 acres of grain crops each year. They included oats, wheat, and corn. The oats and corn were mainly for the farm animals, while the wheat and some of the corn were ground into flour and cornmeal for the family. Hubert had a large family to feed.

Around the first week of September school started for Carl and it was also time to get the cured tobacco ready for market.

Tying the cured tobacco into hands and getting it ready for market was a special process and took time to master.

The barns of tobacco had all been stored in the pack house for the last few weeks and had dried out. The pack house had a basement underneath it where Hubert and Carl could hang the tobacco to bring it back into order by adding moisture to make it soft and pliable again. Carl remembers having to hang a hundred or so sticks in the basement every day after school.

Carl's Grandma Rierson and Aunt Genny, who both lived with them at the time, worked in the tobacco during the day. Hubert was also there, however he may have been preparing the land for the grain crops, oats, and wheat, which needed to be planted between mid-September and early October.

All of Hubert's children were old enough to help in tying the tobacco and Loretta, Brenda, and Barbara also helped every afternoon after school and at night.

After removing the tobacco from the sticks it was sorted into grades and tied into hands. The tobacco hands had the stems at the top and the leafy part at the bottom. A pretty golden colored wrapper leaf was wrapped and secured around the top of the hand.

After tying the tobacco into hands, they were put on slick tobacco sticks. This made it easy to remove the hands and store them in baskets when they got to market. A lot of effort was made to neatly stack the tobacco on the baskets before the tobacco auction. Back then it was thought the tobacco would sell at a higher price the better it looked on the warehouse floor.

Taking the tobacco to the market was Hubert's favorite event of the year. After the sale he loved going to the little window at the market where they cashed the checks. He knew this was payday!

Late fall and early winter were spent hand cutting and splitting more wood for the wood cook stove and the heating stoves. The family needed a lot of wood to last them through the winter.

Like many farmers of the time Hubert had a lot full of hunting dogs. The dogs stayed with Hubert and Carl wherever they went. They may be running a rabbit while the two were plowing in a field. Sometimes Hubert and Carl would stop their work to listen and watch the dogs work a rabbit. Then Hubert would whistle and the dogs would come running. Sometimes Hubert would point to where a rabbit had gone into

This is the scene inside a tobacco warehouse in the 1950's. The hands of tobacco are neatly stacked on baskets on the warehouse floor.

a thicket and the dogs would dive in after it. Hubert would just grin and go back to work.

Tobacco farming was hard work during these times. All of Elias and Alma's children and most of their grandchildren grew up helping in any way they could in the fields or at the tobacco barns. There was a job for everyone from small children to the adults, and each job was equally important to the family.

Carl recalls, "We had it good on the farm. Daddy and Grandpa Young were easy to work with. Daddy was always at home. He didn't send us to the field, he went with us. He had no modern equipment, just the basics. We didn't have a lot of extra things, but we did have what we needed. We got along with each other, knowing we were loved and well cared for by our parents and grandparents."

Carl Young standing at a Young get-together last year. He was discussing the old days with his first cousin, Gary Young. Both grew up helping their fathers and Grandpa Elias Young on his farm during the 1950's.

Members of the Young family priming tobacco in a field in the 1950's. You can see they have pulled the bottom half of the leaves off the stalk. They will come through this same field and pull the remaining leaves in the following weeks.

From left Barbara, Annie Mae, Brenda, and Annie Mae's Mother Grandma Rierson stringing tobacco. You can see the tall stack of logs in the background that was used to heat the barn. As the end of the log would burn up they would push it farther into the fire to keep the inside of the barn at a constant temperature.

Arthur Goins, Clyde Young, and a family friend, Robert Jefferies, take a break at the end of a long row of priming tobacco.

Grandma and Grandpa Young at the tobacco barn with their granddaughter Brenda stringing tobacco.

Gary, Ken, Clyde, and Carl Young priming tobacco at one of their family farms in Oak Ridge, NC.

Above is a painting, by Richard Hedgecock, of Louis Dollarhite using Elias Young's horse drawn cultivator behind a team of mules. Louis enjoys using his mules to plow tobacco fields the same way Elias did in the first half of the 1900's.

Grandpa Young preparing a tobacco barn in the late 1950's. He loved spending the night tending the fire and was a master of the art of curing tobacco in a wood fired barn. Even into the 1960's when they began using oil to heat and there was no longer a need to spend 24 hours a day at the barn Grandpa Young would often spend these nights sleeping at the barn with one of his grandsons.

Allen Young is the youngest grandson of Raymond and Ruby Young. He graduated from Kendall College of Art & Design in Grand Rapids, MI. While in school he met his wife, Stephanie, who is also a graduate of Kendall College. He is a furniture designer at a residential design firm in High Point, NC. Two years ago Allen and Stephanie moved into Raymond and Ruby's home place in Oak Ridge, NC. In his spare time Allen enjoys working in the garden at their small hobby farm, collecting antiques, and spending time outdoors. He has always had an interest in family history and this sparked his interest in writing a book with Jimmy about the Young family. It has been a great project filled with stories, memories, and mountains of pictures. Allen and Stephanie cannot wait for their growing family to share some of the same experiences as generations of the Young family have before them.

Jimmy Flynt is the son of Opal and Pete Flynt and Elias and Alma Young's grandson. Over the years Jimmy has enjoyed the hobby of writing books. He helped his mother, Opal, write her book, "Gold Were The Days" – a story about Opal and the Young Family growing up during the Great Depression. Opal's book was a great inspiration in writing this book, "Growing Up Young". Jimmy has also written "A Winner's Life – Coach Jack Blaylock"; the story of the Kernersville and East Forsyth High School baseball and basketball coach, "The Treasure Of Them All"; the story of Lorillard Tobacco Company, and "The Last Fan Of Jimmie Foxx"; a story about the forgotten most powerful slugger in the history of Major League Baseball. Jimmy would like to thank his wife, Judy for allowing him the free time to write this book.

www.ingramcontent.com/pod-product-compliance
Lightning Source LLC
Chambersburg PA
CBHW080103010626
45794CB00014B/2971